LANDLORD AND TENANT SERIES

Rent Review

LANDLORD AND TENANT SERIES

Rent Review

by

Jill Alexander

BLACKSTONE
PRESS LIMITED

This book has been printed digitally and produced in a standard specification
in order to ensure its continuing availability

OXFORD
UNIVERSITY PRESS

Great Clarendon Street, Oxford OX2 6DP

Oxford University Press is a department of the University of Oxford.
It furthers the University's objective of excellence in research, scholarship,
and education by publishing worldwide in

Oxford New York

Auckland   Cape Town Dar es Salaam Hong Kong   Karachi
Kuala Lumpur Madrid Melbourne Mexico City   Nairobi
New Delhi Shanghai Taipei Toronto
With offices in
Argentina Austria Brazil Chile Czech Republic France Greece
Guatemala Hungary Italy Japan South Korea Poland Portugal
Singapore Switzerland Thailand Turkey Ukraine Vietnam

Oxford is a registered trade mark of Oxford University Press
in the UK and in certain other countries

Published in the United States
by Oxford University Press Inc., New York

A Blackstone Press Book

ISBN   1-84174-130-2

Antony Rowe Ltd., Eastbourne

Contents

1.1 General purpose of rent review clauses   1.2 Construction of rent review clauses   1.3 Rectification of rent review clauses

2.1 Introduction   2.2 Content of rent review clauses   2.3 The main types of market rent review clauses   2.4 Trigger notice type of review   2.5 Form of trigger notice   2.6 Effect of an invalid trigger notice   2.7 Counternotices   2.8 Effect of an invalid counternotice   2.9 Service of trigger and counternotices   2.10 Delays: time of the essence   2.11 Effect of time being of the essence   2.12 Delay: time not of the essence   2.13 No notice procedure: automatic reviews   2.14 Agreeing a revised rent   2.15 Upwards only reviews   2.16 Rent review dates   2.17 Rent review periods   2.18 Valuation date

Acknowledgements

This book reproduces two paragraphs from *The RICS Guidance Notes for Surveyors acting as Arbitrators and Independent Experts in Commercial Property Rent Reviews* (pp. 112 and 114). This material is reproduced by kind permission of the Royal Institution of Chartered Surveyors, which owns the copyright.

The rent review clauses (Appendices 1 and 2–11) are taken from the *Encyclopaedia of Forms and Precedents* and are reproduced by kind permission of The Butterworths Division of Reed Elsevier (UK) Limited.

Abbreviations

AGA	authorised guarantee agreement
CA	Court of Appeal
HL	House of Lords
LPA	Law of Property Act 1925
RICS	Royal Institution of Chartered Surveyors
s.	section
ss.	sections
VAT	value added tax

Table of Cases

ix

Table of Statutes

Table of Secondary Legislation

CHAPTER ONE

Introduction to Rent Review

1.1 GENERAL PURPOSE OF RENT REVIEW CLAUSES

Leases generally last for a considerable period of time, and while it is possible for the rent to remain the same over the entire term, with the rise in both inflation and property values, it is unlikely to happen. The position was explained as long ago as 1977 by Lord Salmon in the House of Lords case of *United Scientific Holdings Ltd* v *Burnley Borough Council* [1978] AC 904, at 948:

> In a period of acute inflation, such as we have experienced for the last 20 years or so, and may well continue to experience for many years to come, what is a fair market rent at the date when a lease is granted will probably become wholly uneconomic within a few years. Tenants who are anxious for security of tenure require a term of reasonable duration, often 21 years or more. Landlords, on the other hand, are unwilling to grant such leases unless they contain rent revision clauses which will enable the rent to be raised at regular intervals to what is then the fair market rent of the property demised. Accordingly, it has become the practice for all long leases to contain a rent review clause providing for a revision of the rent every so many years. Leases used to provide for such a revision to be made every 10 years. Now the period is normally seven and not infrequently every five years. To my mind, it is totally unrealistic to regard such clauses as conferring a privilege upon the

landlord or as imposing a burden upon the tenant. Both the landlord and the tenant recognise the obvious, *viz*, that such clauses are fair and reasonable for each of them. I do not agree with what has been said in some of the authorities, namely, that a rent revision clause is for the benefit of the landlord alone and not at all for the benefit of the tenant. It is plainly for the benefit of both of them. It is for the benefit of the tenant because without such a clause he would never get the long lease which he requires; and under modern conditions, it would be grossly unfair that he should. It is for the benefit of the landlord because it ensures that for the duration of the lease, he will receive a fair rent instead of a rent far below the market value of the property which he demises. Accordingly, the landlord and the tenant by agreement in their lease provide that at stated intervals during the term the rent should be brought up to what is then the fair market rent.

The rent review clause is intended to resolve what is essentially a conflict between the interests of the landlord and the tenant. Originally, this was the tenant's need for the security a long lease can provide and the landlord's desire to ensure that the rent payable throughout the term remains competitive and protected from inflation. Nowadays, modern tenants do not necessarily always want the commitment of a long lease, whereas landlords do. Many landlords are finance companies or pension funds who want a long-term arrangement to ensure a certain return on their investment. Tenants, on the other hand, often want the flexibility of shorter terms.

The general purpose of a rent review clause was more recently explained by Sir Nicolas Browne-Wilkinson V-C in *British Gas Corporation v Universities Superannuation Scheme Ltd* [1986] 1 WLR 398, as being

... to enable the landlord to obtain from time to time the market rental which the premises would command if let on the same terms on the open market at the review dates. The purpose is to reflect the changes in the value of money and real increases in the value of the property during a long term ... and not so as to confer on the landlord a windfall benefit which he could never obtain on the market if he were actually letting the premises at the review date.

The rent review clause is considered by many to be the most important provision in the lease, and it is certainly one that the parties will refer to throughout the term.

1.2 CONSTRUCTION OF RENT REVIEW CLAUSES

1.2.1 General

Rent review clauses have become more complex and sophisticated over the years and have been the subject of much judicial consideration. One of the reasons parties litigate in relation to rent review clauses is the financial consequences of one construction of a clause as opposed to another. Also with the volume of litigation, a clause which appeared clear at the outset can have a different meaning by the time of review because of intervening court decisions. Equally, one of the parties may want a different meaning from that originally intended to deal with unforeseen events which might financially prejudice its position. While the parties could agree to alter the wording to reflect the change, this is unlikely to happen as one party's gain will almost invariably be the other party's loss. Therefore, the only course left is to seek the court's judgment on an issue of construction.

Leases are construed by the courts under the same principles as apply to commercial contracts. Recently there has been a change in approach, but basically what the court will try to do is to ascertain the intentions of the parties as demonstrated by the wording of the rent review clause. Lord Simon of Glaisdale, in *Wickman Tools Ltd* v *Schuler AG* [1974] AC 235 (quoting from *Norton on Deeds*), said: 'The question to be answered always is "What is the meaning of what the parties have said?" not "What did the parties mean to say?", it being a presumption, to rebut which no evidence is allowed, that the parties intended to say that which they have said'. The parties cannot give evidence of what their intention actually was, therefore reference to the parties' intentions is meant objectively and not subjectively, in that the court will try to establish the intention that reasonable people would have if placed in the particular situation and not the intentions of the actual parties (*Reardon Smith Line Ltd* v *Yngvar Hansen-Tangen* [1976] 1 WLR 989). In any event, rent review clauses are often being construed years after the lease was granted and after assignment by the original parties, so that the courts can consider only what was actually drafted as the original parties will not be involved in the process.

The process of construction mentioned above may not be appropriate in all cases. Rather than putting a question of construction to the court, it may be that one of the parties feels that a mistake was made which was incorporated in the lease. In such a case, the injured party could apply to the court for rectification (see 1.3 below).

3

1.2.2 Extrinsic evidence

The next issue is the question of extrinsic evidence and whether it can be used to prove the intentions of the parties. The traditional approach to extrinsic evidence is demonstrated in the case of *Prenn* v *Simmonds* [1971] 1 WLR 1381, where Lord Wilberforce stated:

> In my opinion, then, evidence of negotiations, or the parties' intentions, and *a fortiori* of [one party's] intentions, ought not to be received, and evidence should be restricted to evidence of the factual background known to the parties at or before the date of the contract, including evidence of the 'genesis' and objectively the 'aim' of the transaction.

Lord Wilberforce's reason for this approach was that to admit such evidence would not be helpful, as until a final agreement was reached the parties' positions would be changing. The factual background referred to by Lord Wilberforce in the *Prenn* case is also known as 'the matrix', as can be seen in *Basingstoke and Deane Borough Council* v *The Host Group Ltd* [1988] 1 WLR 348, at 353, where Nicholls LJ said:

> ... it is axiomatic that what the court is seeking to identify and declare is the intention of the parties to the lease expressed in that [rent review] clause. Thus, like all points of construction, the meaning of this rent review clause depends on the particular language used interpreted having regard to the context provided by the whole document and the matrix of the material surrounding circumstances.

Therefore, the traditional approach was that recourse to extrinsic evidence was allowed in limited circumstances as it was recognised that contracts were not construed in a vacuum. However, that traditional approach to extrinsic evidence was greatly extended in the more recent case of *Investors Compensation Scheme Ltd* v *West Bromwich Building Society* [1998] 1 All ER 98. There, Lord Hoffman said that 'Interpretation is the ascertainment of the meaning which the document would convey to a reasonable person having all the background knowledge which would reasonably have been available to the parties in the situation in which they were at the time of the contract'. The background knowledge he refers to includes absolutely anything which would have affected the way in which the language of the document would have been understood by a reasonable man, the only limitations being evidence of the parties' negotiations and knowledge that was not 'reasonably available to the parties'.

Lord Lloyd dissented on this, and early indications are that such a wide definition of surrounding circumstances does not meet with judicial approval. In *Scottish Power plc* v *Britoil Exploration Ltd, The Times*, 2 December 1997, Staughton LJ said that 'Such a wide definition of surrounding circumstances, background or matrix seemed likely to increase the cost [of litigation] to no very obvious advantage'. He then added a plea that surrounding circumstances should be confined to what the parties had in mind, and what was going on around then at the time when they were making the contract.

The issue of the parties' subsequent actions was not addressed in the *Investors* case and so the position remains that the subsequent actions of the parties will not be admissible as an aid to construction (*Wickman Tools Ltd* v *Schuler AG* [1974] AC 235).

1.2.3   One-off contracts

The courts tend to look at rent review clauses as one-offs, and therefore a decision interpreting one rent review clause is not used as direct authority for the interpretation of another similar but not identical clause. See *Equity & Law Life Assurance Society* v *Bodfield Ltd* [1987] 1 EGLR 124, 125, CA, where Dillon LJ said 'that to refer to authorities on other documents merely for the purpose of ascertaining the construction of a particular document is to be deplored as a wrong approach and likely to lead to confusion and error'. However, he did approve of certain guidelines laid down in *British Gas Corporation* v *Universities Superannuation Scheme Ltd* [1986] 1 WLR 398, which illustrated a more purposive approach to the construction of rent review clauses, but went on to say that 'however valuable guidelines are, the function of the court in each particular case is to construe the particular rent review clause which is in issue in the case'.

Given the sheer number of cases brought to the courts, some consistency in approach is definitely required. This appears to have been the view of the Court of Appeal in *St Martins Property Ltd* v *Citicorp Investment Bank Properties Ltd* [1998] EGCS 161, CA, where Aldous LJ referred to an earlier case and said that while it was not normally apposite to construe a clause of a lease by reference to a decision on construction of a clause in another lease which is not identical, in his view the case of *Lynnthorpe Enterprise Ltd* v *Sidney Smith (Chelsea) Ltd* [1990] 2 EGLR 131 did support his conclusion, and it would therefore be odd to construe the clause in the instant case differently to the clause in the *Lynnthorpe* case.

1.2.4 Purposive or commercial purpose approach

1.2.4.1 Introduction

The primary rule of construction is that if the meaning of the words is clear, the court will give effect to them unless there is a clear contrary intention. If this literal approach results in a meaning which is contrary to 'commercial common sense' then the courts have expressed a liking for the 'purposive' or 'commercial purpose' approach. When dealing with a commercial contract, Lord Diplock took a fairly robust line in *Antaios Compania Naviera SA* v *Salen Rederierna AB* [1985] AC 191, when he declared 'if detailed semantic and syntactical analysis of words in a commercial contract is going to lead to a conclusion that flouts business common sense, it must be made to yield to business common sense'. Nicholls J discussed the commercial purpose approach in the construction of rent review clauses in the Court of Appeal case of *Basingstoke & Deane* v *Host Group Ltd* [1988] 1 WLR 348, at 353, where he said:

> ... what the court is seeking to identify and declare is the intention of the parties to the lease expressed in that [rent review] clause. Thus, like all points of construction, the meaning of this rent review clause depends on the particular language used, interpreted having regard to the context provided by the whole document and the matrix of the material surrounding circumstances. We recognise, therefore, that the particular language used will always be of paramount importance. Nonetheless, it is proper and only sensible, when construing a rent review clause, to have in mind what is normally the commercial purpose of the clause.

1.2.4.2 The commercial purpose of a rent review clause

In following the commercial purpose approach, the court will have to determine what the common purpose of a rent review clause is. In the *Basingstoke* case (1.2.4.1 above), Nicholls J said that the purpose of a rent review clause was not in doubt; he then referred to Sir Nicolas Browne-Wilkinson's speech in *British Gas Corporation* v *Universities Superannuation Scheme Ltd* [1986] 1 WLR 398, at 401, when he said:

> There is really no dispute that the general purpose of a provision for rent review is to enable the landlord to obtain from time to time the market rental which the premises would command if let on the same terms on the open market at the review dates. The purpose is to reflect the changes in the value of money and real increases in the value of the property during a long term ... and not so as to confer on the landlord

a windfall benefit which he could never obtain on the market if he were actually letting the premises at the review date.

See 1.1 above.

1.2.4.3 The operation of the commercial purpose approach

There are many examples throughout this book of the operation by the courts of the commercial purpose approach to the construction of rent review clauses. One aspect of the rent review clause in particular illustrates the effective use of this approach. The aspect referred to is a common reference in a rent review clause, being that the amount of rent payable under the actual lease must be excluded when determining the reviewed rent. The basis of most rent review provisions is that the reviewed rent will be that which would be obtained on a hypothetical lease of the premises at the review date on the terms of the actual lease, other than rent. Landlords argued that the effect of using the words 'other than rent' was that the hypothetical lease had to exclude not only the rent but also the rent review provisions. This meant that higher rents would be achieved, as a lease without a rent review provision would be more valuable than one with such a clause. Initially the courts agreed with the landlords, and the controversial first decision on that was *Westminster Bank plc v Arthur Young McClelland Moores & Co.* [1985] 1 WLR 1123. Later cases followed the same line until the decision in *British Gas Corporation v Universities Superannuation Scheme Ltd* [1986] 1 WLR 398, which was approved by the Court of Appeal in *Equity & Law Life Assurance Society plc v Bodfield Ltd* [1987] 1 EGLR 124. The Court in the *British Gas* case took a purposive approach to the question when they said that to exclude all provisions as to rent produced a result so manifestly contrary to commercial common sense that it could not be given literal effect (see 3.8.1 for further discussion).

1.2.4.4 Limitations to the commercial purpose approach

There are limitations to the commercial purpose approach. The court, when faced with clear and unambiguous terms, must apply those terms even if the result is contrary to commercial sense. In *British Gas* (see 1.2.4.3 above), Sir Nicolas Browne-Wilkinson stated: 'Of course, the lease may be expressed in words so clear that there is no room for giving effect to such underlying purpose. Again, there may be special surrounding circumstances which indicate that the parties did intend to reach such an unusual bargain.' Similarly, in *MFI Properties Ltd v BICC Group Pension Trust Ltd* [1986] 1 EGLR 115, Hoffman J said that it was not disputed that the language of the parties must be construed in the context of the document as a whole and against the commercial background of the transaction. He went on to say:

> But there will also be cases in which the language used by the parties shows beyond doubt that they intended an assumption for which, to a third party who knows nothing of the negotiations, no commercial purpose can be discerned. In such circumstances the court has no option but to assume that it was a *quid pro quo* for some other concession in the course of negotiations. The court cannot reject it as absurd merely because it is counter-factual and has no outward commercial justification.

Clearly, the courts cannot re-write the language used by the parties in order to make the contract conform to business common sense (*Co-operative Wholesale Society Ltd* v *National Westminster Bank plc* [1995] 1 EGLR 97). In the *Co-operative* case Hoffman LJ went on to say that 'language is a very flexible instrument and, if it is capable of more than one construction one chooses that which seems most likely to give effect to the commercial purpose of the agreement'.

Notwithstanding what has just been said, the commercial purpose approach is not favoured by all, as is illustrated by the case of *The Melanesian Mission Trust Board* v *Australian Mutual Provident Society* [1996] NPC 188, where the court favoured the more traditional, literal approach when they said:

> The intention of the parties is to be discovered from the words used in the document. Where ordinary words have been used they must be taken to have been used according to the ordinary meaning of these words. If their meaning is clear and unambiguous, effect must be given to them because that is what the parties are taken to have agreed to be their contract. Various rules may be invoked to assist interpretation in the event that there is an ambiguity. But it is not the function of the court, when construing a document, to search for an ambiguity. Nor should the rules which exist to resolve ambiguities be invoked in order to create an ambiguity which, according to the ordinary meaning of the words, is not there. So the starting point is to examine the words used in order to see whether they are clear and unambiguous. It is of course legitimate to look at the document as a whole and to examine the context in which these words have been used, as the context may affect the meaning of the words. But unless the context shows that the ordinary meaning cannot be given to them or that there is an ambiguity, the ordinary meaning of the words which have been used in the document must prevail.

As can be seen from the above, the language of the document is still of paramount importance. Only if the language is unclear or ambiguous can recourse be made to the commercial purpose approach.

1.2.5 Presumption of reality

Tied into the purposive approach is an approach to construction based on reality. This presumption applies in the absence of clear, contrary words or necessary implication (*Co-operative Wholesale Society Ltd v National Westminster Bank plc* [1995] 1 EGLR 97). The presumption is that the hypothetical lease should be as similar to the actual lease as possible, as in *Norwich Union Life Assurance Society v Trustee Savings Banks Central Board* [1986] 1 EGLR 136, where Hoffman J said that 'there is . . . a presumption that the hypothesis on which the rent should be fixed at review should bear as close a resemblance to reality as possible'. This can be put in a different way, i.e. that the presumption of reality means that when a reviewed rent is being assessed on the basis of the hypothetical letting, the tenant should not pay for something he does not have (*Pearl Assurance v Shaw* [1985] 1 EGLR 92). A recent application of the presumption of reality can be seen in *St Martins Property Ltd v Citicorp Investment Bank Properties Ltd* [1998] EGCS 161, CA, where the point was made that this approach will be adopted only if and to the extent that the lease is ambiguous.

The presumption of reality does, of course, have its limitations, as the valuer will be bound by the lease to base his assessment of the reviewed rent on some assumptions and disregards which are contrary to reality (*MFI Properties Ltd v BICC Group Pension Trust Ltd* [1986] 1 EGLR 115). An example of such an assumption is that the tenant has complied with the repairing covenant in the lease (see 3.4.3.1). The effect of this is that if the tenant has not so complied, and this would affect the value of the rent in a detrimental way, then it will be ignored for rent review purposes. This is obviously fair, albeit that it does not reflect reality. An example of a disregard is a disregard of any improvements (see 3.13.4). In the absence of such a disregard the improvement paid for by the tenant would be rentalised, and thus the tenant would effectively pay twice, once for the actual improvements and then again through the increase in rent. Again, it is only fair that there is a departure from reality in that instance.

These general principles and approaches can be seen in operation in the case law referred to throughout this book.

1.3 RECTIFICATION OF RENT REVIEW CLAUSES

When mistakes are made in drafting rent review clauses, they are not usually noticed until the first rent review takes place. Rectification may be available where the lease does not reflect what the parties agreed. Rectification is an equitable remedy and therefore its availability is at the discretion of the court. While a full discussion of the remedy is beyond the scope of this book, a brief overview will be given.

The primary principle before rectification will be ordered is that there must be clear evidence of a mistake (*Lansdown Estates Group Ltd* v *TNT Roadfreight (UK) Ltd* [1989] 2 EGLR 120), and the mistake must generally be common to both parties. An illustration is *Boots The Chemist* v *Street* [1983] 2 EGLR 51, where the lease provided for reviews every seven years whereas there was evidence (from the travelling draft) that they should be held every five years. Also in *Equity & Law Life Assurance Society Ltd* v *Coltness Group Ltd* (1983) 267 EG 949, where rectification was granted where a memorandum recorded that the rent was agreed until the expiration of the lease, whereas it should have provided that it was agreed until the next review date. What is important to note is that rectification will not generally be available where the parties have agreed on a provision but have failed to realise its full implications and the clause then does not achieve what was intended.

Only exceptionally will rectification be available for unilateral mistake. If fraud is involved then it may be available. Otherwise, certain requirements have to be established before it will be available in such circumstances. These requirements were laid down in *A. Roberts & Co. Ltd* v *Leicestershire County Council* [1961] Ch 555 and approved by the court of Appeal in *Thomas Bates & Son Ltd* v *Wyndham's (Lingerie) Ltd* [1981] 1 WLR 505. The requirements are:

(a) that one party (A) erroneously believed that the document sought to be rectified contained a particular term or provision, or possibly did not contain a particular term or provision which, mistakenly, it did contain;

(b) that the other party (B) was aware of the omission or the inclusion and that it was due to a mistake on the part of A;

(c) that B has omitted to draw the mistake to the notice of A; and

(d) that the mistake must be one calculated to benefit B.

If these requirements are satisfied then the court may regard it as inequitable to allow B to resist rectification to give effect to A's intention on the ground that the mistake was not, at the time of execution of the document, a mutual mistake.

Review provisions were omitted entirely in the case of *Central & Metropolitan Estates Ltd* v *Compusave Ltd* [1983] 1 EGLR 60, although there was evidence that the parties had agreed to the inclusion of rent review provisions. Rectification was ordered as it would be against conscience to allow the lessee, which must have suppressed its knowledge of the lessor's mistake, to take advantage of the omission. In *Stavrides* v *Manku* [1997] EGCS 58, rectification was ordered where rent review dates had been omitted carelessly. *Kemp* v *Neptune Concrete* [1988] 2 EGLR 87, is an example of circumstances where rectification was not ordered. In that case the draft lease initially provided for a six-year term with a rent review after the third year. Later, in the course of negotiations, it was agreed that the term would be extended to 12 years, but a second review was not mentioned and was ultimately not included in the executed lease. When the landlord's solicitors realised the mistake, they asked the tenant to agree an amendment, which he refused to do, and so the issue eventually came before the Court of Appeal. The Court refused to rectify the lease because (*inter alia*) a 'mistake' had not been made by the landlord when executing the deed as there was no mistake in the actual drafting of the lease; the mistake was in the negotiations as the parties had at no time considered the question of adjusting the rent review provisions.

Under s. 63(1), LPA 1925, the right to have the lease rectified passes to successors in title (*Boots The Chemist* v *Street* (1983) 268 EG 817). However, rectification is not available against a purchaser for value without notice of the claim for rectification (*Smith* v *Jones* [1954] 2 All ER 823, an unregistered land case). The position in registered land is different. If the claimant is in occupation of the land or in receipt of the rents and profits and the claimant's interest in registered, the claim to rectify the lease may be an overriding interest which will bind a purchaser (*Blacklocks* v *JB Developments (Godalming) Ltd* [1982] Ch 183 and *Nurdin & Peacock plc* v *DB Ramsden & Co. Ltd* [1999] 1 EGLR 119).

CHAPTER TWO

Structures and Forms of Rent Review Clauses

2.1 INTRODUCTION

Generally, leases will stipulate that the tenant will pay an initial rent which will be reviewed after a certain period of time. The lease will then deal with the issue of how the reviewed rent is to be determined. It is obviously open to the parties to agree certain increases in advance, but the most common method of calculating the reviewed rent is based on property market rents. Other methods include rent assessed by reference to:

(a) a published index of prices. Under this method the rent is linked to an index chosen by the parties, and the rent will increase or decrease in line with that index and therefore it protects the parties from the effects of inflation;

(b) tenant's turnover. Here the tenant pays rent based upon the amount of turnover of the tenant's business;

(c) equity rents, where the tenant sublets the property and the landlord receives a percentage of the rents which the tenant receives from the subtenants;

(d) rent payable under a headlease, i.e. when a sublease is granted the parties will often link the rent to that payable under the headlease.

This book mainly considers the most common form of rent review, based on property market rentals, but chapter 6 discusses some alternative review methods.

2.2   CONTENT OF RENT REVIEW CLAUSES

Rent review clauses generally should deal with the following issues:

(a)   When will a review take place (including a consideration of whether a review has to take place, or not)?

(b)   How will the rent review process be initiated? (Will formal notice be required or is it automatic?)

(c)   Must the rent review be initiated by a certain time; and if it must not, will the landlord be entitled to review late?

(d)   If the parties fail to agree on a revised rent, will a third party determine the new rent; if so, how will he be appointed and on what basis will the revised rent be determined?

(e)   Subsequent to the third party's award, what steps are required to be taken?

Issues (a)–(c) are considered in this chapter; issue (d) is considered in chapters 3 and 4; and issue (e) is considered in chapter 5.

2.3   THE MAIN TYPES OF MARKET RENT REVIEW CLAUSES

When drafting a rent review clause based on market rents, the draftsman has to decide on the machinery for setting the review in motion. Previously, the approach favoured was for the landlord to notify the tenant in writing of the proposed new rent and the review would follow a timetable. That approach was known as the 'trigger notice' method. It became less popular over time due to the many instances where the timetable was not adhered to and the difficulties that then ensued. The approach that became and remains the most common is what is known as the 'automatic review' method, under which there is no set timetable to be followed and the parties simply have to agree on a new rent. Both of these approaches are considered below.

2.4   TRIGGER NOTICE TYPE OF REVIEW

It is not essential, but it is possible, to initiate a rent review by the service of a notice called a 'trigger notice'. Trigger notice type reviews were used in the past, but for practical purposes they are now obsolete. Where service of a notice is required, great care must be taken as this issue has been the subject of much litigation. The advantage of trigger notices is that they formally announce the commencement of the rent review process. The disadvantage is that they usually lay down a set timetable to be followed which can lead to dispute when delays occur and the clause fails to specify how such delays will affect the process. It is usually recommended that notices should be avoided, but as long as the clause specifies the effect of non-compliance with the specified timetable then it can successfully be used.

Rent review clauses based on trigger notices can take different forms. Some merely require one party to advise the other party that a review is desired. A more sophisticated form of notice is one which is usually given by the landlord and includes a proposed revised rent which the tenant will be deemed to accept unless it indicates to the contrary. From the tenant's point of view, the fact that only the landlord can start off the review machinery is not usually a problem, as leases generally have what are known as 'upwards only' review clauses and so the rent can only increase (or stay the same) and not decrease, and therefore it is in the landlord's interest to initiate the review if property values have increased. If they have not increased, the landlord will not initiate the process, but this will be of little concern to the tenant as the tenant could not gain anything from a review due to its upwards only nature (see 2.15 for a discussion of upwards/downwards reviews). However, if the review is upwards or downwards and rental values have fallen, the landlord may decide that it is not in his best financial interests to serve a notice. The tenant, on the other hand, will want a review he or she is likely to get a reduction in his or her rent.

During periods of economic growth, it would be hard to envisage a time when the landlord would not want to initiate a review; and accordingly, when many leases were drafted the parties or their advisers would not have considered the possibility that it might not be in the landlord's best interests to so act. However, the property recession in the 1990s resulted in both landlords and tenants looking very carefully at the rent review clause to see, first of all, if the clause was in fact upwards only or if it could be interpreted as working downwards and, secondly, if it could be assessed downwards, was the landlord obliged to initiate the process or could he simply continue to enjoy the financial benefits of the pre-recession rents? The first issue is discussed at 2.15 and the second issue was addressed by the Privy Council in *Sunflower Services Ltd* v *Unisys New Zealand Limited* [1997] NPC 21. In that case, the rent could be reviewed upwards or downwards and the relevant clause provided that 'the Lessor *may* give notice in writing to the Lessee setting out the amount which the

Lessor considers to be the full current market annual rent of the Premises'. The facts were that the rent would decrease on review, and therefore the landlord refused to serve a notice to trigger the review provisions despite being requested to do so by the tenant. It was held that none of the provisions obliged the landlord to trigger the review and that the tenant could not force him to do so. By way of contrast, in the case of *Addin* v *Secretary of State for the Environment* [1997] 14 EG 132, the landlord refused to send a trigger notice as the rent under the lease could be (and was likely to be) assessed downwards. The court, adopting the commercial purpose approach (see 1.2.4), held that the rent was to be reviewed as the lease stated that the yearly rent '*shall*' be the higher of £148,500 or such sum as shall be assessed as the current open market rent, which contemplated that there would be an assessment. As ever, each case will be determined on the basis of the actual wording of the clause.

Even if there is an automatic review (see 2.13), the landlord may be able to frustrate the rent review process by refusing to do something that is essential for the process to work, such as refusing to refer the matter to a third party for determination (see 4.1). An example (taken from the *Encyclopaedia of Forms and Precedents*) of a modern form of a rent review clause with a review triggered by notice is given in Appendix 1, but below is an example of the part of that clause dealing with the trigger notice.

Example 1
Example of part of a rent review clause dealing with a trigger notice

The Rent for any review period is to be either—

1   the Rent specified in a notice given by the Landlord to the Tenant at any time [not earlier than 6 months before the review date to which it relates] ('a review notice'), or
2   the Rent agreed between the parties in writing within 3 months after the date of service of a review notice in substitution for the sum specified in that review notice, or
3   at the election of the Tenant made in a written counternotice served on the landlord within 3 months after the date of service of a review notice, the Rent determined by an arbitrator.

Time is to be of the essence in relation to all stipulations as to time in this paragraph.

Notes:
Paragraph 1: The reference to the notice being served 'not earlier than 6 months before the review' can be included if the landlord so desires, but the landlord must ensure that the notice does not go too early (i.e. before the six-month period begins). There is no reference to the notice having to be served by a particular time (e.g., 'not later than 3 months from the review date') and therefore if the words in brackets are excluded the landlord has no time restrictions and cannot inadvertently lose his right to review. Where there are time restrictions and these are missed, this can lead to the landlord being unable to review at that review date (see 2.10 and 2.11).
Paragraph 2: The parties have three months after the review to agree a revised rent.
Paragraph 3: If the tenant does not accept the landlord's proposal for the reviewed rent then the tenant can elect to have the question decided by an arbitrator, but must do this within three months of the landlord's notice. The final sentence of the clause states that time is of the essence; the full effect of this statement is discussed below (see 2.11), but basically in the context of this paragraph what it means is that if the time limit is missed then the tenant will not be able to serve a late counternotice and will have to accept the rent stipulated in the landlord's notice.

As an alternative to the above, the clause can require the tenant to serve a counternotice specifying a reviewed rent if the landlord's rent is unacceptable. An example of such a clause follows:

Example 2
Example of part of a rent review clause requiring the service of a counternotice

The Landlord may at any time (without being under obligation so to do) within the period of twelve months before or after any of the review dates serve on the Tenant a notice in writing (hereinafter called 'a Rent Notice') specifying an increase of the rent payable hereunder from the relevant review date to an amount specified in a Rent Notice and thereupon the following provisions shall have effect:

(1) The Tenant within 28 days after the receipt of a Rent Notice may serve on the Landlord a counternotice specifying the rent which the tenant is willing to pay from the relevant review date and calling upon the Landlord to negotiate with the Tenant the amount of rent to be paid hereunder as from the relevant review date.

(2) If the Tenant shall fail to serve a counternotice within the said twenty-eight days he shall be deemed to have agreed to pay the increased rent specified in the Rent Notice as from the relevant review date.

(3) If the Tenant shall serve a counternotice then the Landlord and the Tenant shall forthwith consult together and use their best endeavours to reach agreement as to the amount of the rent to be paid hereunder as from the relevant review date but failing agreement within fifty-six days after the service of such counternotice (or within such extended period as the Landlord and the Tenant shall mutually agree) the question of whether any and if so what increased rent should be payable hereunder shall be referred to the arbitration of a single arbitrator in the manner hereinafter mentioned.

Note
This clause was taken from the case of *Patel* v *Earlspring Properties* [1991] 2 EGLR 131, CA (see 2.5 and 2.7 below).

2.5 FORM OF TRIGGER NOTICE

2.5.1 General

Most leases will provide that the notice must be in writing, and it was stated *obiter* by Lord Russell in *Dean and Chapter of Chichester Cathedral* v *Lennards Ltd* (1977) 35 P & CR 309 that where the lease did so provide then a written notice would be essential if the notice was to be valid. Similarly, it was held in *Museprime* v *Adhill Properties Ltd* [1990] 2 EGLR 196, that an oral counternotice was ineffective where there was a requirement that it be in writing.

Some leases will specify the form the trigger notice is to take, in which case it will be good practice to follow that prescribed form. It may not prove fatal to the validity of the notice, however, if the notice is not in the prescribed form as the court may hold that the provision is not of the essence of the contract in that it is not mandatory but directory. A mandatory provision is one which must be fulfilled in all its strictness, and failure to perform it means that the whole thing fails. A directory provision does not require that degree of strictness; even though it is not complied with, the whole does not fail; it could still be regarded as valid and effective (*Dean and Chapter of Chichester Cathedral* v *Lennards Ltd*).

2.5.2   Test for validity of notices

The general test for the validity of notices is whether the notice makes it clear that the server wishes to activate the rent review process. Put in a slightly different way, the test applied by the courts when determining whether any notice is ineffective is whether the reasonable recipient is in any reasonable doubt as to the effect of the notice (*Mannai Investment Co. Ltd* v *Eagle Star Life Assurance Co. Ltd* [1997] AC 749).

2.5.3   Typographical errors

A mere typographical error will not invalidate a notice. See *Durham City Estates* v *Felicitti* [1990] 1 EGLR 143, CA, where the first notice specified the wrong review date and a certain sum as the new rent. The second notice had the same sum in words as the first notice, but an incorrect sum expressed in figures. The court held that the notice was valid as the test was whether the tenant would be misled as to what figure was required by the landlord, and on receiving the second notice the tenants would have assumed correctly that the sum stated in figures contained a typographical error and that the sum stated in words was the intended figure. On a similar point, in *Fox & Widley* v *Guram and another* [1998] 03 EG 142, the rent review date was incorrect but it was held that the misstating of the rent review date was plainly a typographical error which misled nobody.

2.5.4   Requirement to propose a new rent

If the trigger notice is required to propose a new rent but fails to do so, this will not automatically invalidate the notice (see *Dean and Chapter of*

Chichester Cathedral v *Lennards Ltd* (1977) 35 P & CR 309, where the court stated that the notice should not be held invalid simply because of the omission of one bit of machinery, their view being that the inclusion of the proposed rent was a directory provision and not of the essence of the contract). However, in *Commission for the New Towns* v *Levy & Co.* [1990] 2 EGLR 121, the requirement in the rent review provisions that the proposed rent be specified was held to be mandatory and the failure to specify the proposed rent resulted in the notice being invalid. The judge distinguished the *Chichester Cathedral* case on a number of issues, but in particular held that the provision in the rent review clause which stated that the notice 'shall specify the yearly rent' contrasted with the much less forceful clause in the *Chichester Cathedral* case, which merely stated 'upon either party giving to the other at least 3 months' written notice . . .'.

Whether the approach adopted in the *Levy* case is the correct one is perhaps less clear after the decision in *Patel* v *Earlspring* [1991] 2 EGLR 131, CA, which concerned a counternotice rather than a trigger notice. In *Patel*, the tenant's counternotice did not specify a rent when the rent review clause provided 'the Tenants within twenty-eight days after the receipt of a Rent Notice may serve on the landlord a counternotice specifying the rent which the Tenant is willing to pay . . .'. The landlords, relying on the *Chichester Cathedral* case, claimed that the notice was invalid as the provision requiring the rent to be specified was a mandatory provision. However, Woolf LJ said: 'That case does not appear to me to be in any way relevant to the facts of this case. What is required to be in a rent notice which starts the machinery running is not necessarily the same thing which is required in a counternotice.' That being the case, he did not feel it was appropriate to comment either one way or the other as to the correctness of the decision in that case. He also made the point that it is dangerous to try to apply one authority given in relation to a different rent review clause in different circumstances to another situation. Woolf LJ went on to hold that the counternotice was valid as the clause in this case was not mandatory, and what was done by the tenant was clearly sufficient to indicate that he was not prepared to accept the rent proposed by the landlords.

Thus a provision that the notice should specify a rent is likely to be mandatory if the rent review machinery cannot be operated without a figure being specified. So, where the rent review provisions are of the type whereby the landlord serves a notice specifying a rent and the tenant, if he rejects that figure, then has to serve a counternotice objecting to that figure and electing for the matter to be determined by an arbitrator, and if no counternotice is served, the landlord's proposal will be accepted; then if no rent is specified the rent review cannot operate. However, if the rent review is not of that type and can operate without the figure being specified (as in the *Chichester Cathedral* case) then it will not matter whether the figure is specified or not. The rent review provisions in the *Levy* case were not of the former type, but the court nevertheless held that the notice was invalid because of the clear wording of the clause. Therefore, ultimately, whether such a requirement is of the essence of a particular lease will depend on the construction of that particular lease.

2.5.5 Must rent be reasonable?

Where the rent review clause requires the landlord to specify a rent in the notice, there is no requirement that the rent stipulated in the notice be reasonable (*Amalgamated Estates v Joystretch Manufacturing* [1981] 1 EGLR 96; *Davstone (Holdings) Ltd v Al-Rifan* (1976) 32 P & CR 18; and, more recently, *Fox & Widley v Guram and another* [1998] 03 EG 142, where the court confirmed that landlords were entitled to propose such rent under the lease as they liked and there was nothing in the lease that would result in an implied term that the figure specified must be a bona fide and genuine pre-estimate of the rent). Often for tactical reasons the proposed rent will be higher than the actual market value, but a careless tenant could find that he is bound to accept it if there is a requirement to serve a counternotice and he fails to do so. Some rent review provisions may provide that the proposed rent be a figure which 'in the opinion' of the landlord is the open market rent. The question may then arise as to whether the figure reflects the genuine opinion of the landlord; and if it does not then the notice may be invalid as it could be argued that there was a false or fraudulent misrepresentation. This was mentioned in *Davstone (Holdings) Ltd v Al-Rifan* (above) but the point was left open. To avoid any potential claim of fraudulent misrepresentation the landlord should base his proposal on the advice of its surveyor, who should have based his proposal on evidence of comparable properties. The surveyor may, of course, be proved to be wrong in his estimation, but that in itself would not make the notice invalid in the absence of fraud. If the notice contains a figure which the tenant then accepts, the landlord cannot then alter the figure unless he can set the agreement aside on other grounds (*Centrovincial Estates plc v Merchant Investors Assurance Co.* [1983] Com LR 158).

2.5.6 Use of 'subject to contract' and 'without prejudice'

Care must be taken when drafting the trigger notice to avoid the potential invalidity of notices which employ the phrases 'subject to contract' and 'without prejudice', the use of which could lead the recipient to believe that the letter was merely a preliminary to review and not an actual notice. These phrases have become so commonplace that they are often included without any thought as to their effect, or indeed relevance. In *Shirlcar Properties Ltd v Heinitz* [1983] 2 EGLR 120, CA, the notice was held to be ineffective. In that case the rent review clause provided that the rent was to be the open market rent and was to be determined as follows:

(a) specified in a notice in writing signed by or on behalf of the Lessors and posted by recorded delivery post in a prepaid envelope addressed to the Tenant at the demised premises at any time before the beginning of a clear period of two quarter days . . . immediately preceding the review date . . .

(b) agreed between the parties before the expiration of three months immediately after the posting by recorded delivery of such notice in substitution for such sum or

(c) determined at the election of the tenant (to be a counternotice in writing served by the tenant upon the Lessors not later than the expiration of the said three months) by an independent surveyor appointed by the parties jointly . . .

A letter was prepared by the landlord's agents which stated:

. . . We act on behalf of your landlords, Shirlcar Properties Ltd, and have been instructed to deal with the rent review on the above premises due as at the 29 September 1981. The rent required as from the review date is £6,000 pa exclusive, and we look forward to receiving your agreement.

Below the agent's signature were the words 'subject to contract'. It was held that it was not an effective notice as it could not be said that the tenants, on receiving the letter, would necessarily and reasonably have inferred that it was an effective trigger notice. A tenant on receiving the letter would be left in doubt as to whether the figure given was a firm figure specified under the rent review clause, or was merely being put forward as a provisional figure which the landlord could revise if agreement was not reached. Due to the doubt about its meaning, the letter was held to be ineffective. The notice would have been effective if the words 'subject to contract' had been omitted.

The phrase 'without prejudice' has also been held to invalidate a notice (*Norwich Union Life Insurance Society v Tony Waller* [1984] 1 EGLR 126). However, and perhaps exceptionally, it has been held that the use of both 'subject to contract' and 'without prejudice' did not invalidate a notice (*Royal Life Insurance* v *Phillips* [1990] 2 EGLR 135) as the judge stated that in this particular situation a reasonably minded recipient would appreciate that it was a notice activating a rent review. In that case the tenant had so appreciated and had sent a counternotice, the invalidity issue being raised only after the tenant had sought professional advice. All uncertainty can be avoided by not using those phrases.

2.5.7 Misleading correspondence

The parties and their agents must also be careful not to inadvertently send correspondence that could be treated as being a trigger notice. In *Norwich Union Life Insurance Society* v *Sketchley plc* [1986] 2 EGLR 126, the rent review clause provided:

> (a)   The Landlord shall be entitled by notice in writing given to the Tenant at any one time after the commencement of the fourteenth year of the term hereby granted to call for review of the initial market rent ... and if upon any such review it shall be found that the then current market rent ... is greater than the initial market rent then ... the initial market rent shall be increased to the then current market rent ... (c) Such revision shall in the first instance be made by the Landlord and the Tenant or their respective surveyors in collaboration but if no agreement as to the amount of the then current market rent at the review date shall have been reached between the parties hereto or their surveyors within three months after the date of the Landlord's notice ... the question as to the then current market rent of the premises at the appropriate date and as to whether there shall be any increase in the rent ... and if so what the amount of the increased yearly rent shall be shall if the Landlord shall so require by notice in writing given to the Tenant within three months thereafter but not otherwise be referred ... to a surveyor ... and his determination will be final and binding on the parties.

A letter from a surveyor was sent to the tenant, which stated:

> We have been instructed by your landlords, Norwich Union Insurance Group, to negotiate with you in connection with the rent review contained in your lease which becomes effective as at September 29 1982. It is our client's proposal to increase the rental to £11,500 per annum exclusive with effect from this date. We look forward to hearing from you at your earliest convenience that this increase is acceptable to you.

The argument put forward by the landlord was that the letter was only inviting the tenant to negotiate, it was not invoking the rent review provisions. That argument was rejected by Scott J, as the rent review clause required the parties to negotiate. It was held to be a valid notice as the test for deciding whether it was a valid notice was satisfied, being whether a tenant reading it would think that it was intended to set in motion the rent review procedures. Time was of the essence in this case, and the landlord failed to comply with the time limit to refer the matter to a surveyor for determination and therefore lost its chance to revise the rent.

The decision in this case has to be contrasted with the earlier decision in *Norwich Union Life Insurance Society* v *Tony Waller* [1984] 1 EGLR 126 (see 2.5.6). The plaintiff in both cases is clearly the same, and the leases were on much the same terms and related to a parade of shops. In the *Tony Waller* case, Harman J held that a letter headed 'without prejudice' but otherwise in virtually the same form as the letter sent in the *Sketchley* case, was not an effective notice. The distinguishing feature of the two cases is the absence of the words 'without prejudice' in the *Sketchley* case. The judge in the *Sketchley* case was also referred to *Shirlcar Properties Ltd* v *Heinitz* [1983] 2 EGLR 120, CA (see 2.5.6), where Lawton J said:

Since there is an argument both ways about this matter and as, in my judgement, it is an argument which is reasonable on both sides, it seems to me that it cannot be said that the tenants, on receiving this letter, would necessarily and reasonably have inferred that it was an effective trigger notice for the purpose of the lease. There is doubt about its meaning and as there is a doubt it seems to me that the letter was ineffective for the purposes of the rent review clause in the lease.

In response to that the judge said that he accepted that where a notice from one party will require action from the other party, i.e., the recipient of the notice, in order that the latter may protect his position the document which is said to constitute notice must be sufficiently clear in its terms as to avoid the recipient being led into an error as to its intended effect. However, he did not see why so strict an approach is necessary where it is the author of the notice, not the recipient, who is going to have to take action consequent upon the notice to protect his rights. The letter in this case was in his judgment an effective notice. He went on to say that whether, if it had been a notice requiring action to be taken by the recipient tenant to protect his rights, it would have been sufficiently clear in its terms to constitute an effective notice, was another matter and would raise different considerations.

Example 3
Example of a trigger notice

To: (*name of tenant*)
of   (*address*)

Lease made on (*date*) between (1) (*name of original landlord*) and (2) (*name of original tenant*) ('the Lease') of (*describe premises*) ('the Premises')

I, (*name of current landlord*), the [current] landlord of the Premises, GIVE YOU NOTICE under (*number of appropriate provision of the lease*) of the Lease that I wish the rent payable under the Lease to be reviewed in accordance with (*number of appropriate provision of the lease*) of the Lease [as at (insert rent review date under the lease)] [and in accordance with (*number of appropriate provision of the lease*) of the Lease, I SPECIFY a reviewed rent of £ ... per year [exclusive of VAT]]

Dated: Signed:
                                   (*signature of, or on behalf of, the landlord*)

(*on duplicate*)

Received a notice of which the above is a true copy

Dated: Signed:
                                    (*signature of, or on behalf of, the tenant*)

Note
This type of trigger notice includes a provision specifying the reviewed rent; if the lease does not require the reviewed rent to be specified then this is not necessary.

2.6   EFFECT OF AN INVALID TRIGGER NOTICE

Clearly, if an invalid trigger notice is served the landlord will generally want a valid notice to be served. The question then to be addressed is whether this is possible. If time is of the essence in relation to serving the trigger notice then it will not be possible to serve another notice outside the specified time frame and the landlord will have lost his ability to review the rent at that review date (see 2.10 and 2.11 below for a discussion of time being of the essence). However, if time is not of the essence, generally another notice can be served (see 2.12 below for a discussion of delay when time is not of the essence).

2.7 COUNTERNOTICES

2.7.1 Introduction

After receipt of the trigger notice, some rent review clauses require the recipient, who is usually the tenant, to serve a counternotice within a set period of time specifying the rent which the tenant is willing to pay if he or she does not agree with the rent suggested by the landlord; others require the tenant to elect to have the rent determined by a third party (see the examples in 2.4 above). The former type of clause can be very dangerous for a tenant, who may be forced to accept a high rent simply because he or she failed to realise the significance of the trigger notice and did not serve a counternotice within the stipulated time limit. Where time is of the essence, the tenant will be unable to serve a late counternotice and will have to accept the figure suggested by the landlord, irrespective of its reasonableness or otherwise.

Accordingly, when acting for a tenant, it is imperative that any reference to time being of the essence in relation to service of a counternotice should be deleted. If agreement cannot be reached on this and the tenant is forced to accept such a term, its significance must be clearly explained to the tenant, in writing, and the tenant should insist that any disagreement about the rent should be determined by an arbitrator rather than by an expert as the court can extend the time for service of counternotices under the Arbitration Act 1996 (see 2.11).

2.7.2 Form of counternotices

2.7.2.1 General

The lease may prescribe a particular form that the counternotice is to take. It may require the tenant to stipulate that the tenant does not agree with the landlord's suggested rent, or it may require the tenant to elect to have the rent determined by an independent third party. If the former is required then very little is needed for there to be a valid counternotice. In *Barrett Estate Services* v *David Greig (Retail)* [1991] 2 EGLR 123, a statement by the tenant that he considered the landlord's proposal 'to be excessive' was held to be sufficient.

2.7.2.2 Counternotice specifying rent

Some leases may require the tenant to specify in the counternotice the rent which he or she would be willing to pay. In *Patel* v *Earlspring Properties* [1991] 2 EGLR 131, CA, in response to a letter from the landlord proposing a new rent, the tenant replied by letter and asked the landlord to reconsider the new rent. The lease provided that the tenant 'may' serve a notice specifying the rent which the tenant was willing to pay and it was thus held that the tenant's letter was a valid counternotice under the lease. The court said that the decision in *Commission for the New Towns v Levy & Co.* [1990] 2 EGLR 121 did not apply (see 2.5.4). In *Patel* it was said that 'What is required in a rent notice which starts the machinery running is not necessarily the same thing which is required in a counternotice.' In the *Patel* case there was no mandatory requirement to specify the counter rent as long as the letter indicated that the tenant was not prepared to accept the proposed rent.

2.7.2.3 *Counternotice electing for a third party determination*

The counternotice may require the tenant to elect for a third party determination. In such cases the test for a valid counternotice was laid down in *Amalgamated Estates v Joystretch Manufacturing* [1981] 1 EGLR 96, CA, where it was stated that 'the tenant must make it clear to the landlord that he proposed to have the rent decided by arbitration in accordance with the provisions of the lease'. In a number of cases the courts have had to consider whether a letter simply objecting to the landlord's proposed rent could be considered as being a counternotice electing to have the rent determined by a third party. Such letters clearly did not meet the test laid down in the *Joystretch* case and early case law held them not to be valid counternotices (see *Edlingham v MFI Furniture Centres* [1981] 2 EGLR 97, applied the *Joystretch* test but added that the notice must be unequivocal). In *Edlingham*, the tenants unsuccessfully claimed that they had sent a valid counternotice as they had written to the landlord in response to the landlord's trigger notice and their letter had said: 'Will you please accept this letter as counternotice to the effect that we consider that the rent of £50,000 is excessive and will appreciate it if you will kindly forward to us comparables on which you based this figure.' The court held that there was nothing in the letter to indicate that the tenants wanted to go to arbitration. The landlord was left without any clear indication as to what the tenants wanted to do. Later decisions held the test was not whether the notice was 'unequivocal' but whether it was 'clear', and this now seems to be the preferred test (*Nunes v Davies Laing Dick* (1985) 51 P & CR 310). In *Nunes*, the tenant's agent wrote: 'I am instructed by the tenants to give you hereby formal notice that the open market rental is £12,000 per annum and call on you under the terms of the above Lease to agree this. Please confirm that this is accepted as good notice.' This was held to be a valid notice despite there being no direct reference to electing for a third party determination. The judge referred to the fact that the letter had been headed up 'In the matter of the Rent Review' and described itself as a 'formal notice' and asked for confirmation that it was 'due notice'. The judge went on to say that therefore, it must have been clear to anyone receiving the letter that the tenant's agent was giving formal notice. The judge rejected the *Edlingham* test that the notice must be unequivocal. In *Glofield Properties Ltd v Morley* [1988] 1 EGLR 113, the letter was described as a 'formal objection and counternotice' and was held to be a valid counternotice.

The later case law seems more willing to make notices valid as long as it is clear what they are trying to achieve. It must be remembered, however, that it is of limited use to consider previous decisions of the court in other cases of construction as they are not binding in a later case. (See *Prudential Property Holdings v Capital Land Holding* [1993] 1 EGLR 128, where it was stated by Colyer QC that 'precedent is not wholly compelling or conclusive, although it may provide illustration or inspiration for arguments as to the instruction and effect of leases' (see also 1.2.3). However, he did go on to adopt the approach taken in *Oldschool v Johns* (1980) 256 EG 381, which he said was looked upon with approval in the *Joystretch* case, being that in order to be a counternotice the document must either state that it is a counternotice under the relevant clause, or it must state clearly that the tenant is exercising his election to have the rent fixed independently.)

2.7.2.4 Use of 'subject to contract'

As with notices (see 2.5.6), it is better practice to avoid the use of the phrase 'subject to contract' as it may lead to the invalidity of the counternotice. This was what happened in *Sheridan v Blaircourt Investments* [1984] 1 EGLR 139, where a letter from the tenants was headed up 'without prejudice and subject to contract' and was held to be invalid. In *Sheridan*, the tenant was required to serve a counternotice electing to have the matter determined by a third party, and the court felt that the letter from the tenant was wholly insufficient to alert the landlord to the fact that the tenant wished to exercise his right of election. The judge said that even if the letter had been adequate in itself, the heading would have made it inadequate. However, by way of contrast, in *British Rail Pension Trustee Co. v Cardshops* [1987] 1 EGLR 127, a letter headed 'subject to contract' which stated that the parties were prepared to agree a rent of £24,000, was held to be a valid counternotice. The landlords, relying on the *Sheridan* case (above) and the *Shirlcar* case (2.5.6 above), claimed that the counternotice was invalid. The judge, referring to *Sheridan*, pointed out that this case did not involve an election for determination by a third party but simply required the tenant to state the amount which was, in the tenant's opinion, the market rent; and, referring to *Shirlcar*, said the clause in this case did not trigger a rent review. The counternotice in this case simply started a period during which the parties were required to enter into negotiations, and if they failed to agree then there was a reference to a referee. It was said that the heading could be explained either as a mistake, or as intended to ensure that the letter was not taken as an offer capable of acceptance.

As can be seen from the case law, it is difficult to say for certain what effect the use of 'subject to contract' will have — much will depend on the wording of the lease.

Simple mistakes can be easily avoided by referring back to the lease and ensuring that the counternotice does reflect its requirements. Clients should be advised to seek professional help in drafting a counternotice to avoid the danger of invalidity.

Example 4
Example of a counternotice electing for third party determination

To: (*name of landlord*)
of: (*address*)

Lease made on (*date*) between (1) (*name of (original) landlord*) and (2) (*name of (original) tenant*) ('the Lease') of (*describe premises*) ('the Premises')

I, (*name of current tenant*), (the [current] tenant of the Premises), GIVE YOU NOTICE that I [elect (or where the lease does not use the term 'elect' require)], in accordance with (*number of appropriate provision of the lease*) of the Lease, that the reviewed rent [payable from (*rent review date*)] under the Lease is to be determined by an [arbitrator (*or as required*) expert].

Dated: Signed:
                                             (*signature of, or on behalf of, the tenant*)

(*on duplicate*)
Received a notice of which the above is a true copy.

Dated: Signed:
                                             (*signature of, or on behalf of, the landlord*)

Example 5
Example of a counternotice specifying a rent

To: (*name of landlord*)
of: (*address*)

Lease made on (*date*) between (1) (*name of (original) landlord*) and (2) (*name of (original) tenant*) ('the Lease') of (*describe premises*) ('the Premises')

I, (*name of current tenant*), (the [current] tenant of the Premises), GIVE YOU NOTICE in accordance with (*number of appropriate provision of the lease*) of the Lease that I am willing to pay as the reviewed rent under the Lease the sum of £(. . .) per year [exclusive of VAT].

Dated: Signed:
                                        (*signature of, or on behalf of, the tenant*)

(*on duplicate*)
Received a notice of which the above is a true copy.

Dated: Signed:
                                        (*signature of, or on behalf of, the landlord*)

2.8   EFFECT OF AN INVALID COUNTERNOTICE

A counternotice may be invalid because it is not served within the time limit specified in the lease, or because it does not contain the provisions required by the lease. Often mistakes occur because the tenant itself serves the counternotice rather than seeking legal advice. The effect of such failure largely depends on whether time was of the essence of the service of the notice. If time was not of the essence then the tenant can simply serve another notice, but this will not generally be the case where time is of the essence. See 2.10 and 2.11 below.

2.9   SERVICE OF TRIGGER AND COUNTERNOTICES

2.9.1   General

The terms of the lease usually specify the method for service of notices, with the provisions of s. 196, LPA 1925 often being expressly incorporated into the lease. Section 196 of the 1925 Act contains presumptions that apply to notices to confirm when they will be treated as having been sufficiently served. It provides:

(1)   Any notice required or authorised to be served or given by this Act shall be in writing.

(2)   Any notice required or authorised by this Act to be served on a lessee or mortgagor shall be sufficient, although only addressed to the lessee or mortgagor by that designation, without his name, or generally to the persons interested, without any name, and notwithstanding that any person to be affected by the notice is absent, under disability, unborn, or unascertained.

(3)   Any notice required or authorised by this Act to be served shall be sufficiently served if left at the last-known place of abode or business in the United Kingdom of the lessee, lessor, mortgagee, or other person to be served, or, in case of a notice required or authorised to be served on a lessee or mortgagor, is affixed or left for him on the land or any house or building comprised in the lease or mortgage, or, in case of mining lease, is left for the lessee at the office or counting-house of the mine.

(4)   Any notice required or authorised by this Act to be served shall also be sufficiently served, if it is sent by post in a registered letter [or by recorded delivery] addressed to the lessee, lessor, mortgagee, mortgagor, or other person to be served, by name, at the aforesaid place of abode or business, office, or counting-house, and if that letter is not returned through the post-office undelivered; and that service shall be deemed to be made at the time at which the registered letter would in the ordinary course be delivered.

(5)   The provisions of this section shall extend to notices required to be served by any instrument affecting property executed or coming into operation after the commencement of this Act unless a contrary intention appears.

The words in square brackets in s. 196(4) were added by the Recorded Delivery Service Act 1962.

2.9.2   Section 196(3), LPA 1925

Under s. 196(3), a notice will be sufficiently served if left at the last-known place of abode or business in the United Kingdom; or under s. 196(4) a notice will be sufficiently served, if it is sent by registered post or recorded delivery post addressed to the relevant party, at the place of abode or business and if that letter is not returned undelivered. If a notice is sent by ordinary post it will not comply with s. 196(4), but if it is received then it will be sufficiently served under s. 196(3) (see *Stylo Shoes Ltd v Prices Tailors Ltd* [1959] 3 All ER 901, where s. 23(1) of the Landlord and Tenant Act 1927 was considered, the provisions of which are similar to s. 196).

In *Kinch v Bullard* [1998] 4 All ER 650, the provisions of s. 196(3), LPA 1925 were considered. In that case a notice had been sent by first class post addressed to the relevant party and delivered to their address. The court held that the natural meaning of s. 196(3) was that if a notice could be shown to have been left at the last-known abode or place of business of the addressee, that constituted good service, even if the addressee did not actually receive it.

2.9.3   Section 196(4), LPA 1925

Under s. 196(4), service is deemed to be made at the time when the registered letter or recorded delivery letter would be delivered in the ordinary course; and if delivery is to business premises then it will have to be on a normal working day to ensure that someone can sign for it. See *Stephenson & Son v Orca Properties Ltd* [1989] 2 EGLR 129, where delivery was attempted on a Friday but no one was there to sign for it. When delivery was eventually made on the Monday, it was too late and the notice was ineffective.

In *Midland Oak Construction Ltd v BBA Group Ltd*, (unreported) February 1983, CA, the provisions of s. 196 were expressly incorporated but the rent review clause also stated that service was to be by recorded delivery post addressed to the tenant at its registered office. The notice was delivered by hand to the premises. The Court of Appeal held it to be effective as the lease provision was overriden by the express incorporation of s. 196. It appears from the case law that the vital issue is whether the notice was in fact delivered and actually received; if it was then the notice is likely to be effective as that is the whole purpose of notice provisions.

2.9.4   Implied incorporation of s. 196, LPA 1925

If s. 196 is not expressly incorporated in the lease, can it be impliedly incorporated? Section 196(5) provides:

> (5)   The provisions of this section shall extend to notices required to be served by any instrument affecting property executed or coming into operation after the commencement of this Act unless a contrary intention appears.

A lease is clearly 'an instrument affecting property', but it is arguable whether a notice under a rent review is 'required' to be served. The other provisions in s. 196 refer to notices 'required or authorised' to be served by the Act. While there is no authority on the point, and strictly speaking rent review notices are not notices required to be served in the sense that there is no obligation to serve them, they are required to be served in the sense that the parties intended such notices to be served. In *Davstone Holdings Ltd v Al Rifai* (1976) 32 P & CR 18, at 28, it was accepted that s. 196 did apply to rent review notices. However, this is not entirely settled, and therefore if the parties wish to be sure that s. 196 applies then it should be expressly incorporated.

2.9.5   Where s. 196 is not incorporated

Where s. 196 does not apply there are no special rules relating to the service of notices under a rent review clause. The general law will therefore apply, with the basic principle being that giving a notice means causing a notice to be received (*Sun Alliance & London Assurance Co. Ltd v Hayman* [1975] 1 WLR 177). It will be a question of construction of the lease terms whether a notice has been properly served. Whether the method of service specified in the lease is mandatory (in that the notice will not be valid if it is not followed), or permissive (in that the notice will still be valid even if the lease provisions are not followed) will also be a question of construction. A provision which states that notices 'may' be served in a certain way is more likely to be considered permissive than a provision that states that notice 'shall' be served in a certain way. Having said that, in *Midland Oak Construction Ltd v BBA Group Ltd*, (unreported) February 1983, CA, the rent review provision stated '... it shall be such annual sum as shall be (a) specified by notice in writing signed by or on behalf of the lessor and posted by recorded delivery post' and paragraph (a) was held to be permissive. It is probably best to draft non-mandatory methods of service in case one form of notice proves ineffective, so that the alternative method(s) could be used.

2.9.6   Validity of notices

Notices should be addressed to the correct person and served on him. Care must therefore be taken when dealing with companies to ensure that the company and not a subsidiary or associated company is served. In *Midland Oak Construction Limited v BBA Group Ltd* (above), the notice was served on a subsidiary of the tenant who was in occupation of the premises, and it was held that this was not acceptable as there was not sufficient evidence to show that the subsidiary company had been authorised to accept the notice on behalf of the tenant. If there was sufficient evidence of authority then the position would be different. If a notice is addressed to the directors of a company, it will be valid if it is clear that it is a notice to the company (*Hawtrey* v *Beaufront Ltd* [1946] KB 280).

If a notice is to be served on an agent or a solicitor then this should be expressly provided for to ensure the validity of the notice. The agent must have authority to accept service. If an agent serves a notice then again the agent must have the authority to do so. In *Cordon Bleu Freezer Food Centres* v *Marbleace* [1987] 2 EGLR 143, two inconsistent notices were served on the tenant by different agents and the court had to consider if the agents had authority to serve the notices. On the facts, it was held that only one of the agents had authority and thus one of the notices was invalid. The effect of this was that the landlord had applied out of time for the matter to be determined by a third party, and as a result the rental suggested by the tenant became payable, that sum being approximately half of what the landlord wanted.

2.10 DELAYS: TIME OF THE ESSENCE

2.10.1 General

Where rent review clauses provide a timetable the question inevitably arises as to the consequences of failing to comply with it. The lease may specifically deal with the situation, and as a matter of good practice should do so; but if it does not then the presumption is that time is not of the essence (*United Scientific Holdings* v *Burnley BC* [1978] AC 904) and failure to meet a time limit will not prevent a review taking place. If parties do want time to be of the essence in respect of all or any part of the procedural steps then they must clearly state that to be the case. Usually, nowadays it is considered better practice for landlords to avoid time limits and their related problems altogether. However, the use of time limits can be an advantage, in that the tenant knows exactly when a review will take place and can plan its business accordingly.

If the parties want to follow a timetable for all or some of the steps in the rent review process, the draftsman must make it very clear in relation to which steps time is to be of the essence. So, for example, often a lease will not make time of the essence for service of the landlord's trigger notice, but will make it of the essence for service by the tenant of a counternotice. The result is that a tenant who delays will be deemed to accept whatever rent was fixed by the landlord in his notice without recourse to a third party for determination. While this practice was 'deplored' by Templeman LJ in *Amalgamated Estates* v *Joystretch Manufacturing* [1981] 1 EGLR 96, it still occurs and tenants must try, where possible, to avoid such a provision.

In *United Scientific*, Lord Diplock held that the presumption that time is not of the essence can be rebutted if there are contraindications:

(a)   in the express words of the lease; or
(b)   in the interrelation of the rent review clause and other clauses; or
(c)   in the surrounding circumstances.

It should be noted that even if a lease was granted before the *United Scientific* decision, it will still be construed and the intention of the parties deduced on the basis of the law as laid down in that case and not on the basis of the law as it was thought to be at that time (*Henry Smith's Charity Trustees* v *AWADA Trading & Promotion Services Ltd* [1984] 1 EGLR 116).

2.10.2   Contraindications in the express words of the lease

2.10.2.1   Phrases that make time of the essence
Using the words 'time is of the essence' is the clearest way of rebutting the contrary presumption, but sometimes those words are not included and the courts have had to consider whether other phrases have the effect of making time of the essence. For example, in *Drebbond Ltd* v *Horsham District Council* (1978) 37 P & CR 237 and in *Norwich Union Life Insurance Society* v *Tony Waller* [1994] 1 EGLR 126, the clause provided that if no agreement was reached then if the landlord required by notice in writing given to the tenant within three months thereafter, 'but not otherwise', the question was to be referred to a surveyor. The words 'but not otherwise' were held to make time of the essence. In *Touche Ross & Co.* v *Secretary of State for the Environment* (1983) 46 P & CR 187, CA, Dillon LJ said it was undesirable that questions of whether time is of the essence of a rent review clause should depend on minute differences of language, but it is possible that small differences of language will lead in some cases to opposite conclusions. In the *Touche Ross* case the question of what was a fair market rack rental was to be referred to a surveyor 'as soon as practicable and in any event not later than three months after service of a trigger notice', and time was held not to be of the essence. The *Touche Ross* decision was followed in *Thorn EMI Pension Trust Ltd* v *Quinton Hazell plc* [1984] 1 EGLR 113.
   If the words 'time is of the essence' are absent, the court will look at the rent review clause as a whole to see whether the presumption of time not being of the essence has been rebutted. There are many cases on this, but it is very difficult to enunciate clear principles from them as fairly minor differences in drafting can lead to different results. Other expressions have

lead to time being held to be of the essence where, for example, language is used which indicates that the time limit is final. In *Mammoth Greetings Cards* v *Agra* [1990] 2 EGLR 124, rent was to be 'conclusively fixed' by the landlord's trigger notice if the tenant failed to serve a counternotice in time, and time was held to be of the essence. In *Lewis* v *Barnett* (1982) 2 EGLR 127, CA, the rent review provision stated that if the landlord failed to make an application for the appointment of a surveyor within a certain period of time then the review notice was to be 'void and of no effect'. The Court of Appeal held that those words amounted to a 'contraindication' as required in *United Scientific* and therefore the notice was invalid.

2.10.2.2 Time of the essence in respect of all steps in the process

If time is expressly stated to be of the essence in respect of any one step of the process but not in respect of any other or others, this is generally seen as meaning that time is not of the essence in respect of those other provisions (*Amherst* v *James Walker (Goldsmith and Silversmith) Ltd* (1980) 254 EG 123). At times it has been unclear with regard to which parts of a clause time is to be of the essence, and this is a question of construction for the courts. As is common, case law provides conflicting authority. In *Bradley (C.) & Sons Ltd* v *Telefusion Ltd* (1981) 259 EG 337, a clause in the lease provided that the reviewed rent should be:

> ... such amount as shall be agreed between the Landlord and Tenant by a date not later than six months prior to the commencement of the (relevant) rent period as representing the current market value at such date of the demised premises or in the absence of agreement (time to be of the essence of this provision) as shall be determined by an Arbitrator as sole arbitrator ... to be nominated by the President ... of the Royal Institution of Chartered Surveyors ... and so that in case of any arbitration ... the Arbitrator shall make his determination by a date three months prior to the commencement of the (relevant) rent period ...

It was held that time was of the essence only in relation to the requirement that the arbitrator make his award three months prior to the commencement of the relevant rent period. The positioning of the words lead the court to conclude that the parties could not have intended the words to affect the whole clause or the provision relating to agreement between the parties as that would render them meaningless.

The decision in *Bradley* v *Telefusion* was followed in *Art and Sound* v *West End Litho* [1992] 1 EGLR 138, where very similar wording was used. However, by contrast, in *Kings (Estate Agents) Ltd* v *Anderson* [1992] 1

EGLR 121, the wording of the rent review clause was virtually identical to that in *Bradley* but the court was able to distinguish that case because in *Kings* the clause omitted to make reference to the fourth (and relevant) rent review. Therefore there was no time limit to which time could be of the essence. The judge's view (*obiter*) was that if the arbitration provision had mentioned the fourth rent review then he would have had great difficulty in agreeing with the judge in the *Bradley* case. He read the provisions in *Bradley* as meaning that time was of the essence in respect of the provision which required the parties to reach agreement, which meant that if agreement was not reached by the time specified there would be no more time allowed for agreement and the landlord would have to apply for arbitration. Similarly, in *Shuwa Ashdown House Corporation* v *Grayrigg Properties* [1992] 2 EGLR 127, the approach in the *Kings* case was preferred but again that view was expressed *obiter*. Accordingly, however unpopular, lower courts would have to follow the *Bradley* decision.

2.10.2.3 Condition precedent
Sometimes the rent review clause provides that a provision is a condition precedent, and there is conflicting authority as to whether such an expression makes time of the essence. In *Chelsea Building Society* v *R & A Millett (Shops) Ltd* [1994] 1 EGLR 148, it was held that the words 'It shall be a condition precedent to the determination of the full market rental value of the premises that the Lessor shall give the Lessee during the first six months of the fifth tenth and fifteenth or twentieth year . . . of the said term notice in writing' made time of the essence. Rattee J said:

> . . . the words of the clause express what might almost be called the clearest possible intention on the part of the parties to the lease that the lessor should not have a right to have the rent reviewed at any given review date unless the lessor first gave notice within the first six months of the relevant year of the term. To say that the giving of such a notice within such a time is a condition precedent of the lessor's right to have a new market rent determined is equivalent to saying that that right of the lessor shall not arise unless he gives notice as required by the relevant clause within the specified period.

The *Chelsea Building Society* case did not follow the decision in *North Hertfordshire District Council* v *Hitchin Industrial Estate Ltd* [1992] 2 EGLR 121, where the clause provided that the rent could be varied at certain times and that '(c) It shall be a condition precedent to any such variation of rent as aforesaid that the Council or the tenants shall be served twelve months' written notice . . . of their intention to vary the rent'. Here it was held that the reference to 'condition precedent' did not make time of the essence. This case can be distinguished from the *Chelsea* case, as in the former the clause did not actually require service of the notice within any particular time limit. All that was required was that notice should be 12 months' notice, without any requirement as to the date by which that 12 months' notice should be given. Also, unlike the *Chelsea* case, the rent review could be triggered by either party.

2.10.2.4   Deeming provisions

General   The next area of difficulty relates to so-called 'deeming provisions'. These are clauses which state what the consequences will be if there is default. So, for example, a clause which provides that if a tenant does not serve a counternotice he will be deemed to have agreed the figure proposed by the landlord, is a 'deeming provision'. Another example is where a tenant is required to specify a rent in a counternotice and that rent will be 'deemed' to be the market rent unless the landlord applies for the appointment of a surveyor within a certain time limit. The Court of Appeal considered such a provision in *Henry Smith's Charity Trustees* v *AWADA Trading & Promotion Services Ltd* [1984] 1 EGLR 116, and held that such a provision made time of the essence. Slade LJ said: 'Any form of expression which clearly evinces the concept of finality attached to the end of the period or periods prescribed will suffice to rebut the presumption'.

The Mecca case   The decision in *Henry Smith's Charity Trustees* v *AWADA Trading & Promotion Services Ltd* was distinguished by the majority of the Court of Appeal in *Mecca Leisure* v *Renown Investments* [1984] 2 EGLR 137, where time was held not to be of the essence in respect of service by the tenant of a counternotice, where the rent review clause provided that if the tenant failed to serve a counternotice within the specified period he would be deemed to have agreed to pay the rent specified in the landlord's notice. The relevant clause provided:

> That at any time during the three months commencing nine months before and ending six months before the expiration of the fifth tenth fifteenth twentieth and twenty-first years of the term hereby granted the Lessor may serve on the Lessee a notice in writing (hereinafter called 'a Rent Notice') providing for an increase of the rent payable hereunder as from the expiration of the year of the term then current as the case may be (hereinafter called 'the review date') to an amount specified in the Rent Notice and thereupon the following provisions shall have effect: (i) The Lessee within twenty-eight days after the receipt of the Rent Notice

may serve on the Lessor a counter-notice calling upon the Lessor to negotiate with the Lessee the amount of rent to be paid hereunder as from the review date (ii) if the Lessee shall fail to serve a counter-notice within the period aforesaid it shall be deemed to have agreed to pay the increased rent specified in the Rent Notice as from the review date (iii) If the Lessee shall serve on the Lessor a counter-notice calling upon the Lessor to negotiate with it as aforesaid then the Lessor and the Lessee shall forthwith consult together and use their best endeavours to reach agreement as to the amount of rent . . .

Eveleigh LJ said:

It is [also] important in deciding questions of construction to distinguish between principle on the one hand and argument on the other. That there is a presumption against time being of the essence in rent-review clauses is principle; that where a particular rent-review clause contains a 'deeming' provision this will nevertheless suffice to make time of the essence of that clause is argument. As such, it can validly be used in respect of any rent-review clause containing similar provisions: it does not necessarily follow that it will succeed in every such case.

He went on to say that

The effect, therefore, of the *Henry Smith's Charity* case is in my opinion that, although the fact that a rent-review clause does contain a 'deeming' provision is a contraindication which may be sufficient to rebut the general principle, whether it does so or not remains in the end a matter of the proper construction of the particular clause concerned. . . . In my opinion the potential detriment to the tenant, if time is held to be of the essence of the material part of the clause, if he serves his notice a day or a week late and is thus fixed with perhaps a wholly unreasonable rent specified in the landlord's trigger notice, far outweighs any potential harm to the landlord from any tardiness on the tenant's part. If, having served his original notice, the landlord receives no timeous counternotice from the tenant, the remedy is in his own hands: all he need do is to serve a further short notice on the latter making time of the essence of the procedure.

Browne-Wilkinson LJ in his dissenting judgment said that in order to avoid fine distinctions, he was not prepared to distinguish this case from the *Henry Smith's Charity* case. While accepting that the rent review clause in that case was more detailed than that in *Mecca* and had certain features which were not present in *Mecca*, he did not think that the right answer could depend on comparatively small differences in drafting. He went on to say he would have allowed the appeal in the hope that clarity and consistency in the relevant law would be maintained.

The position post-Mecca   The conflicting decisions mentioned above make it very difficult to know whether time is of the essence in respect of any provision, and cases subsequent to *Henry Smith's Charity* and *Mecca* have not helped clarify the point (see *Taylor-Woodrow Property Co. Ltd v Lonrho Textiles Ltd* [1985] 2 EGLR 120; *Phipps-Faire Ltd v Malbern Construction Ltd* [1987] 1 EGLR 129; *Greenhaven Securities Ltd v Compton* [1985] 2 EGLR 117; and *Bickenhall Engineering Co. Ltd v Grandmet Restaurants Ltd* [1994] EGCS 146, CA). What is clear is that the existence of deeming provisions will not automatically be sufficient to rebut the presumption that time is not of the essence; whether the presumption is rebutted will depend on all the circumstances of the case (*Power Securities (Manchester) v Prudential Assurance Co.* [1987] 1 EGLR 121). In *Power Securities*, Millett J said:

Where the parties have not only required a step to be taken within a specified time but have expressly provided for the consequences in case of default, this provides an indication, of greater or less strength, that time is to be of the essence, but it is not necessarily decisive. Whether it is so or not must depend on all the circumstances of the case, including the context and wording of the provision, the degree of emphasis, the purpose and effect of the default clause and any other relevant provisions.

He went on:

Since 1978 the parties or their legal advisers must be taken to know that, unless they evince an intention to the contrary, the presumption is that time is not of the essence of any limit specified in the rent review clause. Failure to negate that presumption by express words might well be thought by some to indicate an intention to accept the presumption; but whether this be so or not, it certainly cannot be taken to evince an intention to displace it.

This issue was considered most recently by Neuberger J in *Starmark Enterprises Ltd v CPL Distribution Ltd* [2000] 46 EG 196, where the clause under consideration was (almost) identical to the clause in *Mecca*. In his judgment Neuberger J reviewed the authorities but felt bound to follow the reasoning of the majoirty in *Mecca*. Referring to the confusion that exists as a result of the Court of Appeal decisions in *Henry Smith's Charity* and *Mecca*, he said it would be desirable that the present perceived uncertain state of the law be determined by the House of Lords sooner rather than later.

2.10.3   The interrelation of the rent review clause and other clauses

2.10.3.1   General
It was suggested in the *United Scientific* decision (see 2.10.1) that if there is an interrelation between a rent review clause and a break clause this could rebut the presumption that time is not of the essence. The reasoning behind this is the presumption that the break clause would be intended to give the tenant the opportunity to break the lease if he found the new rent to be unacceptable. This intention would be frustrated if time was not of the essence of the review process, as the landlord could delay the review until after the period during which the tenant could exercise the break option. Accordingly, in *Al Saloom* v *Shirley James Travel Service Ltd* (1981) 42 P & CR 181, CA, where there were rent review and break clause provisions (and these were in the same clause) and the last date for service of a trigger notice was also the last date upon which the lessee could give notice to determine the lease, there was clear interrelation which made time of the essence. What is clear from the case law is there must be an interrelationship between the rent review clause and the break clause before time will be of the essence; the mere existence of a break clause will not make time of the essence.

The *Al Saloom* case was followed in *Legal & General Assurance (Pension Management) Ltd* v *Cheshire Council* [1983] 1 EGLR 121 (where the provisions were in different sub-clauses). In *Edwin Woodhouse Trustee Co. Ltd* v *Sheffield Brick Co. plc* (1983) 270 EG 548, Finlay J said that the fact that the break clause and the rent review provisions were separately set out was not a point of great significance. However, in that case time was not of the essence as there was no provision for a landlord's 'trigger notice' (the rent review being of the automatic type, see 2.13) and no interrelation between the two provisions.

2.10.3.2   The Metrolands case
Even if there is an interrelationship between the rent review and break clauses, that may not be sufficient to rebut the presumption that time is not of the essence. In *Metrolands Investments Ltd* v *J.H. Dewhurst Ltd* [1986] 1 EGLR 125, CA, the rent review provision provided for the rent to be agreed between the parties, and failing agreement to be determined by

arbitration. The decision of the arbitrator was to be obtained before the expiration of the first half of the 14th year of the term (19 August 1981). The break clause provided that if the tenant wanted to end the lease at the end of the 14th year of the term (18 February 1982), it had to serve written notice between 19 August 1981 and 18 November 1981. No attempt to agree a rent or go to arbitration was made before 19 August 1981, and the tenant did not attempt to operate the break clause before 19 November 1981.

The landlord wrote to the tenant on 2 December 1981 indicating that it wanted a review, and the tenant replied that it was too late. The court said that there was the clearest possible correlation between the rent review clause and the break clause. The relevant dates were clearly fixed by the draftsman in the contemplation that any necessary decision of the arbitrator would be obtained at the very latest before 19 August 1981, which was to be the start of the three-month period (19 August 1981–18 November 1981) during which the tenant was to be free, if it thought fit, to serve a notice to determine the lease. The draftsman manifestly envisaged a timetable by virtue of which the lessee would know the rent which would be payable for the last seven years of the term by the time when it came to make its decision whether or not to exercise its right to determine the lease. However, the court went on to say that though there was the clearest interrelation between the timetable embodied in the rent review clause and that embodied in the break clause, such interrelation in the context of this particular lease was not a 'contraindication' sufficient to rebut the initial presumption of construction that the timetable specified in the rent review clause for the obtaining of the arbitrator's decision was not of the essence of the contract. The court gave two reasons for this conclusion:

(a) that the actual obtaining of the arbitrator's decision was to a substantial degree outside the lessor's control; and

(b) any potential hardship to the tenant which might otherwise arise through tardy action by the landlord in initiating the rent review procedure could be eliminated, or at least substantially mitigated, by the tenant initiating such action itself.

It would seem, therefore, that the landlord would need fully to control the event as to which time was to be of the essence, before the court will hold the presumption to be rebutted.

2.10.3.3 *The case law reviewed*
The case law was reviewed by the Court of Appeal in *Central Estates Ltd* v *Secretary of State for the Environment* (1995) 72 P & CR 482. In that case the

lease contained a break clause permitting either party to determine the lease by six months' notice at the expiration of the first 21 years of the term (which was 28 September 1992). Under the rent review clause, either the landlord or the tenant could also require a review by serving a notice not less than 12 months before the rent review period on 29 September 1992. If the rent was not agreed within six months of the service of the rent review trigger notice, the rent was to be referred to an independent surveyor for determination. On 12 April 1992, the landlord wrote to the tenant requiring the rent to be reviewed, and the tenant contended that the notice was too late and the rent could not be reviewed as time was of the essence. Time was held to be of the essence by the Court of Appeal after referring to earlier authorities on the interrelationship of break and rent review clauses. The Court said that the cases fell into three categories:

(a) Where the rent review is triggered by a notice from the landlord only, is upwards only and is followed by a period in which the tenant, to whom alone the right to determine is given, may consider whether or not to serve a notice to determine the term. The cases within this category are *C. Richards & Son Ltd v Karenita Ltd* (1971) 221 EG 25, where time was held to be of the essence; *Samuel Properties (Developments) Ltd v Hayek* [1972] 1 WLR 1296, where time was not of the essence because the break clause contained a provision extending the period during which the tenant could exercise his right to surrender if the reviewed rent had not been ascertained by the time stipulated in the rent review clause; and *Coventry City Council v J. Hepworth & Son Ltd* (1982) 46 P & CR 170, where time was held to be of the essence.

(b) Where a review notice is to be served not later than the last date on which a break notice might be served. The review notice might be served only by the landlord in respect of an upwards only rent review, and the break notice might be served only by the tenant. The relevant case law in this category is *Al Saloom v Shirley James Travel Service Ltd* (1981) 42 P & CR 181 and *Legal & General Assurance (Pension Management) Ltd v Cheshire County Council* (1983) 269 EG 40 where time was held to be of the essence.

(c) Where either party might trigger the rent review, which is upwards or downwards, but only the tenant might serve a notice to determine the lease. See *Stephenson v Orca Properties Ltd* [1989] 2 EGLR 129, where time was held to be of the essence.

The case of *Metrolands Investments Ltd* v *J.H. Dewhurst Ltd* [1986] 1 EGLR 125, CA (considered at 2.10.3.2 above) was in a separate category because the rent review was not of the trigger notice type.

Morritt LJ went on to say that the clear trend of all these cases supported the proposition that the presumption is displaced and time is of the essence if the timetable laid down by the lease allows a period after the service of the review notice in which to consider whether or not to serve a break notice, for if time is not of the essence the period allowed for the service of the break notice, as to which time is of the essence is eliminated or eroded. The essential question, he said, 'is whether the terms of this lease give rise to any meaningful distinction'. He then referred to the *Metrolands* decision, where part of the Court's reasoning for holding that time was not of the essence was that the tenant could initiate the rent review procedures (as it could here). Morritt LJ did not accept that as a distinction which points to a different result. He said:

> A tenant will seek a rent review if he thinks that the rent should be reduced; likewise the lessor will seek a review if he thinks it should be increased. Neither will seek a review just for the sake of it. In each case the other party is entitled to give notice to determine the lease. Thus as the rent review may be both up and down and either party may trigger its operation and give notice to determine the term the effect of the timetable contained in the lease is to confer on both parties that which in the first category of cases to which I have referred was conferred on one of them only, namely the tenant. In my judgment, this mutuality requires that time should be of the essence for the service of the rent review notice by whichever party it is served, in the same way and for the same reasons as in the cases in the first category, time is of the essence of the landlord's notice triggering the rent review because of its relation to the tenant's right to determine the term.

2.10.4 Surrounding circumstances

There is little authority on time being of the essence because of 'surrounding circumstances' and *United Scientific* (see 2.10.1) did not give any insight into its meaning. D.N. Clarke and J.E. Adams, in *Rent Review and Variable Rents* (3rd edn, Longman), discuss the view that one of the key issues is whether 'surrounding circumstances' will be those that exist at the time the lease was granted and are in the lease, or whether later circumstances can be considered. Their view is that 'surrounding circumstances' would be restricted to those in existence at the time of the lease was granted and reflected in the lease terms. This must be so since the question is one of construction of the lease.

2.11 EFFECT OF TIME BEING OF THE ESSENCE

Unless the parties agree to extend time limits (and any such agreement should be recorded in writing), where time is of the essence and any time limit has been missed, late observance will not be allowed. Accordingly, if time is of the essence in serving a trigger notice then the landlord will lose his ability to have the rent reviewed if he fails to abide by the timetable. The court cannot step in and determine the rent, even if it could be ascertained by the court, as that would fly in the face of the clearly expressed requirement of strict compliance with the time provisions (*Weller* v *Akehurst* (1981) 42 P & CR 320). Equally, if a tenant fails to serve a counternotice in time then the landlord's proposed rent will stand.

Where the rent is to be determined by an arbitrator (but not an expert), time may be extended under s. 12, Arbitration Act 1996 in respect of arbitrations begun after 31 January 1997. The court will extend the time only if it is satisfied:

(a) that the circumstances are such as were outside the reasonable contemplation of the parties when they agreed the provision in question, and it would be just to extend the time; or

(b) that the conduct of one party makes it unjust to hold the other party to the strict terms of the provision in question (s. 12(3)).

An application under s. 12 was considered in *Fox & Widley* v *Guram and another* [1998] 03 EG 142, where the tenants unsuccessfully sought an extension of time for the serving of a counternotice in order to bring arbitration proceedings. In holding that the tenants had failed to establish that they satisfied the requirements of s. 12(3)(a) or (b), Clarke J said it was right to take account of the underlying purpose of the Arbitration Act 1996, and it was plain from the Advisory Committee's report on the Arbitration Bill that the purpose of the Act was to restrict the circumstances in which the court would have power to extend time.

Section 12 was also considered in *Harbour & General Works Ltd* v *Environment Agency*, (unreported) 22 February 1999. This case did not relate to a rent review, but the reasoning will be applicable to rent reviews. Coleman J said that the correct approach was

... to start from the assumption that when the parties agreed to the time-bar they must be taken to have contemplated that if there were any omission to comply with its provisions in not unusual circumstances arising in the ordinary course of business, the claim would be time-barred unless the conduct of the other party made it unjust that it should. Narrowly overlooking a time-bar due to an administrative oversight is far from being so uncommon as to be treated as beyond the parties' reasonable contemplation.

It is clear from this case that the courts will not readily intervene where deadlines have not been observed and time is of the essence.

2.12 DELAY: TIME NOT OF THE ESSENCE

2.12.1 Unreasonable delay

If there is a very long delay by the landlord then the tenant may feel that the landlord's right to a review should be lost in respect of that particular review. A much delayed rent review can place the tenant in a difficult position, as the new rent will usually be payable retrospectively (with interest) and therefore the tenant may have to find a large sum of money which he or she had not planned for.

It was suggested in the *United Scientific* case (see 2.10.1) that an unreasonable delay which caused prejudice or hardship to the tenant would result in a loss of the right to a particular review. While some subsequent cases followed that *dictum*, when the matter came before the Court of Appeal in *London & Manchester Assurance Co. Ltd v G.A. Dunn & Co.* (1982) 265 EG 39 and *Amherst v James Walker (Goldsmith & Silversmith) Ltd* [1983] Ch 305, the arguments based on unreasonable delay failed and the prevailing view was that mere delay, no matter how lengthy, would not destroy the right to a review. However, the right to review may be lost through estoppel. Both the *Amherst* and the *Dunn* decisions referred to this, and in *Amherst* Lawton LJ said: 'He [the landlord] would have been estopped if the tenants could have proved that by his words or conduct he had represented that he did not intend to ask for the payment of a higher rent and in reliance on that representation they had altered their position to their prejudice.' Estoppel, however, is difficult to prove.

2.12.2 Abandonment

Another argument for delay leading to the loss of the right to review is the concept of abandonment. There is conflicting authority on whether abandonment could apply: in *Dunn* it was stated that a long, inexplicable delay could amount to sufficient evidence for abandonment; and in *Amherst* it was suggested that a right to review could not be lost through abandonment. From the above, what is clear is that a landlord will not easily lose his right to a review.

2.12.3 Notice making time of the essence

Where a lease contains time limits but time is not expressly of the essence, and the landlord fails to comply with any such time limit, the tenant can make time of the essence by serving notice on the landlord (*United Scientific Holdings* v *Burnley BC* [1978] AC 904). By serving such a notice a tenant will know with certainty when or if the review will take place. Once the notice is served, the landlord will either serve the trigger notice and thus start the review process, or he will not and will lose his right to review at that time because time will have been made of the essence. If there are no time limits in the rent review clause then such a notice could not be served by the tenant (*London & Manchester Assurance Co.* v *Dunn* (see 2.12.1 above)). Also, a notice cannot be served in circumstances where it is open to either the landlord or the tenant to take a step in the process, because if the landlord fails to take the required step then it is open to the tenant to do so (*Factory Holdings Group Ltd* v *Leboff International Ltd* [1987] 1 EGLR 135).

The notice can be served only where the landlord fails to comply with a particular time limit and the tenant is unable to take the required step. The issue then is whether the tenant has to wait a reasonable time before serving his notice. In *United Scientific* there were conflicting views, but the majority felt that the tenant should wait a reasonable time and it is therefore perhaps prudent to do so, albeit that this brings another problem in determining how long a reasonable period is! That approach was not followed by the Court of Appeal on a case on notices to complete (*Behzadi* v *Shaftesbury Hotels* [1991] 2 All ER 477), where it was held that the innocent party did not have to wait until there had been unreasonable delay by the party in breach before serving a notice. However, the notice had to give a reasonable period of time in which to complete or perform the obligation. Given that there is no compelling authority directly on the point, it is perhaps advisable to wait a reasonable time before serving notice.

Example 6
Example of a notice making time of the essence

To: (*name of landlord*)
of: (*address*)

Lease made on (*date*) between (1) (*name of (original) landlord*) and (2) (*name of (original) tenant*) ('the Lease') of (*describe premises*) ('the Premises')

I, (*name of current tenant*), (the [current] tenant of the Premises), refer to (*number of appropriate provision of the lease*) of the Lease which requires a trigger notice ('the Notice') (*or insert the relevant type of notice as described by the Lease*) to be served by you. I GIVE YOU NOTICE requiring you to serve the Notice within 21 days of receipt of this notice (time being of the essence) and if you fail so to do, the rent shall not be reviewed as at (*insert relevant rent review date*).

Dated: Signed:
                              (*signature of, or on behalf of, the tenant*)

(*on duplicate*)
Received a notice of which the above is a true copy.

Dated: Signed:
                              (*signature of, or on behalf of, the landlord*)

2.13   NO NOTICE PROCEDURE: AUTOMATIC REVIEWS

Many rent review clauses do not require the service of a trigger notice to initiate the review process and merely provide that the revised rent will be that which is agreed between the parties. This does not imply a term that there must be an attempt to agree (*Wrenbridge Ltd* v *Harris (Southern Properties) Ltd* (1981) 260 EG 1195).

In default of agreement the revised rent will be that determined by an expert or arbitrator (see chapter 4). These are known as automatic reviews. The rent review process does, of course, still have to be started, so some form of action is required; but the clear advantage of automatic reviews is the complete avoidance of the problems associated with notices and missed time limits. These problems are that the landlord may lose his right to review if he fails to serve a trigger notice in time (see 2.10 and 2.11); and the tenant may have to accept the landlord's proposed rent if he fails to serve a counternotice in time (see 2.10 and 2.11); and there is a risk that the trigger/counternotice may be invalid, in not being either properly drafted

47

or served (see 2.9). With the automatic review, a review cannot be lost simply because of missed deadlines. However, it leaves the timing of the review uncertain. If a tenant wants some control of the process then a provision could be included in the lease allowing the tenant to initiate the rent review process.

There are many precedents for automatic reviews. The Law Society/ RICS have produced model forms, and these are reproduced in Appendix 2. Further examples from the *Encyclopaedia of Forms and Precedents* are in Appendix 3. The relevant part of the clause is contained in the example below.

Example 7
Example of an automatic review with determination by arbitration

Six months before each review date, time not being of the essence of the contract, the Landlord and the Tenant must [explore the possibility of (or as required) open negotiations with a view to] reaching agreement as to the Rent for the following review period and the Rent for that period may be agreed at any time or, in the absence of agreement, is to be determined by an arbitrator [not earlier than the relevant review date] (or as required). The Rent for any review period may be agreed at any time or, in the absence of agreement, is to be determined by an arbitrator [not earlier than the relevant review date].

Note
Many leases with automatic reviews will have the second alternative as it has no time scale at all and therefore avoids any potential argument that time may be of the essence.

Example 8
Example of an automatic review with determination by an expert

Six months before each review date, time not being of the essence of the contract, the Landlord and the Tenant must [explore the possibility of (or as required) open negotiations with a view to] reaching agreement as to the Rent for the following review period and the Rent for that period may be agreed at any time or, in the absence of agreement, is to be determined by an expert [not earlier than the relevant review date] (or as required). The Rent for any review period may be agreed at any time or, in the absence of agreement, is to be determined by an expert [not earlier than the relevant review date].

Note
Many leases with automatic reviews will have the second alternative as it has no time scale at all and therefore avoids any potential argument that time may be of the essence.

2.14 AGREEING A REVISED RENT

In almost all leases it is open to the parties to agree a revised rent; and if agreement can be reached, time and money will be saved. It is unusual nowadays to provide a time limit within which agreement has to be reached, but generally the clause will allow either party to apply for an independent third party to be appointed not earlier than six months before the review date which gives some time restraints to work to. Once agreement has been reached it should be formalised to avoid either party resiling. The agreement should be in writing, and there should be no reference to the agreement being 'subject to contract' as this will result in the agreement not being enforceable (*Henderson Group plc v Superabbey Ltd* [1988] 2 EGLR 155; see 5.2).

2.15 UPWARDS ONLY REVIEWS

2.15.1 General

Given that the general purpose of the rent review clause is to ensure that the rental value keeps in line with inflation, it would seem fair that reviews are upwards or downwards. However, many leases drafted in the 1980s contained upwards only rent review clauses, and it has become accepted practice for that to be the case. The effect of an upwards only rent review clause is that if rental values have fallen since either the grant of the lease or the last review, the rent will remain the same — it will not fall below the figure that is being paid prior to the review. Clearly, upwards only clauses benefit only the landlord, but they were nevertheless accepted by tenants at a time when the possibility of a downwards review seemed unlikely. For many tenants that view proved expensive when the property market slumped in the late 1980s and early 1990s, and tenants (particularly in London) were burdened with rents which far exceeded the current market value. The result has been to see tenants bring court actions in an attempt to argue that the review should be upwards or downwards.

2.15.2   Absence of clear wording

Usually, the lease will expressly provide that the rent will be the greater of (i) the current rent, and (ii) the reviewed rent. However, there have been a number of recent cases in which there were no express words indicating clearly an 'upwards only' review and where the court has had to decide the position. In *Royal Insurance Property Services* v *Cliffway* [1996] EGCS 189, the review clause allowed only the landlord to initiate rent reviews by notice specifying an 'increase of the rent', which would then be deemed to be agreed as the 'increased rent' if the tenant failed to serve a counter-notice. The court said that it was clear from the lease that the review machinery was solely geared to 'increases', and therefore the review was upwards only despite the lack of express wording to that effect. Similarly, the Court of Appeal in *Standard Life Assurance* v *Unipath Ltd* [1997] 2 EGLR 121, held that the clause was an upwards only clause where the rent was to be reviewed after five years to 'such increased sum as might be substituted' under the provisions for review. The review provisions allowed the landlord to initiate a review and provided for 'such increased rent' to be paid as from the expiry of each five-year period 'until the lease rent is further increased'.

The Privy Council considered whether a review provision was upwards only in *Melanesian Mission Trust Board* v *Australian Mutual Provident Society* [1997] 41 EG 153. The rent review provision provided that the tenant would pay 'Base Rent at the rate specified in Item 9 of the first Schedule or where increased in accordance with the express provisions of this Lease at the increased rent'. It was held that it was an upwards only review. In *Great Bear Investments Ltd* v *Solon Co-operative Housing Services Ltd* [1997] EGCS 177, clause 6.2 of the rent review clause provided for the revised rent to be 'the rent previously payable hereunder or such rent' as would be determined by an expert. Under clause 6.7, where the reviewed rent was agreed or determined after the relevant review date, the tenant, being obliged until then to pay at the rate applicable before the review date, became liable to pay 'by way of additional rent a sum equal to the difference (if any) between the reviewed rent and the rent actually paid for the period commencing on the relevant review date'. Rental values fell over the first five years of the lease, and the tenant contended that since either party could initiate the rent review, the party who initiated it could choose between the two alternatives in clause 6.2 and thus make the clause an upwards and downwards rent review clause. The landlord contended that clause 6.2 should be read as if the words 'whichever is the higher' had been inserted and took out a construction summons to determine the point. The court agreed with the landlord and stated that it was clear that a mistake had been made and that clause 6.2 was unworkable without some machinery for deciding which of the two alternatives should apply.

2.15.3 Upwards/downwards review

In *Harben Style Ltd* v *Rhodes Trust* [1995] 1 EGLR 118, *Royal Bank of Scotland plc* v *Jennings* [1997] 19 EG 152 and *Addin* v *Secretary of State for the Environment* [1997] 14 EG 132, the landlords accepted that the clause could result in either an upwards or a downwards review, and the approach they then took to avoid a downward review was to refuse to apply for the appointment of a valuer and thus frustrate the review (see 4.2).

2.15.3.1   The Harben case
In *Harben*, the lease was granted in 1978 for a 20-year term, and during the first five years the rent was £10,000 per annum. The lease provided that the rent was to be the 'market rent', and it was defined as

> ... such yearly rent as may be agreed in writing between the landlord and the tenants to be the market rent for the same review period or in default of such agreement as aforesaid before the review date relative to the same review period as may be determined to be the market rent as aforesaid by a surveyor appointed by the President for the time being of the Royal Institute [sic] of Chartered Surveyors at the request in writing of the landlord provided always (a) that the market rent for the review period when determined by a surveyor appointed as aforesaid shall on no account be less than £10,000 per annum ...

There was also a clause which provided that if the reviewed rent was not ascertained at all, or not ascertained until after the beginning of the review period, the tenants were to pay rent at the preceding year's rate until the rent was ascertained; and after the rent was ascertained the tenant was to pay the excess, if there was any. On a true construction of the lease it was accepted that the yearly rent payable during any review period may be greater or less than that which was payable during the period of the term immediately preceding the review period, subject only to the minimum provision referred to in proviso (a), being £10,000.

2.15.3.2 The Jennings case

Similarly, in the *Jennings* case there was no mention of any 'increase' — the rent was to be the initial rent which was then to be reviewed to the best yearly rent obtainable. The rent review clause provided that 'the revised rent may be agreed between the Landlord and the Tenant or in the absence of agreement determined by a specialist valuer ... the revised rent to be determined by the valuer ... shall be as in his opinion represents the best yearly rent reasonably obtainable for the Demised Premises'. The rent review clause did not take into account the possibility that property values might fall and that the revised rent would turn out to be less than the rent that had been previously paid. There was no provision for the repayment by the landlord to the tenant of the excess amount of rent that would have been paid if the revised rent was lower than the rent that had previously been paid. It was conceded that such a term would have to be implied.

2.15.3.3 The Addin case

In *Addin*, the rent had been reviewed in 1988 to £440,000, but subsequent to that rental values had fallen. The rent review clause provided that for each rent review period the rent 'shall be the higher of the sum of £148,000 or such sum as shall be assessed as the current open market rent'. At the review in 1995, the open market rent was likely to be less than the then current rent of £440,000, and the rent could be reduced on review as the provisions were upwards/downwards.

Despite the potential financial loss to tenants, many landlords still try to insist on upwards only reviews. Where they are accepted, their effect should (ideally for the tenant) be tempered by a break clause to allow the tenant to get out of the lease at review should he or she so wish. If a tenant manages to negotiate an upwards or downwards review then it is essential that the rent review is either of the automatic type, or that it can be triggered by either the landlord or the tenant and that reference to a third party can be by either party. If that is not the case, the landlord could simply refuse to operate the review machinery, as was seen above.

2.16   RENT REVIEW DATES

The parties will agree on the review dates and the draftsman will then insert them into the lease. This appears a simple enough exercise, but care must be taken to avoid any uncertainty as to the actual dates on which the reviews will take place. For example, if a clause states that the rent will be reviewed in 'every fifth year of the term' and the lease was granted in 2000 but the term was expressed to commence in 1999, will the review be in 2005 or 2004? The principles of law to be applied were laid down in *Bradshaw* v *Pawley* [1980] 1 EGLR 49:

Where a lease creates a term of years which is expressed to run from some date earlier than that of the execution of the lease, the relevant law may be summarised as follows.

(1)   The term created will be a term which commences on the date when the lease is executed, and not the earlier date.

(2)   No act or omission prior to the date on which the lease is executed will normally constitute a breach of the obligations of the lease.

(3)   These principles do not prevent the parties from defining the expiration of the term by reference to a date prior to that of the execution of the lease, or from making contractual provisions which take effect by reference to such a date, as by defining the period for the operation of a break clause or an increase of rent.

(4)   There is nothing in these principles to prevent the lease from creating obligations in respect of any period prior to the execution of the lease.

(5)   Whether in fact any such obligations have been created depends on the construction of the lease; and there is nothing which requires the lease to be construed in such a way as to avoid, if possible, the creation of such obligations.

Those principles were applied in *Beaumont Property Trust* v *Tai* [1983] 1 EGLR 122, where the lease was executed on 17 December 1979 but ran from the commencement of the term which was 25 March 1976. The lease provided:

To hold the same ... unto the lessee for a term of 25 years from the 25th day of March 1976 yielding and paying therefore to the company:— (a) during the first five years (from the date of the lease) of the said term a yearly rent of two thousand five hundred pounds ...

The question for determination was whether the rent review would be on 25 March 1981 or 25 March 1984. It was held that the lease clearly stated that the term of the lease at its maximum would expire 25 years after 25 March 1976, but within that total period of 25 years there would be possible breaks at five-yearly intervals. The first five-year period was not affected by the later execution of the lease, still expiring five years after 25 March 1976. The problem in this case was caused by the words in brackets, 'from the date of the lease', which in the court's view were put in the wrong place; they should have been inserted after the words 'yielding and paying'.

To avoid uncertainty, the draftsman should specifically state what the rent review dates will be (see (a) below), or state the date from which the review periods should be calculated (see (b) below):

(a) Specific review dates: '1 January 2005, 2010, 2015 and 2020';
(b) Specific review periods: '1 January 2005 and every fifth anniversary of that date'.

If using specific dates, as in (a) above, the draftsman must be aware of the potential impact on the hypothetical lease and its review provisions. There is no impact if rent is reviewed on the basis of an assumption of a hypothetical letting for the residue of the actual term. However, where the hypothetical lease is for a longer term than the residue of the contractual term of the actual lease, this could mean that the hypothetical lease would have a long period without any review. The consequences of this can be illustrated by an example. If a 25-year lease, which commenced in 1995, were to be reviewed in the years 2000, 2005, 2010 and 2015, and the hypothetical lease is for 20 years from any particular rent review date, this would mean that by the fourth review in 2015 there would be an assumption of a lease expiring in 2035 with no further rent review. The impact of that is that unless there was a term to the contrary, the rent would be assumed to remain the same for the final 20 years of the lease, which would increase the rent achievable in 2015.

In respect of (b) above, the further point to note is that if the 'term' is defined as including any period of holding-over, or extension or continuation of the contractual term, whether by statute or common law (most modern leases will be so defined), then expressing the review dates in that form could mean that reviews will occur during any period of statutory continuation (*Willison* v *Cheverell Estates Ltd* [1996] EGLR 116; see 2.17 below). It is essential that instructions are sought as to whether this is required.

A further concern relates to retrospective commencement dates, which are fairly common when a landlord desires uniformity across a development with all leases commencing on the same date. In this situation, if the lease provides for rent reviews to take place on the anniversary of the commencement date of the lease, and the tenant's actual lease is not granted until after that date, this will obviously shorten the period before the first review. This will have to be explained to the tenant.

2.17 RENT REVIEW PERIODS

At present parties generally agree on five-yearly reviews, but it is open to them to agree any period for review that they wish. However, sounding a cautionary note, non-standard provisions can lead to difficulties for the valuer in assessing the rent payable as there may be insufficient comparable transactions to utilise when assessing the new rent. Rent reviews can take many months to resolve and involve the parties in considerable expense; therefore if reviews are more frequent than every five years, those factors would become more onerous. Frequent reviews also prevent the tenant from being able to make long-term financial projections, which obviously affects its overall business strategy.

Some leases will provide for a review in the final year of the lease, and the reason this is done is that the lease may be subject to a statutory continuation once the contractual term has expired under the Landlord and Tenant Act 1954, Part II. If the lease does come within the 1954 Act scheme then the landlord could apply for an 'interim rent' to be paid under s. 24A, but case law shows that an interim rent will be less than the rent obtainable on a valuation based on market rentals as the valuation is based on a yearly tenancy (*Charles Follett Ltd* v *Cabtell Investment Co. Ltd* [1987] 2 EGLR 88, CA). Also, the interim rent will not be payable on the expiry of the contractual term as the landlord will have to apply to court for an interim rent to be fixed.

Tenants will generally object to a review in the final year as one of the purposes of an interim rent being fixed has been described as providing a cushion for the tenant against a large increase on renewal (*Charles Follett Ltd* v *Cabtell Investment Co. Ltd*). Also, the review will only be on the basis of a hypothetical letting for a fixed term, which does not accord with the reality of the tenant's situation, as at the time of review the term is uncertain and the tenant's only right is to a new tenancy. A further argument against this type of review is that if the landlord achieves a good rent it will be in a strong bargaining position and may then even delay negotiations for a new lease. Additionally, it could result in added expense for the tenant through there being extra negotiations, first at the time of the review at the end of the lease, then for an interim rent and lastly for the rent under the new lease.

As discussed in 2.16, if a review in the final year is not wanted the parties must ensure that it does not occur through careless drafting. If the method of drafting shown in (b) above is used, and the lease defines the term as including any period of holding-over, or extension or continuation of the contractual term, whether by statute or common law, then it could be argued that the rent can be reviewed every five years, whether under the contractual term or any statutory continuation. See *Willison v Cheverell Estates Ltd* [1996] 1 EGLR 116, CA, where the definition of the term did not include a reference to any period of continuation and as a result the court held that the landlord could not operate the rent review during a statutory continuation. However, it seems that if the definition had included such a reference then the outcome might have been different.

2.18   VALUATION DATE

The review date will usually be the date upon which the property is valued for rent review purposes and the date from which the new rent becomes payable. The effect of the review date being different to the valuation date is that if the valuation date is the date of the determination of the revised rent then the rent may have increased from the rent review date to the date of determination of the new rent, which would clearly not be to the advantage of the tenant, particularly given that the reviewed rent will generally be payable as from the review date. The courts favour a construction which results in the review date and the valuation date being the same. See *Glofield Properties v Morley (No. 2)* [1989] 2 EGLR 118, CA, where the rent was to be assessed 'at the time of such determination'. The landlord said that this meant that the valuation date was whatever time the arbitrator made his award, but the tenants argued that the valuation date was the start of the relevant review period. It was held that it was contrary to the whole purpose of a rent review provision that the reviewed rent should be fixed by reference to values prevailing at a date significantly later than the start of the period in respect of which it is payable, therefore the valuation date should be the start of the relevant review period. However, the courts will give effect to a clause which provides for the valuation date and the date the new rent is to become payable to be different (*Prudential Assurance Co. v Gray* [1987] 2 EGLR 134).

In the *Prudential* case, the lease was a reversionary sub-underlease which had been granted on 22 April 1968 for a term of 14 years starting from 24 June 1986. The tenant was to pay an initial rent, which was to be reviewed retrospectively from the commencement of the term. The rent review clause provided that the revised rent was to be 'the yearly rent at which the demised premises might reasonably be expected *at the date of review* to be let in the open market'. The clear purpose of the rent review clause was to protect the landlord against the risk of the rent being below current market rents because it was fixed in 1968 even though the term was not to commence until 1986. The parties could not agree what date 'the date of review' should be. The landlords argued that it meant the date on which the rent is actually determined, and the tenants argued that it meant the date of commencement of the term (24 June 1986), which was the date from which the new rent became payable. The effect of the landlords' construction was that the tenants would have to pay as from the commencement of the term a rent above the market rent at such commencement. The court held that the natural and ordinary meaning of the words 'the date of review' was that they referred to the date of the review, which was the date of the determination of the rent. While the court accepted that its construction produced commercial consequences surprisingly favourable to the landlord, they said that the meaning of the words used was too clear to be affected by such considerations.

In *Parkside Knightsbridge Ltd* v *German Food Centre Ltd* [1990] 2 EGLR 265, the rent review provisions stated:

> The landlords shall be entitled to require by notice in writing to the tenant given on or before 24th June in both or either 1975 and 1982, that the rent hereby reserved and payable hereunder shall be reviewed on the basis of the *then* exclusive rack rent value of the demised premises . . .

The rent review years were subsequently varied to 1982 and 1985. The dispute arose at the 1985 review as to the date on which the rent was to be determined, and the arguments were based on the meaning of the word 'then' in the rent review clause. The landlords contended that the rent was to be determined as at 25 December 1985, which was the date the new rent would become payable. The tenants contended that it was to be determined on 24 June 1985, being the last date the landlord could serve a notice. The judge said that in any lease one would expect that the new rent would be determined as at the date when it first became payable, but that on examination of the clause in this lease it did not seem to him that that was the correct, literal interpretation of the words used. The tenants' contention was based on a literal interpretation of the words used and did not throw up an unfortunate result, and therefore a decision was made in favour of the tenants. See also 3.14.

CHAPTER THREE

Valuation: the Hypothetical Lease

3.1 INTRODUCTION

The central issue to be agreed by the parties or determined by a third party is the revised rent for the property. The revised rent will be agreed or determined through the valuation formula contained in the lease. The formula should result in a revised rent which reflects changes in the value of money and of the property let (*British Airways plc* v *Heathrow Airport Ltd* [1992] 1 EGLR 141). There is no presumption that the revised rent will increase at review (*Bodfield* v *Caldew Colour Plates* [1985] 1 EGLR 110), but most leases will contain an upwards only review clause (see 2.15).

Over the years, valuation formulae have become increasingly complex and have been the subject of extensive litigation. It is therefore advisable to liaise with the client's surveyor when drafting/amending any valuation formula, but particularly where the premises are unusual as a standard formula may not be appropriate in those circumstances.

The basis of most valuations is the hypothetical lease, being the rent which would be obtainable from a hypothetical willing tenant by a hypothetical willing landlord if the premises were available for letting on the open market. The hypothetical lease is based on assumptions (see 3.3–3.12 below) and disregards (see 3.13 below) which describe the hypothetical lease, and which are clearly untrue as regards the actual lease but provide a basis upon which the revised rent can be assessed. Drafting or amending unusual assumptions and disregards need careful consideration as it is very difficult to predict with complete accuracy how they will work, which can then lead to the matter having to be litigated.

It is open to the parties to agree on whatever assumptions and disregards that they wish. However, authority suggests that the hypothetical lease should bear as close a resemblance to reality as possible. See *Norwich Union Life Insurance Society* v *Trustee Savings Bank Central Bank Board* [1986] 1 EGLR 136, where it was stated that if a landlord uses assumptions and disregards in such a way that the hypothetical lease is very generous to a tenant but the actual lease is the opposite, this could result in a higher rent being paid by the tenant on review. However, the problem for a landlord in such circumstances is that the rent may be discounted at review because a tenant would take on an onerous lease only if there was a discount (*Norwich Union Life Insurance Society* v *British Railways Board* [1987] 2 EGLR 137).

When assessing what the rental value of the premises will be, the common approach adopted by valuers is to consider the actual rents that are paid in respect of other, similar properties in the area. These so called 'comparables' assist the valuer in coming to his determination (see 3.14).

An example of the valuation formula is as follows:

Example 9
Example of the valuation formula

The rent at which the demised premises might reasonably be expected to be let by a willing landlord to a willing tenant in the open market on the review date with vacant possession and without taking a fine or a premium for a term equal to the unexpired residue of the term.

3.2   THE VALUE

A number of different phrases are used for valuation purposes. The phrases most commonly met are that the revised rent shall be:

(a)   the market rent; or
(b)   a fair rent or reasonable rent; or
(c)   the best rent or highest rent.

3.2.1   Market rent

Examples of 'market rent' include 'open market rent', 'full market rent', 'yearly rent', 'rack rental' and 'current rack rental'. Usually, the lease will then go on to define the particular phrase, and generally the definition rather than the phrase will be the important element. It would appear that the precise wording will be unlikely to affect the meaning of the phrase. Therefore, in *Royal Exchange Assurance* v *Bryant Samuel Properties (Coventry) Ltd* [1985] 1 EGLR 84, it was held that in the phrase 'full current market rack rental value', 'market' did not add anything of great significance to 'rack' nor 'rack' to 'market', and 'full' added nothing. Then in *Sterling Land Office Developments Ltd* v *Lloyds Bank plc* [1984] 2 EGLR 135, it was held that an 'open market rent' did not have a different meaning to a 'market rent'.

The meaning of 'rack rent' was considered in *Compton Group* v *Estates Gazette* (1978) 36 P & CR 148, where it was held that the primary meaning was the 'full annual value' of the property, but the phrase could mean the maximum rent permitted by law. It is perhaps better to avoid the possible risk of a rent freeze by using the phrase 'market rent'.

In *99 Bishopsgate Ltd* v *Prudential Assurance Limited* [1985] 1 EGLR 72, the court had to consider the meaning of 'fair yearly rent' where an arbitrator had to have regard to current open market lettings with vacant possession before fixing a 'fair yearly rent'. It was held that in that case 'fair' did not mean a rent that was fair as between the particular parties but what the hypothetical tenant would fairly be expected to pay taking the premises from a hypothetical landlord.

The *99 Bishopsgate* case raises a further concern in that the arbitrator 'had *to have regard to* open market lettings' (emphasis added). The difficulty with this is it does not state how much regard is to be had, and the resulting uncertainty is therefore better avoided. It is probably better practice to avoid using 'yearly rent' in case it is given the same meaning as 'yearly letting', which can result in a lower rent being ascertained (see 2.17 above on 'interim rents' under s. 24A, Landlord and Tenant Act 1954).

3.2.2 Reasonable rent or fair rent

There is uncertainty regarding the meaning of 'reasonable rent' and 'fair rent', but it is generally thought that they mean the same thing. Very few leases actually contain references to 'fair rent'. There is some confusion over the exact meaning of 'reasonable' and slight changes in wording can have very different results, as was illustrated in *Ponsford* v *HMS Aerosols Ltd* [1979] AC 63. In *Ponsford*, the majority held that 'a reasonable rent' had a different meaning to a rent that was 'in all the circumstances reasonable'. 'A reasonable rent' is a rent that is reasonable for the premises without regard to what it is reasonable for the particular tenant to pay (an objective test). A rent that is 'in all the circumstances reasonable', on the other hand, means that all the circumstances must be considered, including the landlord's and tenant's circumstances (a subjective test). The effect of the former type of clause in the *Ponsford* case was that improvements made by the tenant were taken into account for valuation purposes, which meant that the tenant had to pay rent on items he had actually paid for in the first place. Effectively, he paid twice, once when the improvements were done and then again at review. It is usual in any event expressly to disregard tenants' improvements at review.

The issue came to be considered again in *ARC Ltd v Schofield* [1990] 2 EGLR 52, where the landlords had an option to renew the lease 'at such rent as may be agreed between the landlords and the tenant, being a fair and reasonable market rent at that time'. Here it was held that the words 'fair and reasonable' could be used subjectively or objectively and it would be a question of construction in every case. In this case the phrase 'fair and reasonable market rent' took its colour from the word 'market' and had an objective meaning.

If a lease has a rent review clause but fails to include a formula for ascertaining the rent, the courts have not followed the majority in *Ponsford* and have a preference for the subjective approach favoured by the minority in that case. In *Thomas Bates & Sons Ltd v Wyndham's (Lingerie) Ltd* [1981] 1 All ER 1077, no formula had been specified and the Court of Appeal said that the arbitrator should assess 'what rent it would have been reasonable for these landlords and these tenants to have agreed under this lease having regard to all the circumstances relevant to any negotiations between them of a new rent from the review date'. A similar approach can be seen in *Central Metropolitan Estates v Compusave* (1983) 266 EG 900.

A further question is whether the phrase 'reasonable rent' allows a valuer to ignore exceptional or freak rents (see 3.2.4 below) which would not be ignored if the valuation was based on the market rent. *Ponsford* relied on the decision in *Cuff v Stone (J. & F.) Property Co. Ltd* (Note) [1979] AC 87, which held that exceptional or freak bids could be ignored, but the question is far from settled.

3.2.3 Best or highest rent

It would seem that 'best rent' or 'highest rent' will not result in a different rent than if the valuation had been based on 'market rent'. In *Daejan Investments Ltd v Cornwall Coast Country Club* (1985) 50 P & CR 157, when considering the phrase 'the highest rent', the court held that the word 'highest' added no more than emphasis. However, there remains a concern that an alternative interpretation by the courts could result in a higher rent being payable, and as such, such terms should be avoided by a tenant.

3.2.4 Special purchasers

Sometimes when the open market rent is being determined the question arises as to whether a bid from a special purchaser — being someone who, because of their particular circumstances, is willing to pay a greater rent in excess of the value of the property (sometimes called an 'overbid') — will be taken into account. An example of a special purchaser would be someone who owns adjoining property and who wants to expand. The special purchaser could be the actual tenant (as in *Secretary of State* v *Reed International* [1994] 1 EGLR 22 (see 3.3 below) and *First Leisure Trading Ltd* v *Dorita Properties Ltd* [1991] 1 EGLR 133, where the tenants also rented adjoining property, and *British Airways* v *Heathrow Airport* [1992] 1 EGLR 141, where the tenant leased a total of eight different buildings at the airport under different leases), or someone else entirely. It would appear from the case law that if there is nothing in the lease excluding a bid from a special purchaser, it could be taken into account, but whether there is such a special purchaser and the effect the special purchaser would have on the value are questions of fact.

3.3 WILLING LANDLORD AND WILLING TENANT

It is usual for the rent review clause to stipulate that the letting is to be by a willing landlord to a willing tenant. If such a provision is not expressly included, it will be implied, as otherwise 'The notion of a letting in the open market between an unwilling lessor and an unwilling lessee (or between a willing lessor and an unwilling lessee) for the purpose of determining a reasonable rent makes no sense' (*Dennis & Robinson Ltd* v *Kiossos Establishment* [1987] 1 EGLR 133).

The willing landlord and tenant are both hypothetical people who do not have any of the individual characteristics of the actual landlord and tenant. Therefore, it will be irrelevant that the actual landlord or tenant is far from 'willing', or that either of them has financial problems (*British Airways* v *Heathrow Airport* [1992] 1 EGLR 141). Having said that, it does not mean that the actual lessee is necessarily excluded from consideration as a potential lessee unless the rent review clause expressly or impliedly makes that direction to the valuer (*First Leisure Trading Ltd* v *Dorita Properties Ltd* [1991] 1 EGLR 133). It will depend on the circumstances whether the valuer is entitled to find that the actual lessee is a potential hypothetical lessee, for example where the actual lessee also lets adjoining property (see *Secretary of State* v *Reed International* [1994] 1 EGLR 22, where the actual tenant occupied adjoining premises and at review the arbitrator concluded that there could be two bidders for the premises — the hypothetical tenant and the actual tenant of the adjoining premises — and as a result of that the rent was increased as the arbitrator believed that the hypothetical tenant would have to make a small overbid in those circumstances). The hypothetical and the real can be easily confused, Bingham LJ said in *James v British Crafts Centre* [1987] 1 EGLR 139, CA:

> Thus the operation of any rent review clause involves a fusion of the actual and the hypothetical. The rent to be determined is that actually to be paid by the actual lessee under the lease in question or his successor in title, but the measure of that rent is determined by reference to what would be paid by a hypothetical willing lessee to a hypothetical willing lessor if the premises were available for letting on the open market, which of course they are not. Depending on the wording of the clause in question, difficulties may arise (as they do here) in determining where the actual ends and the hypothetical begins.

In some instances there may only be one person interested in the particular property, in which case, the valuer will have to decide how to deal with such a case. In *F.R. Evans (Leeds) v English Electric Co. Ltd* (1977) 36 P & CR 185, Donaldson J said:

> The fact that it is very likely that English Electric Co. Ltd would have been the only potential lessee is relevant, but its relevance is indirect. It does not matter whether the only potential lessee was this company or the XYZ Co. Ltd. What matters is that in the state of the market there was not likely to be more than one willing lessee. But the effect of this fact is not decisive because this single potential lessee is to be assumed to be a willing lessee — neither reluctant or importunate, but willing.

3.4 THE PREMISES TO BE VALUED

3.4.1 Introduction

The rent review clause normally provides that the premises demised by the lease will be the premises to be valued for rent review purposes. While this is normal, it is possible to base the valuation on hypothetical premises, as was done in *Lansdown Estates Group v TNT Roadfreight (UK)* [1989] 2 EGLR 120 and *Dukeminster (Ebbgate House One) v Somerfield Property Co.* [1997] 2 EGLR 125, CA. Generally, this would be done only if the premises were unusual and as a result comparables would be difficult to find (see 3.14). That was certainly the position in the *Dukeminster* case, where the rent review clause allowed the landlord to elect to have the rent determined by reference to the notional premises, which were described as a 50,000 square foot warehouse (the actual premises were 250,000 square feet and unique in the area) within a 35-mile radius of Ross-on-Wye. The problem in this case was that the landlord argued that it was entitled to select the precise location of the notional premises within the 35-mile radius (and could therefore opt for a higher rental area). The tenant argued that the notional premises should either be in Ross-on-Wye, or within the 35-mile radius but the rental value would have to be adjusted back to that of a notional warehouse in Ross-on-Wye. The Court of Appeal held that in the absence of clear words, notional premises cannot be taken to be such as to produce a valuation, whether it be too high or too low, which cannot reasonably have been intended to apply to the actual premises. It could only reasonably have been intended that the notional warehouse should be situated in a location comparable to the site of the premises in Ross-on-Wye. Therefore, if the intention is to gear the rent to the highest levels within a certain area, the rent review clause must clearly state that to be the case.

An example from the *Encyclopaedia of Forms and Precedents* of a rent review clause requiring valuation of notional premises is set out in Appendix 4.

3.4.2 Extent of the demised premises

3.4.2.1 *Plans*

Leases generally contain detailed definitions of the demised premises, and these will have to be examined to decide on the extent of the demised premises for rent review purposes. Plans will often be annexed to the lease, and where a plan is used reference can be made to the plan being 'for identification only'. This means that the plan is illustrative only and in the event of a discrepancy between the plan and the verbal description in the deed, the verbal description prevails. Alternatively, the property can be described as being 'more particularly delineated' on the plan, and in that case the plan would prevail in the event of a discrepancy.

3.4.2.2 *Changes to the demised premises*

The demised premises may change during the course of the lease in that new parts may be constructed, and the question then will be whether the new parts are to be included in the valuation. It was held in *Ipswich Town Football Club Company Limited* v *Ipswich Borough Council* [1988] 2 EGLR 146 that this will be determined by the terms of the lease. In the *Ipswich* case, at the date of the review the premises comprised a sports ground and buildings on it which had been constructed at the cost of the tenant. The lease, at various points, distinguished between the sports ground and the buildings, and therefore the court held that the value of the buildings was not to be included. This point was more recently considered in *Braid* v *Walsall Metropolitan Borough Council* [1998] EGCS 41, CA, where it was said that there were compelling reasons for accepting the arguments in the *Ipswich* case, being that, reading the relevant lease as a whole, there was a sustained distinction between the land on one hand and the buildings on the other, and the only legitimate inference from the lease was that on a review the rent was to be assessed by reference to the land alone. In *Braid*, as in *Ipswich*, distinctions had been made between the land and the buildings, and therefore the court held that only the land should be valued.

In *Ravenseft Properties* v *Park* [1988] 2 EGLR 164, the issue was whether the rent was to be determined on the basis of a lease of a piece of land with or without buildings on it. The buildings in question had been built by the tenant, but the court held (following *Ponsford*: see 3.2.2) that the building would be included as there was no express provision to the effect that what was to be valued was something other than the premises as they stood on the review date. Similarly, in *British Airways* v *Heathrow Airport* [1992] 1 EGLR 141, it was stated that it was a question of construction whether account should be had of the buildings on the land. (See Appendix 5 for an example from the *Encyclopaedia of Forms and Precedents* of a rent review clause based on a vacant site without the buildings that have been or are to be erected on the premises.) In the absence of a disregard of tenant's improvements (see 3.13.4), new structures could be included for valuation purposes (as in *Ravenseft Properties* v *Park*), and it is therefore imperative from the tenant's point of view to have such a disregard otherwise the tenant will pay rent on works that have been carried out at his expense.

If a tenant occupies additional property which, while not being included in the lease, is occupied in connection with the leased property then the additional property can form part of the leased property at review (see *Kensington Pension Developments Ltd* v *Royal Garden Hotel (Oddenino's) Ltd* [1990] 2 EGLR 117, where an underlease was granted in pursuance of an agreement to build a hotel and part of the hotel was outside the area of the demised property; it was held that the whole of the hotel was included, even the part outside the demise). Alternatively, part of the original demised premises may be surrendered, in which event only the remaining part would form the demised premises.

3.4.2.3 *Rights included in the demise*
A further consideration is what rights are included in the demise. Generally, the lease will specify what rights are enjoyed, but the parties

may fail to deal with s. 62, LPA 1925. Under this section, rights can pass which were enjoyed merely under licence prior to the grant of the lease. Valuable rights may thus unintentionally pass to the tenant, so s. 62 should generally be excluded and express rights granted as appropriate. Even if rights are not expressly included, one case held that a right of access was assumed where the only access to the property was over adjoining land owned by the tenant, and it was held that for the purposes of that rent review the absence of a right of access should be ignored (*Jefferies* v *O'Neill* (1983) 46 P & CR 376). While the right was implied in that case, it is better practice to ensure that suitable assumptions are expressly included to avoid the argument put forward in the *Jefferies* case that there was no open market for the premises because the only willing tenant was the tenant who occupied the adjoining premises (see 3.13).

Another issue is the status of rights enjoyed under licences or side letters from the landlord, and whether the rights contained in them are to be considered as forming part of the demise for rent review purposes. A right which is of particular relevance in many leases is car parking, which is usually a very valuable right which will affect the potential rental. If it is anticipated that such rights will be granted then the lease should expressly state whether or not they are to be taken into account at review.

3.4.3 Condition and location of the demised premises

In the absence of express provision to the contrary, the demised premises will be valued as they stand on the review date (*Ponsford* v *HMS Aeroscls Ltd* [1979] AC 63 and *Laura Investment Co.* v *Havering London BC* [1992] 1 EGLR 155), which means that the condition of the property and its location will be taken into account. Therefore if either the property or the location either improves or deteriorates in the years between reviews, such improvement or deterioration will be reflected in the rent.

There are limitations to this general principle, which are as follows:

(a) There may be an assumption that the property is in a condition which is consistent with performance of the tenant's covenants, as otherwise the tenant could benefit from his own breach. In particular, if the tenant breaches the repairing covenant, this could have a dramatic adverse effect on rental as any hypothetical tenant would expect a rent-free period or a reduction in rent to compensate for the money he or she would have to pay to remedy the breach. The assumption is usually express, but it may be implied based on the principle of law that no man may take advantage of his own wrong. In *Harmsworth Pension Funds Trustees Ltd* v

Charringtons Industrial Holdings plc (1985) 49 P & CR 297, the tenant was in breach of its repairing covenant; there was no express assumption, but the court held that the disrepair was to be ignored for the purposes of rent review (see 3.8.5 below).

(b) Items which the tenant has brought on to the premises may be excluded for the purposes of ascertaining the rent. What has to be determined first is whether the item is a chattel (and therefore will belong to the tenant and will not be included) or a fixture. The issue then is what constitutes a fixture. Whether an item is a fixture or not depends on the degree and purpose of annexation. The degree of annexation is the degree to which the item is actually attached to the premises; and the purpose of annexation is the intention of the person and whether he or she intended the item to become part of the land or not. If the item could not be removed without causing substantial damage, there is a strong presumption that it is intended to be a fixture. In *Elitestone Ltd* v *Morris* [1997] 2 All ER 513, HL, Lord Lloyd said:

> The nature of the structure is such that it could not be taken down and re-erected elsewhere. It could only be removed by a process of demolition. This, as will appear later, is a factor of great importance in the present case. If a structure can only be enjoyed *in situ*, and is such that it cannot be removed in whole or in sections to another site, there is at least a strong inference that the purpose of placing the structure on the original site was that it should form part of the realty at that site, and therefore cease to be a chattel.

All fixtures at the premises will not, however, form part of the premises for rent review purposes. If a fixture is a tenant's fixture then, in the absence of an express provision to the contrary, it will be ignored for valuation purposes. An item is a tenant's fixture if it was attached to the premises for the purpose of the tenant's trade; or is an item of ornament or convenience; or is an agricultural fixture under the Agricultural Holdings Act 1996, s. 10, or the Agricultural Tenancies Act 1995, s. 8. If the tenant has the right to remove his or her fixtures, it will be assumed that he has done so (*Ocean Accident & Guarantee Corporation* v *Next* [1996] 2 EGLR 84). The concern for the landlord is that the absence of the tenant's fixtures may affect the valuation at review, in that the tenant could receive a discount for fitting out at each review. Landlords wanted to avoid this limitation and included in the lease an assumption that the property 'is fit for immediate use and occupation'. In the case of *Pontsarn Investments* v *Kansallis-Osake Pankii* [1992] 1 EGLR 148, it was held that despite that assumption the tenant could negotiate for a reduction in rent to do fitting out works as the expression meant that the building was free from defects and ready for the tenant to go in and fit it out for his business and commence trading. To avoid this result the assumption became that the premises had been fully fitted out.

In *London & Leeds Estates* v *Paribas* (1993) 66 P & CR 218, CA, the landlords sought a further advantage from the assumption. They argued that the fitting out works had not been carried out at the cost of the willing tenant and that the landlord was entitled to any increase in rental attributable to the hypothetical fitting out works. The Court of Appeal held that the assumption was twofold:

    (a) 'that the demised premises are fit for immediate occupation and use and in a good state of repair and condition'; and

    (b) 'that all fitting out and other tenants works required by such willing tenant have already been completed'.

It was held that the clear purpose of the first part of the assumption was to preclude the actual tenant from arguing before the arbitrator that the hypothetical tenant would be entitled to a discount on account of the actual state of repair of the premises. The purpose of the second part was to preclude the actual tenant from arguing for a discount on the ground that the hypothetical tenant would have required further or different works from those carried out by the hypothetical tenant, with a corresponding reduction in the rent that he would be willing to pay. So the tenant was not required to pay a rent which took into account the fitting out works.

The court in *Ocean Accident & Guarantee Corp.* v *Next* (above) referred to the *London & Leeds* case to support its decision that the function of an assumption 'that the Demised Premises have been fully fitted out and equipped so as to be ready for immediate use and occupation' was to avoid an argument that the hypothetical tenant requires an allowance in reduction of his rent on the basis that the premises are not immediately ready for him to trade. The assumption did not mean that the tenant's fixtures were to be rentalised, and if such a result was required then very clear words would be needed to produce it. In the absence of clear wording, the courts do not appear willing to construe fitting out assumptions as giving any advantage to the landlord other than excluding the possibility of the tenant getting a discount. See also 3.8.2.

(c)   If there is substantial deterioration of an area then in theory such deterioration will be reflected in the rent, since the demised premises will be valued as they stand on the review date. However, in practice, if there is not an upwards/downwards rent review clause, the tenant may pay over the market value as the rent cannot be decreased even if the deterioration means that a decrease is required for the rent to reflect the current market value of the demised premises.

3.5   VACANT POSSESSION

Whether a property is assumed to be let with vacant possession or subject to subtenancies can affect the rental value. The existence of sub-leases may increase or decrease the rental value depending on the circumstances. Most leases will expressly provide that vacant possession of the whole will be assumed, and in the absence of an express provision it is a question of construction in each case whether such an assumption should be implied (*Little Hayes Nursing Home* v *Marshall* (1993) 66 P & CR 90).

While an assumption of vacant possession will generally be implied where the review is to open market rent, in deciding whether that will be the case, the court's function is to ascertain the position from the language used, looked at in light of the surrounding circumstances and what the parties must have intended. The court will consider the circumstances of the original letting and such factors as whether there were sublettings in existence or contemplated at the date of the lease (*Forte & Co. Ltd* v *General Accident Life Assurance Ltd* [1986] 2 EGLR 115, where it was held that while the normal assumption is that there will be vacant possession, different considerations apply when part of the premises is let already and the term will continue beyond the rent review. Where a lease has been granted subject to existing tenancies, it is unlikely that the parties intended the assumption of vacant possession to apply (*Scottish & Newcastle Breweries plc* v *Sir Richard Sutton's Settled Estate* [1985] 2 EGLR 130). However, there have been cases where an assumption of vacant possession has been made even when the premises have been sublet (*99 Bishopsgate Ltd* v *Prudential Assurance Co. Ltd* [1985] 1 EGLR 72, CA; see below).

The effect of an assumption of vacant possession is that the tenant and any subtenants will be assumed to have vacated the property (*F.R. Evans (Leeds) Ltd* v *English Electric Co. Ltd* (1977) 36 P & CR 185). It was held by the Court of Appeal in *99 Bishopsgate Ltd* v *Prudential Assurance Co. Ltd* that it necessarily followed from a letting with vacant possession that rent could be discounted at review if an incoming tenant would be given a rent-free period to fit out the premises. To avoid such discounts, landlords then included an assumption in the rent review clause that the premises were fully fitted out (see 3.4.3).

While an assumption of vacant possession is appropriate where the tenant intends to occupy the whole of the premises, it can cause difficulties where large premises are involved and subtenancies are intended. The ability to ignore subtenancies does not necessarily work in the landlord's favour, as was demonstrated in *99 Bishopsgate Ltd* v *Prudential Assurance Co. Ltd* (above), where the assumption of vacant possession lead the court to the decision that the rental for a 30-floor city office block was to be assessed on a notional letting of the whole building which resulted in a lower rent being achieved (£6,065,000 as opposed to £7,451,000, because there was a discount for rent-free periods to cover the time needed to find subtenants and fit out). If large premises are involved and the tenant will be subletting it or part of it, then in deciding on the rental value the valuer will have to consider market conditions at the review date; and if conditions are such that a tenant would be entitled to receive a discount as compensation for any period that it may take to sublet, such a discount would have to be taken into account when determining the new rent.

The parties should consider at the drafting stage whether subleases are contemplated; and if they are, how they are to be dealt with for rent review purposes. There are a number of possible ways to deal with the vacant possession assumption. 'Ross: Commercial Leases' suggests the following:

(a)   Assume vacant possession of the whole. Where a lease provides for the assumption that the premises are to be let as a whole, this means that the new rent will be based on a single letting of the whole of the property and not on a number of separate leases; this generally reflects the reality of the situation. Such an assumption should not be used where the premises are to be sublet.

(b)   Assume vacant possession of only those parts occupied by the tenant on the review date, and provide that the actual sub-lettings of the remainder existing on the review date are taken into account.

(c)   Assume an entirely artificial level of occupancy, although if any hypothetical sub-lettings are to be assumed the terms of those sub-lettings must be specified so that they can be properly valued.

(d)   Link the rent payable under the headlease with that being paid under the sub-leases.

(e)   Partly link the rent payable under the headlease with that being paid under the sub-leases. For example, provide for the rent

70

payable under the headlease to be a percentage of the open market rent assuming vacant possession and a percentage of the actual rents payable under the sub-leases, in the hope that the latter will reduce the potential unfairness of relying solely upon a market rent basis.

(f) Assume that hypothetical undertenants are immediately available to take underleases of all those parts of the premises that the tenant does not intend to occupy.

3.6 PREMIUMS

It should be assumed that no premium is payable by either party, so that the valuation will ignore any premium which has been paid by either party. If a premium or any other payment by way of inducement has been referred to in the lease then it should be expressly disregarded.

3.7 DURATION OF THE HYPOTHETICAL LEASE

3.7.1 General

The duration of the hypothetical lease must be defined, and in the absence of an express provision it is generally assumed that the term is equal to the unexpired residue of the term on the review date in question as that reflects the reality of the situation (*Norwich Union Life Insurance Society* v *Trustee Savings Banks Central Board* [1986] 1 EGLR 136 and *British Gas plc* v *Dollar Land Holdings plc* [1992] 1 EGLR 135). However, while that will generally be the case, if the unexpired residue does not produce a realistic construction then the court may construe the lease in a different way. This was the position in *Prudential Assurance Co.* v *Salisbury Handbags* (1992) 65 P & CR 129, where a hypothetical lease which was expressed to be on similar conditions to those contained in the actual lease (but expressly excluding any rent review clause) was held to have such a hypothetical term as willing parties would agree at a fixed rent; and in *Millshaw Property Co.* v *Preston BC* [1995] EGCS 186, where the provision stated that the letting was 'for a term of years not exceeding the residue of the term', it was held that, subject to the express provision that the term should not exceed the residue, it was one which the landlord might reasonably be expected to grant and the tenant might reasonably be expected to take, and which produced the best rent which might reasonably be obtainable in the open market.

The duration of the hypothetical lease was considered by the Court of Appeal in *Brown* v *Gloucester City Council* [1998] 16 EG 137. In this case the lease was of vacant land for a term of 125 years from 1989. The parties intended to develop the land but at the first review date no buildings had been erected. The rent review provisions provided that if no building had been constructed at the review date then the rent would be 10 per cent of the aggregate of the rents which 5 notional buildings might reasonably be expected to be let in the open market with vacant possession 'and upon such terms as herein contained'. The parties could not agree on the length of the hypothetical term. If the review was based on the unexpired residue (120 years at that review), then the expert witnesses' view was that no one would take a lease of completed business premises for such a period unless there was a substantial discount from the rent. The result of this would be the tenant would get an unexpected windfall from the rent review clause. The Court of Appeal held that following the decisions of *Norwich Union* and *Dollar Land*, where it was stated that where the hypothetical lease is of the same kind and its subject-matter is the same as the subject-matter of the original lease, then the hypothetical lease should replicate the terms and conditions of the original lease so that, in cases of doubt, the hypothetical term should be the unexpired residue of the term originally granted. However, in *Brown* the subject-matter of the hypothetical lease was not the same as the subject-matter of the original lease and the court, referring to the *Salisbury* case, held that the term was to be such term as the landlord might reasonably be expected to grant and the tenant might reasonably be expected to take in all the circumstances.

A similar issue to that in *Brown* arose in *Westside Nominees Ltd* v *Bolton Metropolitan Borough Council* [2000] EGCS 20. This case involved a sublease of 125 years. The headlease had been granted to the original tenant after it constructed a building on the site. The duration of the hypothetical term was not defined in the lease but the tenant contended that the hypothetical term should be the unexpired residue of the lease (97 years). As in *Brown* this would give the tenant an unexpected windfall as such a long notional term would depress the potential rent. While the court accepted that there was a general rule that, in the absence of contrary indication, it would normally be assumed that the length would be the unexpired residue, this type of case was an exception. Following *Brown*, it was held that the intended duration was for a term that a landlord might reasonably be expected to grant and a tenant might reasonably be expected to take.

The length of the hypothetical lease will affect the valuation. In the past, longer leases attracted higher rents, but economic changes altered that and the position now is that the preferred length of term will depend on the particular property. It is therefore important to seek advice on the preferred length from the client's surveyor before making a decision.

3.7.2 The alternatives

There are at least five duration alternatives to be considered:

(a) *The number of years between each rent review.* Nowadays, with five-yearly reviews being the norm, this is not thought to be appropriate as there will be few comparables for short terms and it does not reflect the original bargain between the parties which was based on a longer term.

(b) *The full term of the actual lease.* If such a provision is desired then the wording must be clear (i.e. 'for a term of 25 years beginning on the relevant review date'). The reason for this is that where the wording is unclear the courts have preferred a construction which results in the hypothetical term being for 'the unexpired residue of the lease', justifying this through the principle of construction which results in the notional term according with reality.

Even where there are express words the court may not give them their literal meaning. In *Toyota (GB)* v *Legal & General Assurance (Pensions Management) Ltd* [1989] 2 EGLR 123, CA, a reversionary lease was granted at the same time as the lease and the reversionary lease was to take effect on the expiry of the existing lease. The rent under the lease was to be valued on the basis of the residue of the term 'hereby granted' but the court said the existence of the reversionary lease was to be taken into account and the notional term was the residue of both the lease and the reversionary lease. If there had been a literal construction, the review to take place after 15 years of the lease would be based on a lease which had only one year to run, whereas there were actually 35 years to run under both leases. In *Lynthorpe Enterprises Ltd* v *Sidney Smith (Chelsea) Ltd* [1990] 2 EGLR 131, the term was stated to be 'equivalent' to the original length of the term, but the court held that the parties had intended that the hypothetical lease was to be on the same terms as those under the actual lease and accordingly the term was the unexpired residue. In *St Martins Property Investments Ltd* v *CIB Properties Ltd* [1998] EGCS 161, the Court of Appeal followed the *Lynnthorpe* decision. In this case the hypothetical leases were to be 'for a term equal in duration to the original term hereby granted', and it was held that the words 'original term' meant 35 years from the commencement of the term, not simply 35 years, and therefore the hypothetical leases were to be of a term equal to the unexpired residue of the term.

(c) *The unexpired residue of the lease, which will obviously decrease at each review.* The concern with this type of provision is that, while it reflects reality, by the last review there is likely to be only a short period of time left to run (for example, on a 25-year term with five-yearly reviews, by the final review there will only be five years left to run of the term), which may make the property less marketable and result in a lower rent being achieved. This problem can be addressed by using alternative (d) below.

(d) *A compromise between (b) and (c) above.* This would involve, say, a term equal to either the unexpired residue, or ten years, whichever is the greater.

(e) *A term which is not based on the actual term.* The parties could leave the issue to be determined at review by stating in the lease that the term will be such a term as would result in the best rent which might reasonably be obtainable in the open market at the time of review. The tenant would probably want to restrict this so that the term would not exceed the length of the original term.

3.7.3 Impact of statutory renewal

The case of *Pivot Properties Ltd* v *Secretary of State for the Environment* (1979) 253 EG 373, confirmed that account was to be taken by a valuer of the possibility of statutory renewal of the hypothetical lease under the Landlord and Tenant Act 1954, as such a renewal was a real possibility in that case. This decision was upheld by the Court of Appeal (*Secretary of State for the Environment* v *Pivot* (1980) 41 P & CR 248).

Taking into account the possibility of statutory renewal was fairly straightforward for the valuer in the *Pivot* case given the particular circumstances, but in other cases it may be more difficult for the valuer to assess whether a renewal is likely. In *Pivot*, the decision lead to a much greater rental valuation than would otherwise have been obtained. As a result, landlords may try to insert an assumption that the lease will be renewed under the 1954 Act. Any such an assumption should be opposed by the tenant and the position left for determination under the general law. The tenants in *Toyota (GB) Ltd* v *Legal & General Assurance (Pensions Management) Ltd* [1988] EGCS 148 managed to have the effect of security of tenure disregarded, in that the lease stated 'there being disregarded all restrictions whatsoever relating to ... security of tenure contained in any statute', and it was held that the effect of those words was that one left out of account the provisions of Part II of the Landlord and Tenant Act 1954. Nicholls LJ agreed with the lower court judge when he said: '... the general context evinces an intention to have regard to the rights at common law of the hypothetical tenant without regard to statutory intervention concerning rent or security of tenure'.

Where the notional period of the lease is long, the possibility of statutory renewal will have little impact on valuation.

3.8 TERMS OF THE LEASE

Most leases will go on to provide the further terms of the hypothetical lease, but if they do not then the terms will be those of the actual lease. See *Basingstoke & Deane BC v Host Group Ltd* [1987] 1 All ER 824, where Nicholls LJ said:

> Of course, rent review clauses may, and often do, require a valuer to make his decision on a basis which departs in one or more respects from the subsisting terms of the actual existing lease. But if and in so far as a rent review clause does not so require, either expressly or by necessary implication, it seems to us that in general, and subject to a special context indicating otherwise in a particular case, the parties are to be taken as having intended that the notional letting postulated by their rent review clause is to be a letting on the same terms (other than as to the quantum of rent) as those subsisting between the parties in the actual existing lease.

The effect of the *Basingstoke & Deane* decision is that if the landlord does not want any of the actual terms of the lease to apply then this must be expressly provided for. This is in accordance with the presumption that the hypothetical lease reflects reality (*Lynnthorpe Enterprises v Sidney Smith (Chelsea)* [1990] 2 EGLR 131, CA). Careful consideration must therefore be given to all the terms of the lease, but particularly to non-standard clauses such as rent discount/rent-free period clauses, and whether these are to be disregarded or not at review.

3.8.1 Exclusion of rent

The amount of rent payable under the actual lease must be excluded from the hypothetical lease, and such an exclusion is implied when a review is to open market rent. However, many leases contain express provision, and in the past a common clause would have the assumption: 'the terms of the lease (other than as to rent) are to apply'.

Difficulties then arose as landlords argued that such a clause also excluded the provisions for rent review. When successful, this resulted in a higher rent being payable as a tenant would generally pay more for a lease which had a fixed rent rather than for one with periodic rent reviews. Despite the fact that such an interpretation is clearly unfair on the tenant, a number of decisions agreed with the landlords' argument. However, it is now unlikely that such clauses will have that effect following the decision in *British Gas Corporation* v *Universities Superannuation Scheme* [1986] 1 WLR 398. That case laid down the correct principles to be applied, being:

(a) words in a rent exclusion provision which require *all* provisions as to rent to be disregarded produce a result so manifestly contrary to commercial common sense that they cannot be given literal effect;

(b) other clear words which require the rent review provision (as opposed to all provisions as to rent) to be disregarded must be given effect to, however wayward the result;

(c) subject to (b), in the absence of special circumstances it is proper to give effect to the underlying commercial purpose of a rent review clause and to construe the words so as to give effect to that purpose by requiring further rent reviews to be taken into account in fixing the open market rental under the hypothetical letting.

However, these are guidelines only, and while they were welcomed and approved in *Equity & Law Life Assurance Society* v *Bodfield* [1987] 1 EGLR 124, CA, it was pointed out that such guidelines do not entitle the court to construe not the clause entered into by the parties but a clause they would have entered into if their lawyers had thought more deeply about how the clause would work in practice. In that case the lease provided that the rent review was to be on the basis of a hypothetical lease on the same terms as those of the lease other than as to duration and rent. The Court of Appeal held that the rent review provisions were excluded from the hypothetical letting by the express exclusion provision.

To make the position absolutely clear the rent review clause should state that the hypothetical lease will contain rent review provisions similar to those in the actual lease. However, if the words of the clause clearly state that rent review provisions are to be disregarded then a court will give effect to them (*Pugh* v *Smiths Industries Ltd* [1982] 2 EGLR 120, where the rent review clause required an assumption of a letting on the terms of the lease 'But excluding therefrom the provisions of this clause'; the hypothetical lease excluded rent review provisions).

The issue of rent review provisions being excluded has been the subject of more recent litigation. In *Prudential Assurance Co. Ltd* v *99 Bishopgate* [1992] 1 EGLR 119, the rent review was on the basis of a hypothetical lease having regard to 'the provisions of the lease (other than the rent hereby reserved)', and the court held that only the amount of rent was excluded, not all the provisions relating to rent. In *Prudential Assurance Co. Ltd* v

Salisburys Handbags Ltd (1992) 65 P & CR 129, the provision stated that the hypothetical lease would be 'on similar covenants and conditions (other than the amount of the rent and the provisions of this present clause for reviewing the rent)' and the court held that the rent review provisions were not to be included.

Example 10
Example of an assumption of terms

The assumption that the hypothetical lease contains the same terms as this Lease, except the amount of the Initial Rent and any rent-free period allowed to the Tenant for fitting out the Premises for his occupation and use at the commencement of the Term, but including the provisions for rent review on the Review Dates.

Note
The 'Initial Rent' will have been defined in the lease.

3.8.2   Rent discounts or rent-free periods

3.8.2.1   General
Many leases provide an incoming tenant with a rent-free period (usually to allow the tenant to fit out), and the claim that is sometimes then made is that the rent to be determined at review should be lower than would otherwise be achieved because the hypothetical tenant will not get the benefit of a rent-free period. Such a claim is usually rejected and rent-free periods will generally be ignored. Additionally, other assumptions are often included in leases to rebut the argument, such as an assumption that the property is fitted out or has had the benefit of a rent-free period for fitting out (see 3.4.3).

3.8.2.2   Inducements
Other problems arise where other inducements (which go beyond rent-free periods to allow fitting out) are given to tenants to encourage lettings. The issue then is whether these other inducements should also be ignored for rent review purposes. At a time when inducements were common, rather than reducing rentals over the lease term, landlords preferred to offer long, rent-free periods with the lease still reflecting the best rent achievable at the time. Landlords felt that this would look better at review. Therefore it was not unusual, for example, for a rent of £150,000

per annum to be referred to in the lease (called the 'headline rent') with the tenant having a year-long rent-free period. Over an initial five-year period the tenant would actually pay only £600,000 (£120,000 p.a.) and not £750,000 (£150,000 p.a.) as indicated by the lease. At review on an upwards only basis, the valuer's starting point would obviously be higher, which would be unfair to the tenant and would not reflect the reality of the situation.

3.8.2.3 Headline rent

Landlords have contended that a disregard of rent-free periods and inducements means that the reviewed rent must be the 'headline rent' currently obtainable in the market, irrespective of the length of the rent-free period or other inducement which the tenant has to be given to secure it. The contrary argument by the tenant is that the only inducements that should be ignored are those granted for fitting out or for subtenants to be found. The construction of four 'inducement' clauses was considered at the same time by the Court of Appeal in the cases of *Co-operative Wholesale Society Ltd* v *National Westminster Bank plc*; *Scottish Amicable Life Assurance Society* v *Middleton Potts & Co.*; *Broadgate Square plc* v *Lehman Brothers Ltd*; and *Prudential Nominees Ltd* v *Greenham Trading Ltd* [1995] 1 EGLR 97. The Court, referring to the presumption of reality, said that they would lean against a construction which would require payment of rent upon an assumption that the tenant had received the benefit of a rent-free period which he had not in fact received. They said:

> ... a clause which deems the market rent to be the headline rent obtainable after a rent free period granted simply to disguise the fall in the rental value of the property is not in accordance with the basic purpose of a rent review clause. It enables a landlord to obtain an increase in rent without any rise in property values or fall in the value of money, but simply by reason of changes in the way the market is choosing to structure the financial packaging of the deal.

Therefore, clear language would be needed before the Court would construe a rent review clause as having the effect of disregarding rent-free periods granted as an inducement.

Considering the cases:

The Co-operative case　In the *Co-operative* case the wording of the clause was as follows:

> The rental value ... for a term ... commencing on the relevant date of review ... on the supposition ... that any rent free period or concession-

ary rent or other inducement ... which may be offered in the case of a new letting in the open market ... shall have expired or been given immediately before the relevant date of review.

Here it was held that the assumption was that the benefits of any rent-free period had been given before the relevant date and thus would be ignored in assessing the open market rent, except to the extent that it would be implied that the hypothetical tenant had moved into the property and could not therefore claim a discount on the basis of needing to fit out. The effect of this clause on the rent, therefore, was that the headline rent derived from the comparables had to be discounted to allow for any rent-free period not attributable to the fact that the hypothetical tenant still had to enter into occupation of the premises. Therefore, the reviewed rent was not to be the headline rent.

The Broadgate case The wording in *Broadgate* resulted in the Court of Appeal being unable to confine the words only to rent-free periods attributable to the tenant having to move in. The *Broadgate* clause stated:

The best yearly rent which would reasonably be expected to become payable ... after the expiry of a rent free period of such length as would be negotiated in the open market between a willing landlord and a willing tenant upon a letting of the premises as a whole by a willing lessor to a willing lessee in the open market ...

The Court held that the hypothetical tenant must be assumed to have (or to have had) the benefit of such a rent-free period, unlike in the *Co-operative* case where the rent-free period was deemed to have expired before the parties negotiated. The Court held that the reference to the rent-free period being 'of such length as would be negotiated in the open market' made it impossible to confine the words to rent-free periods attributable to the tenant having to move in. The effect of this clause on the rent, therefore, was that the open market rent was to be the headline rent.

The Scottish Amicable case In *Scottish Amicable*, the wording of the clause was similar to that in *Broadgate*, in that it said that the new rent was to be the rent which would be payable after the expiry of a rent-free period. However, the Court came to the conclusion that it had a different effect to the clause in *Broadgate*. The clause in *Scottish Amicable* said that the new rent was to be 'the best yearly open market rent (at the rate payable following the expiry of any rent free period or periods at concessionary rents which might be granted on a new letting ... on the relevant review date).'

The Court held that the clause resembled that in *Broadgate* in that it clearly said that the 'New Rent' was to be the rent which would be payable after the expiry of a rent-free period. However, the Court went on to say that the question was, 'what kind of rent-free period?'. The *Broadgate* clause was contrasted with this clause, as this clause did not simply say that it should be whatever rent-free period would be negotiated as between a willing lessor and a willing lessee in the open market. This clause said that it would be the rent-free period which 'might be granted on a new letting'. It was stated that 'a new letting' meant a letting to a new tenant who needed to move in, and therefore a rent-free period did not include a concession given to induce the tenant to pay a higher rent as this would be just as much a characteristic of a renewed letting to a tenant in occupation as of a letting to a new one. The effect of this clause on the rent was that the reviewed rent was not to be the headline rent.

The Prudential case   In the *Prudential* case, the clause stated:

> ... the best rent at which the whole of the premises might reasonably be expected to be let in the open market ... upon the assumption that ... no reduction or allowance is made on account of any rent free period or other rent concession which in a new letting might be granted to an incoming tenant.

It was held that the effect of this clause was that no reduction was to be made or allowance given because a tenant in the real market might be given a rent-free period. However, there was no warrant in the clause for increasing the rent because tenants in the market are being given rent-free periods, and therefore the effect of this clause on the rent was that the review rent was not the headline rent.

There is clearly a reluctance by the Court to construe these clauses in such a way as to give the landlord a financial advantage which is not reflected in property values. The more recent case of *St Martins Property Investments Ltd v Citicorp Investment Ltd* [1998] EGCS 161, CA, confirms the approach based on the presumption of reality favoured by the courts (see 1.2.5). In that case the assumption was that the hypothetical tenant or tenants would not seek a rent-free period or any equivalent reduction in rent, and that any rent-free period should be ignored when considering any comparable rents. The Court said that in contrast to the *Broadgate* case, the clause in this case did not provide unambiguously that the intended rent level was the headline rent level. To allow the landlord to obtain a headline rent, which would be in excess of the market rent, would not accord with the presumption of reality.

Difficulties remain for draftsmen as small differences in language (as above) can lead the court to different decisions. If it is desired to review to the headline rent then the *Broadgate* wording could be used, but even then the court could come to a different conclusion based on the actual terms of the lease in question. Alternatively, the 'plain English' approach could be adopted, but such a suggestion is likely to be met with a certain degree of caution by practitioners because the use of 'plain English' has not yet become widely accepted.

Example 11
Example of a plain English clause for a headline rent

The Rent will be the headline rent on the assumption that the hypothetical tenant has in fact though the real tenant has not had any inducement of any kind available in the market place for taking the hypothetical lease.

3.8.3 Use

The terms of the actual use clause will usually be incorporated into the hypothetical lease unless a specific assumption to the contrary is included, as this accords with the presumption of reality (see 1.2.5). It is possible to state that the use under the hypothetical lease will be different to that under the actual lease, and even if this is not expressly stated it may be implied from the wording of the clause. In *Postel Properties Ltd v Greenwell* (1992) 65 P & CR 239, the use clause in the actual lease stated that the premises were to be used as a retail shop for the sale of high quality chinaware and crystalware, and enamelware and pottery, but the rent review clause was framed more widely and simply stated that the renewed rent was to be that at which the premises might reasonably be expected to be let for retail purposes. It was held that the user under the hypothetical lease was for 'retail purposes' and not the actual use. In *Sheerness Steel Co. v Medway Ports Authority* [1992] 1 EGLR 133, the user clause in the actual lease was very restrictive in that the only use was steelmaking and ancillary operations. The rent review clause referred to the use being 'for industrial purposes' and the court held that the valuation would be based on the latter rather than on the narrower actual use.

Use clauses come in a variety of forms, as discussed below.

3.8.3.1 *Absolute restriction on use*
These clauses restrict the use of the property to a particular use, with the consequence that the landlord has complete control and can refuse any

request for a change. Such clauses are likely to lower the rental at review. The valuer cannot take into account the possibility that the covenant might be waived or modified by the landlord (see *Plinth Property Investments Ltd v Mott, Hay & Anderson* (1978) 38 P & CR 361, where the restrictive user clause resulted in a rent of £89,000 p.a. as against £130,000 p.a. if the use clause had been wider). In *C & A Pensions Trustees Ltd* v *British Vita Investments Ltd* [1984] 2 EGLR 75, the court ignored the literal meaning in favour of a more purposive approach (see 1.2.4). In that case the lessors wrote to the lessees purporting to 'authorise' a change of use which the lessees had not actually asked for. Under the terms of the lease the use clause provided: 'That the lessee will not ... use exercise or carry on or permit to be used exercised or carried on ... any trade or business whatsoever other than such as may be authorised in writing by the lessor.' The court held that the landlord's unilateral waiver was ineffective. That case was referred to in *Tea Tree Properties* v *CIN Properties* [1990] 1 EGLR 155, where Hoffman J said that the landlord's unilateral declaration in the *C & A Pensions* case, while obviously not constituting an actual authority in terms of the lease, must have been evidence, which the valuer was entitled to take into account, of the kinds of user to which the landlord was likely to consent. He went on to say that the valuer should not exclude any potential tenant who might wish to take a lease of the building for any purpose for which it could physically and legally be used.

3.8.3.2   Use restricted to a particular tenant or a particular business of the tenant
Where such clauses restrict the use of the property to use by the original and named tenant, if that use is the only use permitted under the lease then the hypothetical tenant's name will be substituted for that of the original tenant for rent review purposes, as was held by the Court of Appeal in *Law Land Co. Ltd* v *Consumers Association Ltd* (1980) 255 EG 617. In that case the use clause provided that the premises were not, without the prior written consent of the landlord, to be used otherwise than as offices for the Consumer's Association and its associated organisation. If the valuer based his open market valuation on that restriction then a nonsense would be made of the rent review clause since there would only be one potential tenant. This decision was applied in *Sterling Land Office Developments Ltd* v *Lloyds Bank plc* [1984] 2 EGLR 135, where the use clause provided: 'not ... for any purpose other than a branch of Lloyds Bank Ltd'. Here the court went further and inserted new wording, and held that for the purposes of rent review the use clause would be read as 'not to be used for any purposes other than as premises of the hypothetical willing lessee'.

There are limitations to the *Law Land* case. In *James* v *British Crafts Centre* [1987] 1 EGLR 139, CA, it was distinguished on the basis that in *Law Land* leaving a blank in the use clause in which the name of the new hypothetical lessee could be inserted was necessary to determine the open market rent, whereas in the *James* case the existence of the alternative use meant that the hypothetical open market could be assessed. Therefore, if there is an alternative use, the *Law Land* case will not apply.

The courts have not followed the *Law Land* approach where the use is confined to a particular business of the tenant as opposed to a particular tenant. In *SI Pension Trustees Ltd* v *Ministerio de Marina de la Republica Peruana* [1988] 1 EGLR 119, *Law Land* was distinguished. Here the premises could not be used 'otherwise than as offices in connection with the lessee's business of mortgage finance and insurance consultants', and it was held that it should be assumed that the hypothetical tenant would be a mortgage finance and insurance consultant. Thus, the court was not prepared to write a blank for the tenant's business.

3.8.3.3 *Qualified restriction: consent needed*
In this category the use is restricted to a particular use unless the landlord's consent is obtained. There is no proviso that the landlord's consent is not to be unreasonably withheld, and no such proviso is implied (*Guardian Assurance Co. Ltd* v *Gants Hill Holdings Ltd* (1983) 267 EG 678). It would appear that the valuer can take into account that the landlord could consent to a change of use. See *Forte & Co. Ltd* v *General Accident Life Assurance Ltd* [1986] 2 EGLR 115, where certain uses were specified and then the clause provided that the property could be used for such other purpose or purposes as might be authorised by the landlord The court held that the valuer could take into account the fact that the landlord might authorise other forms of user; it was for the valuer to decide whether this was a factor which he could evaluate and, if so, what weight he should give it.

3.8.3.4 *Fully qualified restriction: consent not to be unreasonably withheld*
This type of clause is the most common and provides what the use will be unless the landlord's consent is obtained, such consent not to be unreasonably withheld. The effect at rent review of such a clause is that the valuer has to consider every possible purpose for which the premises could legally and physically be used and every potential tenant for any such purpose (*Tea Trade Properties Ltd* v *CIN Properties Ltd* [1990] 1 EGLR 155).

3.8.3.5 *Use Classes Order*
It is common for the use of the premises to be defined by reference to the Use Classes Order. The Order contains a number of classes of use, and

within each class there is a range of permitted uses. The lease will specify the class permitted under the lease and will generally provide that consent to a change within the class will not be unreasonably withheld. This means that the valuer can value on the basis of a fairly wide user. However, the tenant may then have its rent assessed on a use which is not actually carried on by it.

When using such a formula the draftsman must make it clear whether the reference to the Use Classes Order is to the one existing at the time of the lease, or any later one in existence at review. There is no presumption either way as to whether it was intended that a reference should include a reference to the order for the time being in force, and if it is not clear it will be a matter for construction. In *Brewers Company* v *Viewplan plc* [1989] 2 EGLR 133, the lease referred to Class III of the Use Classes Order 1972, which had been revoked and superseded by the Town and Country Planning (Use Classes) Order 1987. The draftsman had provided for statutory modifications of the Planning Acts and so Morritt J said that the draftsman had been well aware of the necessity to make plain, where intended, that a reference to existing legislation included a reference to any statutory modification. In contrast to the Planning Acts clause, the 1972 Order clause was confined to the 1972 Order alone, and Morritt J went on to say that it was readily understandable that the landlord should wish to confine the benefit to the tenant within a range of which he knew at the time of the lease. This decision was followed in *Worcester City Council* v *A.S. Clarke (Worcester)* [1994] EGCS 31.

The lease may contain an assumption that there is planning permission, but even if there is no express assumption it may be implied. In *Bovis Group Pension Fund* v *GC Flooring & Furnishing Ltd* (1984) 269 EG 1252, the reviewed rent was to be assessed on the basis that the premises 'might reasonably be expected to be let for office purposes', and the Court of Appeal held that the existence of planning permission for office use had to be assumed. However, in *Daejan Investments* v *Cornwall Coast Country Club* (1985) 50 P & CR 157, the permitted use of the property was as a casino but no assumption was made that the hypothetical tenant would have a consent from the Gaming Board permitting the premises to be used as a gaming club. Similar decisions were made in *Trusthouse Forte Albany Hotels* v *Daejan Investments (No. 1)* [1980] 2 EGLR 123 and *Parkside Clubs (Nottingham) Ltd* v *Armgrade* [1995] 48 EG 104. In the latter case there was an assumption that the necessary licences had been granted to the 'Tenant', but the Court of Appeal held that 'the Tenant' was the actual tenant and not the hypothetical tenant, and therefore it could not be assumed that the hypothetical tenant had the necessary licence.

3.8.3.6 Statutory restrictions on use

The general position is that the property will be valued with the benefit of any statutory consents and subject to any statutory provisions that exist on the review date (*Rushmoor BC* v *Goacher* (1985) 52 P & CR 25 and *Railstone Ltd* v *Playdale* [1988] 2 EGLR 153). The valuer cannot take into account the fact that the premises will be/may be used in breach of planning control (*Compton Group Ltd* v *Estates Gazette Ltd* (1978) 36 P & CR 149). However, the valuer may take into account the possibility that planning permission will be granted in the future for development if the wording of the lease allows such a construction (*Rushmoor BC* v *Goacher*). This is sometimes referred to as 'hope value', and in *Rushmoor* it was held that in the circumstances of that case development potential could be taken into account. The clause in question stated that in determining a new rent regard was to be had 'to all the circumstances then existing including any permission for the carrying out of any development of the said piece of land granted pursuant to the Town and Country Planning Acts 1962–1968 or any subsequent legislation or any regulations thereunder'. The tenant's argument that planning was a circumstance to be regarded only if there was planning permission in existence, was rejected.

A concern for tenants relates to the situation where a personal consent may have been obtained by the tenant. The rent review clause may contain an assumption that the benefits of any planning permission and consents are available for the hypothetical tenant. If the personal permission has been obtained through the efforts of the tenant and it enhances the value of the property, the tenant may feel it is unfair for the landlord to get the benefit of any increased rent. However, the landlord may also be caught out by such an assumption in circumstances where a property has planning permission for a wide use but a personal permission is granted to a tenant for a more specialised use; the wider use would result in a greater rent, but the personal permission would be taken into account at review. Thus it may prove fairer to base the valuation on a different, non-personal planning permission even if it does depart from reality.

3.8.3.7 The impact of the clause on valuation

The content of the use clause will affect the valuation of the open market rental at review, with the position being in general that the more restricted the use is the lower the open market rent will be as the group of potential tenants who can comply with the restrictions will be more limited.

While an absolute prohibition can have a considerable effect on the rental value of a property, the impact of any particular use restriction will be a matter for the determination of the valuer. When deciding what type of use clause should be incorporated into the lease, the landlord and tenant will, as ever, have different concerns. If the landlord wants complete control of the use then this has to be balanced against a possible lower rent being achieved at review. The landlord could attempt to get round this by providing that the restriction on use should be disregarded for rent review purposes, but this is clearly unfair to the tenant as the tenant will pay for something he does not have, and therefore such a provision will generally be opposed by the tenant.

3.8.3.8   *The impact of use clauses on alienation*
The use clause must be considered in the light of any clause restricting the assignability of the lease (see 3.8.4 below). If there is a fully qualified use restriction and a clause which allows alienation with the landlord's consent then there will be few valuation problems at review. However, if there is an absolute restriction on user with an absolute restriction on alienation, this can depress the rental at review.

3.8.4   **Alienation**

3.8.4.1   *Alienation covenants*
Such covenants restrict the assignment, under-letting or parting with possession of the lease, or sharing or parting with occupation, and can effect the amount of rent obtainable on review. For example, if a tenant is prohibited from subletting a very large building, this will restrict the number of tenants to those who are willing to take on large premises and may then reduce the rent achievable on review.

Very few leases will contain an absolute prohibition on assignment and under-letting, but the landlord will want to control who his or her tenant is and therefore some restriction is usual. There will be little impact on review if the alienation clause is of the type which is generally acceptable given the type of property. However, adverse consequences are likely to flow if the landlord imposes excessive restrictions which go beyond those necessary to protect the landlord. The type of clause which is generally acceptable is one which allows alienation with the landlord's consent, such consent not to be unreasonably withheld. Even if the clause only states that there can be no alienation without consent, s. 19(1) of the Landlord and Tenant Act 1927 implies the proviso that it must not be unreasonably withheld. Use and alienation covenants should always be read together.

3.8.4.2   *Authorised guarantee agreements*
A new issue which will have to be addressed by valuers over the next few years is the existence of authorised guarantee agreements (AGAs) in

alienation provisions, in leases granted in pursuance of the Landlord and Tenant (Covenants) Act 1995. Many landlords have insisted on AGA provisions, which effectively result in the continuance of the doctrine of privity of contract, albeit for a more limited period. When such leases come up for review, if AGAs are not so widely used at that time then the lease could be seen as onerous, which would result in a discount in the rent. Clearly, a possible way to avoid such a result is to include a disregard of any effect on rent of an AGA. Alternatively, the lease could contain financial tests which prospective assignees have to satisfy; and if they do not satisfy the tests then the landlord could have the option of requiring an AGA.

3.8.5 Repair

Repair clauses come in many forms, but if such a clause imposes an unusually onerous burden on the tenant then this will result in a lower rent at review if the actual lease terms are incorporated into the hypothetical lease (*Norwich Union Life Assurance Society* v *British Railways Board* [1987] 2 EGLR 137). In the *Norwich Union* case the market rent was reduced by 27.5 per cent. The repair clause provided that the tenant was 'to keep the demised premises in good and substantial repair and condition and when necessary to rebuild, reconstruct or replace the same and in such condition yield up the same at the expiration or sooner determination of the said lease'. This repair clause was shown to be more onerous than such clauses for other, similar properties.

A further problem for the landlord occurs where the tenant is in breach of a repair covenant, as the property will be valued in its actual state which will have the effect of reducing the rental, giving the tenant an unfair advantage. Accordingly, to avoid such consequences, most review clauses will provide an assumption that the tenant has complied with its obligations under the lease. However, even if there is no express provision, the tenant cannot take advantage of its own wrong and argue that a reduced rent should be paid even though the reduction would be due to his own default (*Harmsworth Pension Funds Trustees Ltd* v *Charringtons Industrial Holdings Ltd* (1985) 49 P & CR 297; see 3.4.3). Similarly, in *Little Hayes Nursing Home* v *Marshall* (1993) 66 P & CR 90, which related to an option to purchase the property at the open market value, it was held that the premises were assumed to be in the condition they would have been in but for any breach of covenant by the lessees, as a party to a contract is not entitled to take advantage of his own wrong.

Where it is assumed that the premises are in repair, arguments can arise between the parties as to the level of repair that is to be assumed. For example, in *Land Securities plc* v *Westminster City Council (No. 3)* [1995] 1 EGLR 145, the landlord contended that the air conditioning was out of repair and that the tenant was under an obligation to repair it, and that the only way to repair it was in fact to replace it at a cost of £1,350,000. The tenant said that the air conditioning could be repaired and that the premises should be valued as they stood (albeit with the air conditioning repaired, which would give the air conditioning a further life of five years) and not (as the landlord contended) with the installation of a new air conditioning system. The arbitrator agreed with the tenant and as a result reduced the rent by £200,000 p.a. to reflect the actual state of repair which he found complied with the repairing covenant.

3.8.6 Alterations and improvements

The lease will usually contain some type of restriction on the tenant's right to alter the premises. There can be a total prohibition, or a qualified prohibition (in that the landlord's consent is required). Where the restriction is qualified, it is implied under s. 19(2), Landlord and Tenant Act 1927 that consent to improvements will not be unreasonably withheld. If the lease allows the tenant to alter or improve the premises then this will be reflected in the value, and will generally increase the value as a tenant will usually pay more for the ability to carry out improvements. (This is often referred to as 'hope value'.) Usually, the lease will restrict the tenant's ability to do such works and therefore restrict the development potential of the property. If there is a total prohibition then the valuer will be unable to take into account potential development. If consent is needed to make improvements, the valuer will have to decide what effect this has on value. In the case of *Iceland Frozen Foods plc* v *Starlight Investments Ltd* [1992] 1 EGLR 126, the Court of Appeal held that if the rent review clause states that improvements must be disregarded then the valuer is prevented from treating the tenant's right to carry out improvements as giving the tenant a benefit which would result in extra rent being paid.

The *Iceland* decision did not meet with universal approval, and in *Lewisham Investment Partnership Ltd* v *Morgan* [1997] 51 EG 75, Neuberger J distinguished *Iceland* on the facts (although there seems little to distinguish them!). *Lewisham* reflects what was previously understood to be the position — that if a tenant is permitted to carry out improvements, the development potential should be taken into account when assessing the new rent. In *Lewisham*, Neuberger J said that the *Iceland* reasoning 'confuses rentalising improvements with the right to carry out improvement. Improvements are physical things which, under the terms of the instant rent review clause and that in *Iceland*, must not be rentalised; the right to carry out improvements is wholly different'.

3.9 ASSUMPTION THAT COVENANTS COMPLIED WITH

There will generally be an assumption that the tenant has complied with his covenants (see 3.8.5 above on repair), which means that the tenant cannot benefit from his own wrong and the premises will be valued on the basis that the tenant has so complied. The assumption that the tenant's covenants have been complied with is limited, however, in that it is designed to benefit only the innocent party. This is illustrated in *Hamish Cathie Travel England Ltd* v *Insight International Tours Ltd* [1986] 1 EGLR 244, where the lease provided that the rent was to be determined on the basis that the tenant had complied with all the covenants and that no account was to be taken of the effect of improvements (to which the landlord had given consent). The tenant's argument that certain improvements carried out without the landlord's consent should be ignored, since the landlord's consent was required for those improvements and since there was an assumption that the tenant had complied with its covenants, was unsuccessful.

An assumption can also be included that the landlord has complied with his covenants, but most tenants object to such an assumption as the landlord will generally benefit from it and they will then pay rent on something that does not exist through no fault of their own. Given that it has been held that an assumption that the tenant's covenants have been complied with only applies to benefit an innocent party, it seems unfair that a landlord could benefit when he is clearly not innocent. It is not entirely clear whether that will be the court's view in rent review, but in a case under s. 24A, Landlord and Tenant Act 1954, the court said that when fixing an interim rent they would have regard to the actual state of repair of the property and that therefore an assumption was not implied that the landlord had complied with his covenants (*Fawke* v *Chelsea (Viscount)* [1979] 3 All ER 568, CA). The difficulty for the valuer with rent review is that the rent is fixed at review, and therefore if the tenant enforced the covenant against the landlord after review, the tenant would get a repaired property at a rent fixed at a time when it was in disrepair. *Clarke* v *Findon Developments Ltd* (1984) 270 EG 426 (a rent review case), rejected the *Fawke* decision and stated that a valuer cannot, in the absence of express provision, impose a variable rent which will increase when the landlord has complied with its covenants.

Example 12
Example of an assumption that covenants complied with

The assumption that the covenants contained in this Lease on the part of the [Landlord and the] Tenant have been fully performed and observed.

Note
See the above comments on the inclusion of the assumption that the landlord has complied with its covenants

3.10 ASSUMPTION OF REINSTATEMENT OF PREMISES

It is common to have an assumption that if the premises are damaged or destroyed, it will be assumed that they have been reinstated for rent review purposes. On the face of it this does not seem particularly problematic for a tenant who is responsible under a repairing covenant, as it is his or her obligation to keep the premises in good repair and the review will be on the basis of that having been done. Additionally, where the damage or destruction is caused by an insured risk, most leases provide that rent will cease to be paid until the premises are fit for use again. This is less comforting for the tenant than it might at first appear, as the rent will not cease where an uninsured risk has caused the damage or destruction, or where the damage has not resulted in the premises being unfit for use. Also, the period during which rent ceases to be paid is usually limited in time and rent may therefore have to be paid even though the premises are not fit for use.

Tenants can try to exclude the assumption, but landlords are unlikely to accept this; however, they may accept a qualification limiting the assumption to damage or destruction caused by breach of the tenant's covenants or caused by an insured risk. Such a clause provides some protection for the tenant, and it would be very important for such a limitation to be included where the landlord has obligations in relation to rebuilding or repairing.

Example 13
Example of an assumption of reinstatement of premises

The assumption that if the Premises have been destroyed or damaged [by an insured risk or as a result of a breach of covenant by the Tenant] they have been fully rebuilt or reinstated.

Note
The limitation contained in the brackets may be unacceptable to landlords, see above comments.

3.11   ASSUMPTION RELATING TO VAT

Until the introduction of the Finance Act 1989, value added tax (VAT) did not relate to land transactions. However, since that Act land transactions are now within the VAT provisions. The grant of any interest in land is an exempt supply, but an election can be made so that a particular grant will not be exempt. The effect of such an election in relation to leases is that VAT will be charged on rent. This election is known as 'opting to tax', or 'electing to waive the exemption'.

A prospective tenant will always need to know whether the landlord has elected to waive the exemption, and if the election has not been made then the lease will generally contain a provision allowing such an election at a future date. If VAT is charged then this will not be a problem for any tenant who is a taxable person as he or she will be able to set off the VAT paid against any VAT received and reclaim any excess. However, if the tenant is not a taxable person, in that supplies exempt services (e.g., banks, building societies), there will be nothing to set against the VAT it has to pay and consequently the rent is effectively increased by 17.5 per cent (the current rate of VAT).

The fact that some tenants may be unable to recover VAT could have an adverse effect at review, as a tenant who cannot recover VAT may only be willing to pay a lower rent to reduce the impact of the VAT charge. As a result of this, landlords have incorporated an assumption into the lease to protect themselves against any potential disadvantage caused by VAT. The assumption which is commonly drafted is set out in Example 14 below.

Example 14
Example of an assumption relating to VAT

The assumption that the Tenant is able to recover any VAT payable by it onrent and other payments to be made by it under this Lease.

While the example shown is commonly used, it has been suggested that it may not cover all considerations. The issue raised in *Precedents for Conveyancers* is that the clause could result in a tenant claiming a discount at review. The reasoning behind this point is that it could be argued that the false assumption would deter willing lessees, and so the tenant could ask to be compensated for having to accept such a provision. The form of clause suggested in *Precedents for Conveyancers* is set out in Example 15 below and aims to stop the willing lessee claiming that the lease could be disadvantageous.

Example 15
Example of an assumption relating to VAT

The rent shall be reviewed on the following assumptions at the relevant review date ... that the willing lessee and its potential assignees or underlessees of the demised premises suffer no disadvantage at the relevant review date or at any time during the term arising from an actual or potential election by the Landlord to waive exemption in respect of Value Added Tax so far as concerns rent or any other taxable supply received by the Tenant under or in connection with this Lease.

3.12 VARIATION TO THE ORIGINAL TERMS

Throughout the duration of a lease the parties will often vary the terms of the lease, or enter into licences granting consent to alterations or user. The question which then arises is whether the hypothetical lease incorporates only the terms of the original lease, or whether it incorporates the lease as varied. The later deed should expressly state what the review consequences are to be, but if it fails to do so then the terms of the original lease will have to be considered. If the lease provides that the rent is to be reviewed on the terms of 'the lease as they may be varied from time to time', so long as the later deed does vary the lease then the later deed will be incorporated.

In *Pleasurama Properties Ltd* v *Leisure Investments (West End) Ltd* [1986] 1 EGLR 145, CA, a licence had been granted allowing the sub-lessee to convert part of the premises subject to reinstating it at the end of the subtenancy to its former condition. The question was whether that obligation to reinstate should be taken into account in assessing the rent at rent review. The relevant clause in the lease referred to the rent being reviewed on the basis of 'the covenants on the part of the tenant and conditions similar to those herein contained'. There was no specific provision in the lease, or the licence, that the covenant to reinstate contained in the licence should be taken into consideration. If the obligation to reinstate was taken into account then a lower rent would be awarded. Lloyd J stated (*obiter*) that the words 'herein contained' were capable of applying to the lease as varied but that they did not do so in this case. He went on to say that it could not have been intended that the tenant, for whose sole benefit the consent was given, should reap an additional benefit in the form of a reduction in the rent which would otherwise become payable on review. In the case of *SI Pension Trustee Ltd* v *Ministerio de Marina de la Republica Peruana* [1988] 1 EGLR 119, the clause referred to 'the provisions of the lease' and not to 'the provisions as they may be varied from time to time', and this lead the court to the decision that the variations were to be ignored (no reference was made to the *Pleasurama* decision).

In *Lynnthorpe Enterprises Ltd* v *Sidney Smith (Chelsea) Ltd* [1990] 1 EGLR 148, EGCS 60, CA which was upheld on appeal ([1990] 2 EGLR 131), Warner J said that there was no general proposition that a provision in a rent review clause which required it to be assumed that the hypothetical lease contains covenants similar to those in the actual lease is to be construed as requiring any subsequent variation to be ignored. He said that this was the approach taken by the Court of Appeal in a number of cases and is the 'presumption in favour of reality' (see 1.2.5) which requires the terms of the hypothetical lease to reflect any variations (other than perhaps variations personal to a particular tenant) in the terms of the actual lease. This approach was followed in *Commercial Union Life Assurance Co. Ltd* v *Woolworths plc* [1996] 1 EGLR 237, where it was held that options contained in a supplemental lease were to be taken into account in determining the rent at review. In that case the rent was to be reviewed on the basis of '... the same terms and conditions ... as the present demise', and it was held that 'this present demise' referred not to the lease as a document but to the demise created by the lease.

Difficulties can be encountered, then, in deciding whether or not the subsequent deed or licence does actually vary the original lease. If a deed or licence is expressed to be personal to a particular tenant, it will be difficult to prove that it varied the lease (*SI Pension Trustee Ltd* v *Ministerio de Marina de la Republica Peruana*). Also, if the later deed is a licence, it may be difficult to claim that it varies the lease. In the *Pleasurama* case (see above), Lloyd J said: 'I will assume — though I certainly do not accept — that the deed of licence is to be regarded as a variation of the lease.'

3.13   INTRODUCTION TO DISREGARDS

Generally, the hypothetical lease will require the valuer to disregard certain things at review because the parties consider that such matters might increase or decrease the rent. It is entirely at the discretion of the parties what disregards they want, but (as with the assumptions) unusual disregards can lead to difficulty in valuation. Most leases will include express disregards but, there are cases where disregards have been implied. Such cases will be limited to where the absence of an implied term would mean that the lease lacks business efficacy, or does not reflect the parties' intentions. In *Jefferies* v *O'Neill* (1983) 46 P & CR 376, a term was implied which required the valuer to disregard the fact that access to the premises could be obtained only through the tenant's adjoining property, otherwise the rent review provisions would have no practical effect (see 3.4.2.3). The more common disregards are discussed at 3.13.2–3.13.4 below.

3.13.1   Section 34, Landlord and Tenant Act 1954

Nowadays, it is the common view that the rent review clause should specifically state the matters that are to be disregarded, but previously many leases incorporated the provisions of s. 34, Landlord and Tenant Act 1954 (s. 34 is reproduced in Appendix 6). Section 34 of the 1954 Act lays out the factors to be disregarded when the court is determining a rent under a renewed lease. Various problems then arose when interpreting s. 34, one such problem being whether an incorporation of the disregards set out in s. 34 referred to s. 34 as originally enacted in 1954, or the provision as subsequently amended by the Law of Property Act 1969. In one post-1969 lease, the court appeared to assume that the reference was to the amended section (*Euston Centre Properties Ltd* v *H & J Wilson* [1981] 1 EGLR 57), but in *Brett* v *Brett Essex Golf Club Ltd* [1986] 1 EGLR 154, CA, when considering a post-1969 lease, the court came to the opposite conclusion (although it did state that the assumption that the relevant Act was the amended version was the more natural and reasonable assumption in the majority of cases, but not on the construction of this particular lease).

3.13.2   Tenant's occupation

A tenant in occupation may pay more than the going rate in order to avoid the disruption involved in moving; or the tenant's occupation may diminish the value of the premises if the tenant has not been satisfactory and the premises thereby deteriorate (*Scottish Newcastle Breweries plc v Sir Richard Sutton's Settled Estates* [1985] 2 EGLR 130, at 136 E). Accordingly, the effect on rent of the tenant's occupation of the property is commonly disregarded at review. The disregard of tenant's occupation would appear to have a similar effect to the assumption of vacant possession, but the disregard does not require vacant possession to be assumed (*Scottish Newcastle Breweries plc v Sir Richard Sutton's Settled Estates*) and the disregard does not necessarily lead to the exclusion of all evidence of the tenant's previous occupation, only such evidence as effects rents (*Cornwall Coast County Club v Cardgrange* [1987] 1 EGLR 146).

Generally, the disregard will be of the occupation of the tenant, or his subtenant or their predecessors in title. Consideration should also be given to whether the tenant's occupation of adjoining property should be disregarded. If a tenant does occupy adjoining premises and the disregard does not specifically deal with such occupation, it may be argued that such occupation can be taken into account at review (see 3.2.4). This may then increase the rent of the property, as the particular tenant may pay more for the property because of its proximity to its other premises. A contrary argument would be that the valuer is dealing with a hypothetical lease and as such the existence of adjoining premises would not be relevant. While this may be the case, if the tenant does occupy neighbouring properties then the disregard should include occupation of those properties to avoid future argument.

Example 16
Example of a disregard of tenant's occupation

Disregard any effect on rent of the fact that the Tenant, his subtenants, or their predecessors in title have been in occupation of the Premises.

3.13.3   Goodwill

The effect on rent of the tenant's goodwill is usually disregarded, as otherwise a tenant who has built up a successful business will pay extra rent due to his own efforts. Case law has provided a number of definitions of goodwill. In *Cruttwell v Lye* (1810) 17 Ves 335, at 346, Lord

Eldon described it as being 'the probability that the old customers will resort to the old place'. Lord Macnaughton stated, in the case of *IRC v Muller & Co.'s Margarine Ltd* [1901] AC 217, at 223–4, that 'goodwill' was 'the benefit and advantage of the good name, reputation and connection of a business'.

The aim of a provision disregarding goodwill is to exclude reference to any goodwill which comes from the occupier, as opposed to any goodwill which is derived from the actual property itself.

Goodwill disregards usually provide that any goodwill attached to the property due to the carrying on of a business by the tenant or his predecessors in that business will be disregarded. If a particular business started before the commencement of the lease then the disregard should expressly provide that it includes the goodwill relating to before the term.

If the lease does not disregard goodwill but contains a provision disregarding occupation then a disregard of goodwill will usually be implied (*Prudential Assurance Co. Ltd v Grand Metropolitan Estate Ltd* [1993] EGCS 58).

Example 17
Example of a disregard of goodwill

Disregard any goodwill attached to the Premises because the business of the Tenant, his subtenants, or their predecessors in title in their respective businesses is or was carried on there.

3.13.4   Improvements

The position is that when assessing a new rent the valuer must consider the property as it is on the review date; and unless the lease provides to the contrary, the valuer cannot disregard the effect on rent of improvements carried out or paid for by the tenant (*Ponsford v HMS Aerosols* [1979] AC 63, HL; see 3.4.3). Generally, improvements mean a higher rental for the property, and the resulting injustice to the tenant has lead to provisions in the rent review clause which expressly disregard tenant's improvements.

If the lease contains a disregard of tenant's improvements, it must be noted that such a disregard does not require a planning permission obtained to do the works to be disregarded. See *Railstone Ltd v Playdale* [1988] 2 EGLR 153, where Knox J said that there is a strong presumption against either the landlord or the tenant obtaining an advantage which is referable to a factor which has no existence as between the actual landlord and the actual tenant. In this case there was plainly a factor which had existence as between the landlord and the tenant in the shape of the existing planning permission, and unless the clause compelled him to disregard the planning situation Knox J had no doubt that the court would not adopt such an attitude.

The disregard of improvements has a number of elements which are considered below.

3.13.4.1 The meaning of 'improvement'

Before something can be disregarded it needs clear definition. Difficulties in distinguishing a repair from an improvement have lead to a great deal of case law, mainly in interpreting repairing clauses. If the work is a 'repair' then it will be taken into account for valuation purposes, but if it is an 'improvement' and there is an express disregard it will have to be ignored. In *Morcom v Campbell-Johnson* [1956] 1 QB 106, Denning LJ said that an improvement involves the provision of something new for the benefit of the occupier, while a repair is only the replacement of something which is already there even if it is replaced by its modern equivalent. Also, more recently, in *New Zealand Government Property Corp v H.M. & S.* [1982] QB 1145, CA, it was held that an improvement means an alteration or addition to the structure of the property and does not include the installation of tenant's fixtures. Additionally, works which are or become part of the property will not be improvements even where they were paid for by the tenant (*Scottish & Newcastle Breweries plc v Sir Richard Suttons Settled Estates* [1985] 2 EGLR 130, where a building was built according to the design of the tenant, it was not an improvement as it was part of the original building).

It can prove difficult to determine what an improvement actually is as a matter of law; and on a practical level it can be difficult to identify what improvements have already been carried out, as is illustrated in the case of *Young v Dalgety plc* [1987] 1 EGLR 116 where the drawings of the improvements had been lost and the building had thereafter been refurbished. It is clearly important to have accurate records of the 'before' and 'after' state of the property which can then be referred to at review. Such record must be passed from one tenant to the next.

3.13.4.2 The time of the improvements

Generally the lease will provide that only improvements carried out during the lease by the tenant will be disregarded, with the effect that any improvements carried out by the tenant under a previous lease will not be disregarded. Even if the lease does not so provide, this will generally be the case, as works carried out before the grant of the lease will not be considered to be 'improvements' as they will have become part of the property (*Re 'Wonderland' Cleethorpes* [1965] AC 58, HL). Alternatively, it could be argued that works done before the grant of the lease could not be carried out by the 'tenant', only by the 'proposed tenant' (*Euston Centre Properties Ltd v H & J Wilson Ltd* (1981) 262 EG 1079; see 3.13.4.3 below). However, in *Hambros Bank Executor & Trustee Company Ltd v Superdrug Stores Ltd* [1985] 1 EGLR 99, *Re 'Wonderland'* was distinguished on the facts and fitting out works done prior to the grant of the lease were disregarded. In *Re 'Wonderland'* the works had been done many years previously, whereas in *Hambros* the works had been done shortly before the current tenancy by the person who was to become the current tenant and with a view to the grant of the current tenancy. The argument mentioned above that such works would become part of the property was not put forward.

The approach in *Hambros* was followed in *Scottish & Newcastle Breweries plc v Sir Richard Suttons Settled Estates* [1985] 2 EGLR 130, where it was said that if the improvements are referable to the grant of a tenancy under consideration then they are to be disregarded. It is crucial that the disregard is of all tenant's improvements, whenever carried out and whether or not by the person who was the tenant at the time (see 3.13.4.3).

3.13.4.3 The person who carried out the improvements
Under the statutory disregards in s. 34(1)(c), Landlord and Tenant Act 1954 (as amended), the improvements which were to be disregarded were those carried out by 'a person who at the time [they were] carried out was the tenant'. This provision resulted in some injustice to tenants. See *Euston Centre Properties Ltd v H & J Wilson Ltd* [1982] 1 EGLR 57, where improvements carried out by the tenant before the commencement of the term were not disregarded as at the time they were done the person who did them was not considered to be the 'tenant' for the purposes of the disregard. A similar result can be seen in *Brett v Brett Essex Golf Club Ltd* [1986] 1 EGLR 154, CA, where the tenants had built a golf course under a term of their original lease. They were later granted a subsequent lease which disregarded tenant's improvements, but it was held that they were not 'tenants' for the purposes of the disregard. On the grant of the new lease, a new chapter had begun, and it was only in respect of the new lease that the court was concerned. However, in the *Hambros* case (see 3.13.4.2) the slightly different wording lead the court to a different conclusion. The wording of the disregard did not contain a requirement that the improvement had to be carried out during the term. The disregard was of 'any effect on rent of any improvement carried out by the tenant', and since the

work had been done by the person defined in the lease as 'the tenant' it was held to be irrelevant that the works were done before the lease was granted.

Such uncertainties should be avoided by making it clear that improvements carried out by the tenant (even if he is not technically the tenant at the time) prior to the grant of the lease should also be disregarded (see Example 18 at 3.13.4.4 below).

It has been held that works carried out on behalf of the tenant and at its cost fall within the disregard since they have been ordered and paid for by the tenant (*Scottish & Newcastle Breweries plc* v *Sir Richard Suttons Settled Estates* [1985] 2 EGLR 130, where works were carried out by the landlord's contractors). In *Durley House Ltd* v *Cadogan* [2000] EG 183, the tenant entered into a management agreement with a company who then undertook a substantial amount of work on the premises. The question that then arose was whether the works which had been done by the management company would be disregarded at review. The rent review clause incorporated s. 34(2), Landlord & Tenant Act 1954 (see 3.13.1). It was held that work carried out by a contractor or other party by arrangement with the tenant fell within the provision, unless the landlord could identify some factor leading to a contrary conclusion. Neuberger J said:

> ... it seems to me arguable that all that would be required of a tenant to bring himself within section 34(2) is that he either physically effects the works himself or gets a third party to do so. A tenant may well not satisfy section 34(2) in a case where he has got a third party to do the works unless he can establish some involvement in identifying, supervising and/or financing the works resulting in the specific improvements concerned.

The judge went on to say that he had real doubt as to whether a tenant could merely rely on a covenant by a subtenant or licensee to upgrade and refurbish premises, to justify the contention that improvements carried out by them could be treated as having been carried out by the tenant. Carrying out such works, in his view, implied a degree of involvement in their execution. Lastly, the point was made that the s. 34(2) does not require the tenant to have paid for the improvements.

From the above it is important to note that the tenant should ensure that improvements carried out by its subtenants and their predecessors in title and licensees are expressly disregarded, since improvements undertaken by them would otherwise affect the rental value. Disregarding licensees' improvements will be of particular relevance to department stores which have a high percentage of franchisees who may do works that are considered to be improvements.

Sometimes landlords undertake improvements, and the rent review clause must address such an occasion. If the improvements are paid for by the landlord then the landlord will not agree to such improvements being disregarded, but if they are paid for by the tenant, either directly or indirectly through a service charge, then such improvements should be disregarded.

3.13.4.4 *Improvements carried out under an obligation to the landlord*

General Usually, the disregard of tenant's improvements is limited, in that it will not include improvements carried out in pursuance of an obligation to the landlord. This has to be treated with caution, as the obligations do not necessarily have to be contained in the lease and could be in some other contractual document, as in *Godbold v Martin The Newsagents* [1983] 2 EGLR 128 where the landlord granted a licence at the tenant's request to the tenant to carry out certain works. (Landlords commonly grant licences permitting alterations and impose an obligation on the tenant in the licence to do the works in a certain way.) The question that then arose was whether this was 'an obligation'. If it was then it would result in the alterations not being disregarded at review. The courts thus far have been reluctant to construe the licence in such a way, instead holding that the licence did not impose an obligation to do the works but imposed conditions if the tenant chose to do the works (*Godbold v Martin The Newsagents*).

The Court of Appeal in *Historic Houses Hotels v Cadogan Estates* [1995] 1 EGLR 117, CA, considered the effect of licences which contained a covenant that when the works of alteration/improvement were completed, all the provisions contained in the lease were to be applicable to the premises in their then altered state as if the premises in their then altered state had originally been comprised in the lease. The landlords argued that at rent review it had to be assumed that the premises to be valued were the premises as altered, and that the disregard of tenant's improvements was to be ignored in respect of improvements carried out under the licences. It was held that it made no sense to exclude the disregard of tenant's alterations or improvements, and if the disregard was to be inapplicable clearer wording would be needed.

A less favourable result for tenants is illustrated in *Daejan Properties Ltd v Holmes* [1996] EGCS 185, where the *Historic House* case was distinguished. In *Daejan*, there was an absolute prohibition against altering the property but the landlord granted a licence to the tenant allowing certain alterations. The licence provided that it was granted 'to the intent that the works ... shall be deemed to be carried out in pursuance of an obligation to the lessor', and the lease provided that improvements carried out under an obligation to the landlord would not be disregarded. It was held that the improvement carried out under the licence could not be disregarded because of the deeming provision.

Fitting out   A further consideration is where a tenant has an obligation (usually in an agreement to lease) to do fitting out works. If the rent review clause contains an express or implied assumption of vacant possession (see 3.5 above) then to the extent that the fitting out works are tenant's fixtures and fittings they will be ignored for rent review purposes. If there is no such assumption then, because they are carried out under an obligation to the landlord, the fitting out works will not be disregarded unless a clause specifically specifies this to be the case. The parties will have to agree on whether the fitting out works are to be disregarded.

Statutory obligations   Many leases require the tenant to observe statutory obligations, and this too can have an impact on the disregard of tenant's improvements. In *Forte & Co. Ltd* v *General Accident Life Assurance Ltd* [1986] 2 EGLR 115, the tenant did certain works to the property to comply with the Fire Precautions Act 1971, and it was held that those works would not be disregarded as they had been done in pursuance of an obligation to the landlord.

It can be seen from the above that the tenant will want to draft the disregard in such a way that all work done pursuant to any statutory obligation will be disregarded.

Obtaining consents   Most rent review clauses provide that only improvements which have been done with the landlord's consent will be disregarded. Therefore, those done without the landlord's consent will be taken into account. An argument put forward in *Hamish Cathie Travel England Ltd* v *Insight International Tours Ltd* [1986] 1 EGLR 244 was rejected, the argument being that where landlord's consent was required but had been unreasonably withheld, such works should be disregarded. The lease did contain an assumption that the tenant had complied with his covenants. While holding that the landlord's consent had not been unreasonably withheld, the court went on to say that even if consent had been unreasonably withheld the works would not be disregarded as the clause did not contain a term stating that should be the case.

Often, in consenting to alterations the landlord will prepare a licence authorising the works. If such a licence provides that the premises are to be reinstated at the end of the lease then this will also be disregarded (*Pleasurama Properties Ltd* v *Leisure Investments (West End) Ltd* [1986] 1 EGLR 145). Also, if the licence provides that the provisions of the lease should apply to the premises as altered as if the altered premises had been originally comprised in the lease, then the alterations will still be disregarded (*Historic Houses Hotels Ltd* v *Cadogan Estates* [1995] 10 EG 140, CA).

Example 18
Example of a disregard of tenant's improvements

Disregard any increase in rental value of the Premises attributable at the relevant review date to any improvements to the Premises carried out, with consent where required, otherwise than in pursuance of an obligation [except an obligation contained in clause (insert the number of the clause which deals with statutory obligations)] to the Landlord or his predecessors in title either—
  (a) by the tenant, his subtenants, or their predecessors in title during the Term or during any period of occupation before the Term, or
  (b) by any tenant or subtenant of the Premises before the commencement of the Term provided that the Landlord or his predecessors in title have not since the improvement was carried out had vacant possession of the relevant part of the Premises.

Note
The words in square brackets would have the effect of disregarding all work done pursuant to any statutory obligation (see above).

3.14   COMPARABLES

3.14.1   General

The most commonly used method of valuation is comparables. The valuer gathers evidence of the then current rentals paid on properties which are similar to the demised premises and held on similar terms to assist in determining the market rent for the property. This method of valuation works well only when there are sufficient comparables to utilise; so, for example, if the rent of a shop in a shopping mall is to be reviewed then the current rents payable in respect of the other shops in the mall will be relevant. However, where a property is unusual (or even unique) there may be few, if any, comparables to utilise. In such situations the parties may agree to base the valuation on hypothetical premises (see 3.4.1).

Once the valuer has obtained evidence of the rents of comparable premises, it is for the valuer to assess what weight such evidence will have. Valuation is not, however, an exact science and much will depend on the expertise of the valuer.

3.14.2 Post-review comparables

The lease will require the rent to be determined on a certain date ('the review date'; see 2.16 and 2.18) and the question often arises whether the valuer can take into account evidence that has come about after the review date when considering the available comparables. The position is that evidence of rents agreed after the rent review date is admissible. See *Segama* v *Penny Le Roy* [1984] 1 EGLR 109, where Staughton J said:

> If the rent of comparable premises had been agreed on the day after the relevant date, I cannot see that such an agreement would be of no relevance whatever to what the market rent was at the relevant review date itself. If the lapse of time before the agreement becomes greater then, as the Arbitrator saw, the evidence will become progressively unreliable as evidence of rental values at the relevant date. The same is no doubt true of rents agreed some time before the relevant date; but nobody suggested to me that those should be excluded.

3.14.3 Post-review events

The position as far as events occurring after the review date is concerned is that they are inadmissible, except to the limited extent that such events occur between the review date and the date of the post-review comparable if such events affect the rent for the comparable, as the argument is that the hypothetical landlord and tenant could not have known of any such events at the rent review date.

In *Currys Group plc* v *Martin* [1999] EGCS 115, the premises comprised a shop in a shopping centre. The expert had considered the rents of three other units in the shopping centre, one of which had been reviewed after the review date of *Currys'* lease. All three tenants had received substantial inducements, and all three went into liquidation after the review date. *Currys* argued that the events which occurred after the review date should be taken into account (i.e. the liquidations) as they were relevant to the valuation. However, the court held that the expert had been entitled to disregard post-review events which would not have been known to the parties at the date of review. Therefore, economic or political changes which occur after the review date must be ignored.

It is difficult to see the sense in the distinction between post-review 'comparables' and post-review 'events'. The argument that the hypothetical landlord and tenant could not have known of any such events at the rent review date applies to both situations. However, that is the position, and Hill and Redman's *Law of Landlord and Tenant* states that 'the post-valuation date comparable is admissible as evidence of value not because it would be known to the hypothetical lessor and lessee on the valuation date but because it is an indication of the rental value on the valuation date irrespective of such knowledge'.

CHAPTER FOUR

Determination of Rent

4.1 INTRODUCTION

All leases should provide for the parties failing to agree a revised rent. Virtually all leases will provide that on default of agreement, the rent will be determined by an independent third party, usually a surveyor.

Generally, the lease will provide that the independent third party will be appointed by agreement between the parties; and failing agreement, by the President of the Royal Institution of Chartered Surveyors (RICS) or a person acting on his behalf. See Appendix 3, clause 2.2.

4.2 APPLYING TO THE PRESIDENT

The lease should state whether both parties have the right to apply to the President for an appointment, or whether only one party can do so. If only the landlord can apply, the lease should provide that if there is a delay the tenant can apply after a certain period of time has passed. If there is no such provision, the landlord may not opt to have a rent review which could prejudice the tenant if the rent review clause is upwards/downwards and the market has fallen. This problem was encountered in the following cases.

In *Harben Style Ltd* v *Rhodes Trust* [1995] 1 EGLR 18, only the landlord could request the appointment of a surveyor and the landlord refused to do so. The lease provided that if the rent was not ascertained at all then it would continue at the rate payable before the review period. The tenants contended that the landlord could not frustrate the effect of a possible downwards review by the device of declining either to agree on or to apply for the appointment of a valuer, and asked the court to determine the rent as the machinery for rent review had broken down. The court declined to do so as the lease provided for what was to happen if the rent was not ascertained at all in that the old rent would continue. The crucial factor in this case was that there was a rent provided for if the landlord did not choose to apply for the appointment of a surveyor.

In *Royal Bank of Scotland* v *Jennings* [1997] 1 EGLR 101, CA, only the landlord could request the appointment of a valuer and the lease provided that 'If . . . any revised rent . . . has not been ascertained . . . before the first day . . . appointed for payment of rent for the relevant Rental Period, rent shall continue to be payable . . . at a rate equal to the highest rent previously payable hereunder until the first day for payment of rent after the revised rent has been ascertained'. The landlords refused to agree on or to apply for a valuer to be appointed, and the tenants obtained a court order compelling the landlord to apply for the appointment of a valuer. Unlike the *Harben* case, there was no provision detailing what would happen in the event of a rent not being ascertained at all. The lease in *Jennings* did fail to provide for what should happen if the revised rent turned out to be less than the rent that had been previously paid but, it was conceded that an appropriate implied term providing for repayment of any overpayment needed to be added. It was argued by the landlords that they had an option whether or not to invoke the rent review machinery as only they could apply to the President. Sir Richard Scott VC said:

> In my judgment, the issue depends upon whether construing the lease as a whole, the conclusion is justified that the landlord was intended to have that option. If the landlord was intended to have that option, the landlord was entitled to exercise it and to decide whether or not there should not be a rent review. But if the judge below was right in concluding that the provision in question was no more than mere machinery for the carrying out of rent reviews which were intended to happen in any event, then, on authority, there is no reason why the landlord's failure to make the application should be allowed to frustrate the contractual intention discerned from the lease as a whole. The court will in that event if necessary supply machinery to prevent that frustrating refusal from achieving its purpose.

The Court of Appeal dismissed the landlords' appeal wherein they contended that they had the option whether or not to invoke the rent review machinery, and held that the implication to be gained from the lease as a whole was that there would be a rent review for each of the rental periods. The general approach in *Jennings* was followed in *Addin* v *Secretary of State for the Environment* [1997] 14 EG 132, which involved a trigger notice (see 2.15).

4.3   FORM OF APPLICATIONS

The RICS prefers applications to the President for the appointment of an arbitrator or an expert to be made on its own forms, but applications can simply be made in writing. The application will not be processed until the prescribed fee has been paid and a copy of the lease has been received, but that does not mean that an application is not valid without those items. See *Staines Warehousing Co. Ltd* v *Montagu Executor & Trustee Company Ltd* [1987] 2 EGLR 130, where an application had to be made within a set time limit and the issue was whether a letter informing the President of the lease details was a valid application even though no fee had been paid. The application was held to be valid based on the then existing RICS Guidance Notes, even though the application would not be processed until the fee was paid. Useful guidance on the appointment and role of arbitrators and experts is produced by the 'RICS Guidance Notes for Surveyors acting as Arbitrators and Independent Experts in Commercial Property Rent Reviews' (RICS Guidance Note).

4.4   APPOINTING AN ARBITRATOR OR AN EXPERT

4.4.1   Express term

The third party's capacity is very important as it will affect the procedures to be followed. The lease should expressly stipulate in the rent review clause whether the independent third party is to act as an expert or an arbitrator. The very differing roles make it of crucial importance that the choice is clear. A full discussion of the differences between arbitrators and experts is to be found at 4.5 below.

Even where there is clear wording, the courts have been prepared to investigate fully. See *Palacath Ltd* v *Flanagan* [1985] 2 All ER 161, where it was stated that the surveyor would 'act as an expert and not as an arbitrator . . . will consider any statement of reasons or valuation or report submitted to him . . . but will not in any way be limited or fettered thereby [and] will be entitled to rely on his own judgment and opinion', and the court said that such a statement was not conclusive but was a very potent matter to be taken into account. Whether the surveyor was to act as an expert or as an arbitrator would be determined by considering the true construction of the lease.

4.4.2 Ambiguous wording

If the lease is unclear or contains conflicting provisions, the courts will determine the status of the third party. In *North Eastern Co-operative Society Ltd* v *Newcastle upon Tyne City Council* [1987] 1 EGLR 142, the lease provided that the rent was to be

> determined by an independent surveyor agreed between the lessors and the lessees or (in default of agreement) by an arbitrator to be nominated by the President of the Royal Institute of Chartered Surveyors on the application of either party and this lease shall be deemed for this purpose to be a submission to arbitration within the Arbitration Act 1950 . . .

The issue arose as to whether the surveyor appointed by the agreement of the parties was acting as an arbitrator or an expert, and the judge held that he was to act as an expert. The reference to arbitration applied only when the President appointed, accordingly the independent surveyor who was appointed by agreement acted as an expert.

4.4.3 Absence of any reference to capacity

In *Fordgate Bingley Ltd* v *Argyll Stores Ltd* [1994] 2 EGLR 84, the rent review clause failed to state expressly whether the surveyor should act as an expert or as an arbitrator. The lease provided that:

> (3) If the landlord and tenant shall not have agreed the open market rent less than six months before the relevant rent review date, the open market rent shall be determined by a surveyor (hereinafter called 'The appointed surveyor') to be agreed upon in writing by the landlord and the tenant not less than four months before the relevant review date, and in default of such agreement to be nominated by the president for the time being of the Royal Institution of Chartered Surveyors upon the application of the landlord, to be made not less than three months before the relevant rent review date.
>
> (4) The determination of the open market rent by the appointed surveyor (which shall be final and binding on the landlord and the tenant without recourse to the provisions for arbitration herein before

contained), and the fees of the appointed surveyor shall be borne by the landlord and the tenant in equal shares.

. . .

(6) If the landlord and the tenant shall not have agreed the open market rent at least six months before the relevant rent review date, and the landlord shall neglect to make the application referred to in paragraph 3 hereof (unless the parties hereto shall in writing agree otherwise) any notice already given by the landlord to the tenant under the provisions of paragraph 2 hereof shall be void and of no effect.

The landlord failed to apply to the President within the time scale specified in the lease, and applied under s. 27 of the Arbitration Act 1950 (now s. 12, Arbitration Act 1996) for the appointment of an arbitrator out of time (see 2.11). The tenant contended that s. 27 did not apply as the lease provided for the appointment of an expert, not an arbitrator, and consequently the landlord had lost the right to review. The judge said that looking at the lease he found the overall effect clear, and it was held that the surveyor was to act as an expert. The particular considerations were:

(a)   the deliberate non-adoption of any express reference to arbitration in the rent review clause contrasted with other clauses in the lease which did refer to arbitration;

(b)   the rent review provisions did not necessarily presuppose a dispute, even though in many instances in practice no doubt that might arise (the concept of resolution of a difference or dispute is at least some significant indicator that you may have an arbitration rather than a valuation);

(c)   the nature of the exercise — the determination of rent under a rent review — is particularly suitable for expert procedures.

The judge went on to say that there were one or two points that he did not find of any great weight. The use of the word 'surveyor', he said, was of some slight significance, but he did not think it was particularly compelling as it is fairly clear that a surveyor is going to be the right sort of person to deal with the question of the rent review, and that would be true whether it was an arbitration or an expert procedure. The use of the words 'determination' and 'final and binding', he said, had no weight at all, the latter phrase being consistent with either type of procedure. The provision that the fees of the surveyor should be paid in equal shares, he said, had some weight. That provision would be void under s. 18 of the Arbitration Act 1950 if this were an arbitration. However, the judge said that he did not find it necessary to attach weight to that in reaching his conclusion.

4.5 THE DIFFERENCES BETWEEEN AN ARBITRATOR AND AN EXPERT

The main differences are in the following areas:

- Procedure
- Knowledge and expertise
- Costs
- Appeal
- Negligence

4.5.1 Procedure

4.5.1.1 Arbitrator
The arbitrator's powers are contained in the Arbitration Act 1996, which came into force on 31 January 1997 and applies to all applications after that date. The Act contains the general duty of the arbitrator, being:

(a) to act fairly and impartially as between the parties, giving each party a reasonable opportunity of putting his case and dealing with that of his opponent, and

(b) to adopt procedures suitable to the circumstances of the particular case, avoiding unnecessary delay or expense, so as to provide a fair means for the resolution of the matters falling to be determined (s. 33(1)).

The parties are free to agree on the procedure for appointing any arbitrator(s) (called 'the tribunal'), but if they fail to do so ss. 15–18, Arbitration Act 1996 contain detailed provisions. Under s. 15, the parties are free to agree on the number of arbitrators to form the tribunal, and if there is no agreement then the tribunal shall consist of a sole arbitrator. Section 16 provides that if there is to be a sole arbitrator, the parties will jointly appoint an arbitrator; if there are to be two then each party will appoint one; and if there are to be three then each party will appoint one and the two arbitrators will then appoint a third. Section 17 deals with the situation where each party is to appoint an arbitrator and one party refuses to do so; in that situation, the party who has appointed his arbitrator will give notice that he proposes to appoint his arbitrator as the sole arbitrator. Section 18 applies where the procedures in ss. 16 and 17 have failed, and gives the court certain powers including the power to appoint any arbitrator(s).

A further important power is contained in s. 27, which deals with the situation where an arbitrator ceases to hold office, perhaps due to his death. In such a case, the parties can agree on how to deal with the situation, but failing agreement ss. 16 and 18 will apply to fill the vacancy.

Section 34(1) of the Arbitration Act 1996 provides that it is for the tribunal to decide all procedural and evidential matters, subject to the right of the parties to agree any matter. Section 34(2) then contains a non-exhaustive list of the tribunal's powers, including:

(a) when and where any part of the proceedings to be held;

(b) the language(s) to be used;

(c) whether any (and if so what form of) written statements of claim and defence are to be used, when these should be supplied and the extent to which such statements can later be amended;

(d) whether any (and if so which) documents or classes of documents should be disclosed between and produced by the parties, and at what stage;

(e) whether any (and if so what) questions should be put to and answered by the respective parties, and when and in what form this should be done;

(f) whether to apply strict rules of evidence as to the admissibility, relevance or weight of any material sought to be tendered on any matters of fact or opinion, and the time, manner and form in which such material should be exchanged and presented;

(g) whether and to what extent the tribunal should itself take the initiative in ascertaining the facts and the law;

(h) whether and to what extent there should be oral or written evidence or submissions.

In addition to the above, unless otherwise agreed by the parties, s. 38 gives the arbitrator further powers, including the ability to give directions in relation to any property which is the subject of the proceedings and which is owned by or is in possession of a party to the proceedings, for the inspection, photographing, preservation, custody or detention of the property. The arbitrator can also order that samples be taken from, or any observation be made of or experiment conducted upon, the property. This is an invaluable power when dealing with an uncooperative tenant.

If a question of law arises during the arbitral proceedings, the court may be asked to determine the matter, albeit that an arbitrator has power to determine the matter himself. Under s. 45(1), an application can be made to court for the determination of a preliminary issue, but only if:

(a) it is made with the agreement of all the other parties to the proceedings; or

(b) it is made with the permission of the tribunal and the court is satisfied:

(i) that the determination of the question is likely to produce substantial savings in costs, and
(ii) the application is made without delay.

The form of the arbitrator's award is dealt with in s. 52, which provides that if the parties do not agree as to the form then:

(a) it has to be in writing;
(b) it has to be signed by the arbitrators;
(c) it must contain the reasons for the award, unless it is an agreed award or the parties have agreed to dispense with reasons; and
(d) the award must state the seat of the arbitration and the date when the award is made.

An arbitrator's award can, with the leave of the court, be enforced in the same way as a judgment or order of the court (s. 66(1)).

4.5.1.2 Expert
There are no statutory controls over an expert, and therefore if the expert is to follow certain rules or procedures then the lease must contain these (although they rarely do so). If a point of law arises then RICS Guidance Note 4.5.3 states:

... the Independent Expert should ask the parties to consider whether:
(a) they will agree what is the correct answer to the point of law, or one of them will commence proceedings in the Courts to decide it, before he proceeds with his Determination;
(b) they would instead prefer him to take, and proceed on the basis of, legal advice on the point, which he incorporates in his Determination. If he wishes to seek the advice of counsel he may now do so direct ...
(c) he should continue to deal with the reference, but (by their written consent) as an Arbitrator, with or without a legal assessor: he should then proceed as indicated in paragraph 3.2.8 [para 3.2.8 contains the guidance for arbitrators when dealing with disputes involving issues of law].

If all of these courses are rejected the Independent Expert should proceed to decide the point himself on the basis that it forms part of that group of issues referred to him for determination....

There is some opportunity for the parties to appeal against an expert's decision (see 4.5.4.2), but to have any chance of doing so the parties should provide in the lease that the expert's determination should be reasoned, as otherwise if only a figure is provided it will be difficult to show that he failed in his duty to the parties. The independent expert should generally establish at the beginning of the proceedings whether a reasoned determination is required.

4.5.2 Knowledge and expertise

4.5.2.1 Arbitrator

An arbitrator is exercising a quasi judicial function, and therefore must reach a determination based on the evidence provided by the parties. Usually, the arbitrator will have been appointed because of his particular knowledge and expertise, but his role is similar to that of a judge in that evidence will be presented to him and he will make a decision based upon that evidence. An arbitrator cannot rely on evidence that he obtains for himself unless he discloses that evidence to the parties, who then have the opportunity to respond to it. See *Unit Four Cinemas v Tosara Investments* [1993] 2 EGLR 11, where Dunn LJ said: 'It is undoubtedly true that an expert arbitrator can use his own expert knowledge. But a distinction is made in the cases between general expert knowledge and knowledge of special facts relevant to the particular case.' The arbitrator does not have to take account of the views of the expert witnesses (*Lex Services plc v Oriel House* [1991] 2 EGLR 126).

4.5.2.2 Expert

The expert uses his own knowledge and expertise to reach a determination. He may or may not ask the parties to put evidence before him, and will carry out his own enquiries and investigations before reaching a conclusion. If the parties do put evidence before him, he is not bound by it (*North Eastern Co-operative Society v Newcastle upon Tyne City Council* [1987] 1 EGLR 142); however, if the evidence the parties put before him is sufficient, he is under no duty to make his own investigations (*Wallshire Ltd v Aarons* [1989] 1 EGLR 147).

4.5.3 Costs

4.5.3.1 Arbitrator

Sections 59–65 of the Arbitration Act 1996 contain the provisions dealing with the costs of an arbitration and how these should be allocated. Section 59 confirms that 'costs' are:

(a)   the arbitrators' fees and expenses;
(b)   the fees and expenses of any arbitral institution concerned; and
(c)   the legal or other costs of the parties.

The arbitrator has the power to award costs, subject to any agreement of the parties (s. 61(1)). However, under s. 60, if an agreement states that a party is to pay the whole or part of the costs of the arbitration in any event, this will be valid only if made after the dispute has arisen. Costs will be awarded (unless the parties agree otherwise) on the general principle that costs should follow the event, except where it appears that in the circumstances this is not appropriate in relation to the whole or part of the costs (s. 61(1)). This follows the general litigation principle that costs should be awarded to the party who is successful.

The parties are free to agree what costs of the arbitration are recoverable, but if they either completely or partly fail to do so then the provisions of s. 63 apply and the arbitrator determines the recoverable costs. Unless the arbitrator determines otherwise, the recoverable costs are determined on the basis that a reasonable amount shall be allowed in respect of all costs reasonably incurred. Any doubts as to whether costs were reasonably incurred or were reasonable in amount shall be resolved in favour of the paying party (s. 63(5)).

Under s. 64, the arbitrator's recoverable fees and expenses are only such reasonable fees and expenses as are appropriate in the circumstances. If there is any question over the level of the fees, the matter can be determined by the court on the application of any party (s. 64(2)).

Section 65 contains an important provision which could lead to a reduction in unnecessary costs and offer some protection against well-off parties. Under this section, unless otherwise agreed between the parties, the arbitrator can limit the recoverable cost of the arbitration.

'Calderbank offers' must also be considered, as they are relevant in arbitration proceedings. A Calderbank offer occurs where a party makes a 'without prejudice offer to settle except as to costs' in an effort to limit his liability for costs. Under RICS Guidance Note 3.10.6, for a Calderbank offer to be effective it has to contain:

(a)   an unconditional written offer to settle the rent review at a specified rental figure;
(b)   a reasonable offer to pay the other party's costs incurred up to the date of the offer. In rent review disputes it is usually appropriate to propose that each party bears its own costs plus one-half of the arbitrator's fees;

(c) the offer should state that it is made 'without prejudice save as to costs'.

(See *Calderbank* v *Calderbank* [1975] 3 All ER 333.)

Arbitrators have a duty to deal with the issue of costs in their awards (s. 63(3)) and will not consider such matters after the award has been made. Therefore, the party making the *Calderbank* offer must ask the arbitrator to make an interim award, final on all matters except costs.

The *Calderbank* offer can limit the party's costs in that if, for example, a landlord makes a *Calderbank* offer which is not accepted by the tenant and the arbitrator then determines a rent equal to or higher than the landlord's offer, in the absence of special circumstances the arbitrator should order the tenant to pay the landlord's costs and arbitrator's fees which were incurred after the date when the offer ought reasonably to have been accepted.

4.5.3.2 *Expert*

An expert is in a completely different position as regards costs. An expert can award costs only if the power is given to him under the provisions of the agreement. Costs in this context include not only the parties' costs, but also the expert's own fees. If an expert is to determine who shall be responsible for costs then an express condition must be contained in the rent review clause, or in a later agreement made by the parties. If no such clause is included, an expert will usually ask the parties for such a power after he has been appointed.

4.5.4 Appeal

4.5.4.1 *Arbitrator*

Section 67 of the Arbitration Act 1996 contains the procedure to be followed when an aggrieved party wants to challenge an award on the ground that the arbitrator has exceeded his substantive jurisdiction. The court has discretion to confirm the order, vary the award or set aside the award in whole or in part.

Under s. 68, an aggrieved party can apply to the court to challenge an award on the ground of serious irregularity affecting the arbitrator, the proceedings or the award. 'Serious irregularity' means irregularity of one or more of the following kinds which the court considers has caused or will cause substantial injustice to the applicant:

(a) failure by the tribunal to comply with its general duty to act fairly and impartially and to conduct the proceedings in accordance with appropriate procedures (s. 33);

(b) the tribunal exceeding its powers (s. 67);

(c) failure by the tribunal to conduct the proceedings in accordance with the procedure agreed by the parties;

(d) failure by the tribunal to deal with the issues that were put to it;

(e) any arbitral or other institution or person vested with powers in relation to the proceedings or the award exceeded its powers;

(f) uncertainty or ambiguity as to the effect of the award;

(g) the award having been obtained by fraud or in a way contrary to public policy;

(h) failure to comply with requirements as to the form of the award;

(i) any irregularity in the conduct of the proceedings which is admitted by the tribunal or by any arbitral institution vested with powers in relation to the proceedings or the award.

If there is serious irregularity, the court can remit the award to the arbitrator for reconsideration, set the award aside or declare the award to be of no effect.

A party can also, subject to certain limitations, appeal to the court on a question of law arising out of an award under s. 69. The limitations are that an appeal cannot be brought except with the agreement of all the other parties or with the leave of the court. It is very unlikely that all the parties will agree to appeal, and therefore leave of the court will invariably be sought. Section 69 contains provisions similar to but more stringent than its predecessor (s. 1, Arbitration Act 1979), but as an indication of the court's approach under the old law in considering when leave would be granted, the court in *Ipswich Borough Council* v *Fisons plc* [1990] 2 WLR 108 said that there was a presumption in favour of finality and therefore the courts were generally reluctant to grant leave to appeal. In *Ipswich*, Lord Donaldson MR said that the test on granting leave to appeal was that a judge has '... to be satisfied that there was a more or less strong prima facie case for thinking that the arbitrator has erred on a question of law'.

Leave to appeal will now be given only if the court is satisfied on the following matters contained in s. 69(3), being:

(a) that the determination of the question will substantially affect the rights of one or more of the parties,

(b) that the question is one which the tribunal was asked to determine,

(c) that, on the basis of the findings of fact in the award—

(i)   the decision of the tribunal on the question is obviously wrong, or

(ii)   the question is one of general public importance and the decision of the tribunal is at least open to serious doubt, and

(iii)   that, despite the agreement of the parties to resolve the matter by arbitration, it is just and proper in all the circumstances for the court to determine the question.

Both the High Court and the county court can hear appeals under the Act (Allocation and Arbitration Proceedings Order 1996 (SI 1996 No. 3215)). Unlike ss. 67 and 68, s. 69 is not mandatory, which means that the parties can make their own arrangements by agreement, but if they fail to do so then this provision will apply. Under s. 69, the court can confirm the award, vary the award, remit the award to the arbitrator for reconsideration or set the award aside.

Section 70 applies to all applications or appeals under ss. 67–69 and contains supplementary provisions relating to challenges, including time limits within which such challenges must be made. Accordingly, under s. 70(3), an application or appeal must be brought within 28 days of the date of the award, albeit that under s. 79 the court has power to extend that time limit. An aggrieved party must act timeously, otherwise the right to object may be lost (s. 73). Under s. 54, the tribunal can decide what the date of the award will be unless the parties agree otherwise. In the absence of a decision by the tribunal, the date of the award is the date on which it is signed by the arbitrator, or (where it is signed by more than one arbitrator) by the last of them. Under s. 55, the award has to be notified to the parties without delay.

4.5.4.2   Expert

Introduction   Whether a challenge can be made to the determination of an expert depends on the terms of the agreement between the parties. If the rent review provisions clearly state that the issue is to be determined exclusively by the expert, the court cannot intervene. If the rent review provisions do not so stipulate, the court will have the jurisdiction to deal with the relevant issue. Whether the court's jurisdiction has been ousted will depend on the construction of the particular rent review provisions. There is no presumption against construing a contract so it does not oust the jurisdiction of the court on a question of law (*Nikko Hotels (UK) Ltd* v *MEPC plc* [1991] 2 EGLR 102).

Challenging an expert   There are remedies against an expert, but they are much more limited than those available when challenging an arbitrator's award. If there is fraud or collusion then the court can intervene and set aside an expert's determination, even if it was to be conclusive and binding, but such cases will be extremely rare. In the absence of fraud or collusion the position is less straightforward. Challenges may be made either after the expert's determination, or after the matter has been referred to the expert but before he has made his determination. The same principles are applied in both instances.

The courts have in recent years favoured the approach that results in the expert's decision being final. The decision of the Court of Appeal in *Jones v Sherwood Computer Services* [1992] 1 WLR 277, CA, lead to the conclusion that it would be very difficult to set aside an expert's determination. In that case the rent review provisions stated that the expert's determination would be conclusive and final and binding for all purposes. A dispute arose between the parties as to whether the expert's decision could be challenged. Dillon LJ said that the first step must be to see what the parties have agreed to remit to the expert, this being a matter of contract. The next step must be to see what the nature of the mistake was, if there was evidence to show that. If the mistake made was that the expert departed from his instructions in a material respect, either party would be able to say that the decision was not binding. The *Jones* decision was applied in *Nikko Hotels (UK) Ltd v MEPC plc* [1991] 2 EGLR 102, where Knox J said:

> ... if parties agree to refer to the final and conclusive judgment of an expert an issue which either consists of a question of construction or necessarily involves the solution of a question of construction, the expert's decision will be final and conclusive and, therefore, not open to review or treatment by the courts as a nullity on the ground that the expert's decision on construction was erroneous in law, unless it can be shown that the expert has not performed the task assigned to him. If he has answered the right question in the wrong way, his decision will be binding. If he has answered the wrong question, his decision will be a nullity.

It is hard to see how an expert could answer the wrong question, and therefore recourse to the courts seems unlikely under those decisions. Also, if the lease does not require the expert to give reasons for his determination (called a 'non-speaking valuation') and he simply provides a figure, recourse to the courts would be almost impossible. From those cases, it became clear that once an expert had made his determination, a challenge would be extremely unlikely.

Where a challenge was made before the expert's determination, it was first of all held in *Postel Properties Ltd v Greenwell* [1992] 2 EGLR 130, that either party could refer a question of construction of the lease to the court in such circumstances. However, the Court of Appeal did not agree in *Norwich Union Life Insurance Society* v *P & O Property Holdings Ltd* [1993] 1 EGLR 164, which did not involve a rent review clause, but where it was held that the court could not make declarations before the expert had made his determination unless the parties agreed to this. The Court said that the object of the parties in choosing an expert was to obtain a speedy and conclusive determination of the matter. Again, the approach appears to be that the expert's determinations cannot be challenged. However, further authority threw the issue into confusion as it seemed to indicate that there could be a challenge on a point of law. Two such cases did not relate to rent review, or even property. The first was *Director General of Telecommunications* v *Mercury Communications Ltd* [1996] 1 WLR 48, HL, where the court stated that if a determination had been made on the basis of an incorrect interpretation of certain expressions then it could intervene, since there was nothing in the agreement preventing it from doing so. Hoffman J's dissenting judgment was upheld by the House of Lords. In it he said:

> So, in questions in which the parties have entrusted the power of decision to a valuer or other decision-maker, the courts will not interfere either before or after the decision. This is because the courts' views about the right answer to the question are irrelevant. On the other hand the court will intervene if the decision-maker has gone outside the limits of his decision-making authority.
>
> One must be careful about what is meant by 'the decision-making authority'. By 'decision-making authority' I mean the power to make the wrong decision, in the sense of a decision different to that which the court would have made. Where the decision-maker is asked to decide in accordance with certain principles and this may mean having, in a trivial sense, to 'decide' what they mean. It does not follow that the question of what the principles mean is a matter within his decision-making authority in the sense that the parties have agreed to be bound by his views. Even if the language used by the parties is ambiguous, it must (unless void for uncertainty) have a meaning. Accordingly, if the decision-maker has acted upon what in the court's view was the wrong meaning, he has gone outside his decision-making authority.

The other case was *British Shipbuilders* v *VSEL Consortium plc* [1997] 1 Lloyd's Rep 106, which laid down a summary of the legal principles governing the issue of whether an expert's decision could be challenged, as follows:

(1)   Questions as to the role of the expert, the ambit of his remit (or jurisdiction) and the character of his remit (whether exclusive or concurrent with a like jurisdiction vested in the court) are to be determined as a matter of construction of the agreement [under which the expert is appointed];

(2)   If the agreement confers upon the expert the exclusive remit to determine a question, (subject to (3) and (4) below) the jurisdiction of the court to determine that question is excluded because (as a matter of substantive law) for the purposes of ascertaining the rights and duties of the parties under the agreement the determination of the expert alone is relevant and any determination by the court is irrelevant. It is irrelevant whether the court would have reached a different conclusion or whether the court considers that the expert's decision is wrong, for the parties have in either event agreed to abide by the decision of the expert;

(3)   If the expert in making his determination goes outside his remit, e.g., by determining a different question from that remitted to him or in his determination fails to comply with any conditions which the agreement requires him to comply with in making his determination, the court may intervene and set his decision aside. Such a determination by the expert as a matter of construction of the agreement is not a determination which the parties agreed should affect the rights and duties of the parties, and the court will say so;

(4)   Likewise the court may set aside a decision of the expert where the agreement so provides if his determination discloses a manifest error;

(5)   The court has jurisdiction ahead of a determination by the expert to determine a question as to the limits of his remit or the conditions which the expert must comply with in making his determination, but (as a rule of procedural convenience) will (save in exceptional circumstances) decline to do so. This is because the question is ordinarily merely hypothetical, only proving live if, after seeing the decision of the expert, one party considers that the expert got it wrong. To apply to the court in anticipation of his decision (and before it is clear that he has got it wrong) is likely to prove wasteful of time and costs — the saving of which may be presumed to have been the, or at least one of the, objectives of the parties in agreeing to the determination by the expert.

One of the latest cases is *National Grid Co. plc* v *M25* [1999] 1 EGLR 65, which is a decision of the Court of Appeal which did involve a rent review clause. The *National Grid* case referred to *British Shipbuilders*, as containing a useful summary, and the dissenting judgment of Hoffman J in the

Mercury case (which was upheld by the House of Lords) was applied. While *National Grid* related to a challenge before the determination by the expert, the decision also makes it clear that if the expert had made a determination on the basis of a misconstruction of the clause then that determination could have been set aside. In *National Grid*, the Court of Appeal provided some guidance:

(a) The Court said that whether the rent review provisions excluded the jurisdiction of the court to construe the lease was a question of construction of the provisions of each lease. Comparing one case and one document with another gives, at best, very limited assistance.

(b) It was clear from the provisions of the lease in question that the valuer had the exclusive power to determine whether any (and if so what) increase ought to be made to the rent. If that was all the rent review clause stated then the court would have no jurisdiction to intervene, but the lease required the valuer to observe certain agreed contractual directions (normal assumptions and disregards contained in clause 1(4)).

(c) If the valuer did something that he was not appointed to do, he would be acting outside his terms of reference, and he did not have a completely free hand in deciding what increase ought to be made. Whether he was acting within his contractual power depended on ascertaining the correct limits of the power conferred on him by the lease. Those limits were ascertained by a process of construction of the lease, and the terms of the lease did not confer on the valuer, either expressly or impliedly, the sole and exclusive power to construe the lease.

Accordingly, the Court could, in this case, determine the question of construction. The Court of Appeal distinguished the *Norwich Union* case because of the presence in *National Grid* of clause 1(4) which set limits on the expert's powers. No such limitation existed in *Norwich Union*.

Another recent case is *Morgan Sindall plc v Sawston Farms (Cambs) Ltd* [1999] 07 EG 135, where a differently constituted Court of Appeal came to a different conclusion. However, this case involved a challenge to the expert's determination where there was a non-speaking valuation of an option. Robert Walker LJ said:

> The whole point of instructing a valuer to act as an expert (and not as an arbitrator) is to achieve certainty by a quick and reasonably inexpensive process. Such a valuation is almost invariably a non-speaking valuation,

with the expert's reasoning and calculations concealed behind the curtain. The court should give no encouragement to any attempt to infer, from ambiguous shadows and murmurs, what is happening behind the curtain.

These contrasting cases illustrate the uncertainty in this area, a natural consequence of each agreement depending on its own terms, read in its own context (from *National Grid*, above).

What is of crucial importance when drafting a rent review clause is that the parties should make it clear whether the independent expert has exclusive jurisdiction, or whether questions of construction or law can be construed by the court. Simply stating that the expert's decision is 'final and binding' may not be sufficient to persuade the court that no challenge should be made to the expert's determination. Conversely, if there is no reference to the decision being 'final and binding', the court may still on a proper construction of the terms of the agreement decide that no challenge can be made to the expert's decision, as was the case in *Morgan Sindall plc v Sawston Farms (Cambs) Ltd*.

If the determination is set aside, the court cannot determine the value itself and the valuation process will have to be restarted. However, in certain circumstances the court may be able to make a declaration of the valuation, if the court can ascertain from the determination what the actual value should be (*Smith v Gale* [1974] 1 WLR 9).

4.5.5 Liability

4.5.5.1 *Arbitrator*
Arbitrators are immune from being sued for negligence under s. 29 of the Arbitration Act 1996, unless they have acted in bad faith. This immunity extends to their employees and agents. For a discussion of bad faith, see *Melton Medes v Securities & Investments Board* [1995] Ch 137.

4.5.5.2 *Expert*
Given the limited remedies available to challenge the expert's determination (see 4.5.4.2), an aggrieved party's principal remedy is to sue in negligence. There is a heavy burden of proof to be discharged, though. It must be shown that:

(a)   there is a usual and normal practice;
(b)   the defendant departed from that practice;

(c)   the course adopted was one that no competent surveyor acting in a rent review would have taken if he had been acting with ordinary care.

This test was set out in *Hunter* v *Hanley* 1955 SLT 213, at 200, and applied by the House of Lords in *Maynard* v *West Midlands Regional Health Authority* [1984] 1 WLR 634.

No one has yet managed to prove negligence against an expert. A recent case where such a claim was unsuccessfully made was *Currys Group plc* v *Martin* [1999] EGCS 119. There, the expert's determination fixed the rent at £107,000 per annum on the basis of a headline rent (see 3.8.2.3), whereas the tenant contended that the new rent should have been £80,000 and that the expert was in breach of his duty to exercise reasonable skill and care. It was held that the valuation exercise was an art and not a science. Accordingly, it was necessary for the claimant to show that the defendant's determination was one that no reasonably competent surveyor could have reached, and it could not be concluded that it had done so. The defendant's approach was one that would have been adopted by at least some competent surveyors and therefore the claim was dismissed.

4.6   CHOICE OF ARBITRATOR OR EXPERT

The choice of appointing an arbitrator or an expert is clearly one of personal taste, and each has advantages and disadvantages which are summarised below.

It has been common practice to choose an expert, as this was thought to be the better option. The reasoning behind that choice may no longer be as persuasive as it once was but the practice continues.

4.6.1   Procedure

An arbitrator must follow the clearly defined rules of procedure contained in the Arbitration Act 1996, whereas an expert has no set procedures to follow other than any specified in the lease.

4.6.2   Evidence

The parties to an arbitration have the opportunity to present their evidence to the arbitrator and therefore can ensure that their views are known to the arbitrator. An expert is under no obligation to hear evidence from the parties, but will often do so.

4.6.3 Fees

Arbitrators' fees can be taxed under the Arbitration Act 1996, whereas those of an expert have no such limitation. In practice the parties generally agree the level of the expert's fee when one is appointed.

4.6.4 Type of dispute

It is generally thought that in more complex cases — for example, where the valuation is of an unusual property with few comparables — the arbitrator is better suited to deal with such determinations. If the valuation is more straightforward then an expert may be better suited to the task.

4.6.5 Costs

Generally, because of the nature of arbitral proceedings, they last longer and are more formal than valuations by experts, and therefore the costs are greater where an arbitrator is involved. This is not without exception, however, as some experts will hear evidence and have a hearing which will involve a similar level of costs.

4.6.6 Speed

The arbitral process can be slower because the parties have the opportunity to present evidence to the arbitrators. Where the expert is involved such presentations are not always needed, which can speed up the decision-making process. However, where submissions are made there may be no difference in the time taken to resolve the matter.

4.6.7 Appeal

An arbitrator's decision can be the subject of an appeal, but under the Arbitration Act 1996 (and its predecessor in 1979) appeals are less likely than they once were. The ability to challenge the expert's decision, however, is very limited (see 4.5.4.2).

4.6.8 Liability

An arbitrator is immune from liability, whereas an expert is liable in negligence. Given that there has never been a successful case against an expert, this is of limited significance.

CHAPTER FIVE

Post-review and Other Procedural Issues

5.1 INTRODUCTION

After a new rent has been agreed or determined, there are still a number of matters which remain to be dealt with, being:

(a) memorandum recording the new rent;
(b) the amount of rent payable from the review date until the new rent is agreed or determined;
(c) the date upon which the new rent becomes payable;
(d) whether interest is payable;
(e) review of rent review;
(f) rent 'freeze';
(g) stamp duty; and
(h) the effect of new rent on original tenant and guarantors.

5.2 MEMORANDUM RECORDING THE NEW RENT

It is good practice to record the new rent in memoranda which are then exchanged and retained with the lease and other title documents. Alternatively, the memoranda could be endorsed on the lease and the counterpart lease. Many leases will provide that memoranda should be prepared post-review, but in the absence of such a provision they should be prepared in any event. Once prepared, the memorandum should be retained with the other title documents so that on a sale of the landlord's or tenant's interest a prospective purchaser has access to all the relevant information on the lease.

Memoranda are particularly important where there is no other evidence of the new rent, as where the new rent has been agreed between the parties as opposed to having been determined by a third party. This is illustrated by the case of *Esso Petroleum Co. Ltd* v *Anthony Gibbs Financial Services Ltd* [1983] 2 EGLR 112, CA. Under the terms of the rent review clause there was a two-year rent-review period during which a notice calling for a review could be served by the landlords. If the landlords failed to give notice during the review period, they had the right to review the rent on serving a month's notice at any time. The landlords did not serve a notice during the review period and the surveyors for both parties reached agreement that no increase in rent should be made, but no memorandum was prepared to reflect that agreement. The landlords subsequently served a notice requiring a review and the question arose as to whether this could be done. The landlords argued that they could serve such a notice because no notice had been served during the two-year review period. The tenant argued that they could not, since an agreement had been reached by the surveyors as to rent. It was held by the Court of Appeal that there had been no final agreement. All that occurred was an agreement by the surveyors of a rental level which they would be prepared to recommend to their clients, therefore the landlords could call for the later review.

Where the rent has been determined by a third party the memoranda should make reference to that, and copies of all the documentation forming part of the arbitration or expert determination (including the award) should also be retained with the title deeds. If the lease has a guarantor then the lease should provide that he also signs the memoranda to reduce the risk of a claim by the guarantor that he is not liable for the new rent (*Torminster Properties Ltd* v *Green* [1983] 1 WLR 676, see 5.9.2).

Where a mistake is made in the memoranda, whether clerical or otherwise, rectification will normally be available. In *Equity & Law Life Assurance Society Ltd* v *Coltness Group Ltd* [1983] 2 EGLR 118, a memorandum was rectified which incorrectly recorded that the rent was agreed until the expiration of the lease as opposed to the next rent review date (a error).

Examples of memoranda from the *Encyclopaedia of Forms and Precedents* are set out in Appendix 7, and below is an example of a clause in a lease requiring memoranda to be prepared (see Appendix 3 for the full rent review provisions).

Example 19
Example of a clause in a lease requiring memoranda to be prepared

Whenever the Rent has been ascertained in accordance with this schedule, memoranda to that effect must be signed by or on behalf of the Landlord and the Tenant and annexed to this document and its counterpart, and the Landlord and the Tenant must bear their own costs in this respect.

5.3   THE RENT PAYABLE FROM THE REVIEW DATE

It is often the case that the revised rent is not determined until after the review date. Leases generally provide that the current rent will continue to be payable on account until the new rent is agreed or determined. In the absence of an express provision, a term may be implied that the current rent continues (*Weller* v *Akehurst* [1981] 3 All ER 411, where there was no express provision as to the rent that would be payable; the court held that in the circumstances, it was wholly reasonable to suppose that the parties intended that the initial rent was to continue).

The lease could provide that a higher amount than the current rent is payable from the review date (sometimes called an 'interim rent'), but that is not usually done and from the tenant's point of view such a provision is usually best avoided as it may give the landlord free rein to fix an unreasonably high rent, albeit only for a limited period. Where there is a provision for an interim rent, it will become payable as from the review date. Once the revised rent is determined any shortfall would be paid by the tenant and any overpayment would be returned by the landlord to the tenant. The parties would have to decide the method for determining the interim rent, and obviously any such method should be fairly quick and easy if this is to have any benefit to the landlord. If such a clause is included, the tenant should ensure it is protected from an unscrupulous landlord by limiting the amount of rent that can be imposed. Careful drafting is needed to avoid the difficulties encountered in *Panavia Air Cargo Ltd* v *Southend-on Sea Borough Council* [1988] 1 EGLR 111, CA. In this case, the initial rent was £2,700 and the rent review clause provided that the rent was to be agreed between the parties; but failing agreement it was to be determined by a third party. Various time limits were laid down in the schedule, and para. 13 stated that 'as respects the periods of time referred to in this Schedule time shall not be deemed to be of the essence of the contract'. However, para. 14 went on to provide that if for any reason no review took place, or a review was not completed within 12 months of the commencement of any review period then the rent payable would be increased by 25 per cent of the rent currently payable. The tenants contended that time was of the essence as to the 12-month period and that therefore the rent would be increased by 25 per cent (from £2,700 to £3,375, as opposed to a rent of probably £20,000 if the rent review provisions had taken effect) as there had been no review within the 12-month period. The landlords argued that the provision that time was not of the essence applied to the whole schedule, not only to the paragraphs before para. 13. It was held that the wording of the provision made it clear that it applied to the whole schedule. Therefore, the landlords were entitled to have the rent determined by a surveyor in accordance with the provisions in the lease. An example of a clause from the *Encyclopaedia of Forms and Precedents* providing for an interim rent is included in Appendix 8.

The clause should state that the current rent is paid 'on account' as this may reduce the impact of counter-inflation legislation if it is ever reintroduced. By stating that the current rent is paid 'on account', if counter-inflation provisions are re-introduced which restrict rent to that payable when the provisions were brought into force, the rent would be frozen at the revised figure as it would be the revised figure that was payable on the date that rents were frozen, although it would not be determined for some time (see 5.7).

Example 20
Example of a clause providing for rent to be paid on account

If the Rent payable during any review period has not been ascertained by the relevant review date, then rent is to continue to be payable at the rate previously payable, such payments being on account of the Rent for the review period.

5.4   THE DATE UPON WHICH THE NEW RENT BECOMES PAYABLE

The lease will almost always provide that the tenant will be liable for the new rent from the review date, and therefore it will be payable retrospectively (*CH Bailey Ltd* v *Memorial Enterprises Ltd* [1974] 1 WLR 728). The lease should also state when the difference between the old and new rents is to be paid (or any overpayment refunded). This can be the next rental date under the lease after the new rent has been agreed or determined, or some leases provide for it to be paid forthwith upon the new rent being ascertained. If the lease does not contain an express provision dealing with this, it was held by the Court of Appeal in *South Tottenham Land Securities Ltd* v *R & A Millett (Shops) Ltd* [1984] 1 All ER 614, that the rent will become payable on the next rent date following the determination. The effect of this is that rent will not be in arrears until such rent day has passed, and thus any provision requiring interest to be paid on late payments of rent will not be activated until such time (*Shield Properties & Investments Ltd* v *Anglo-Overseas Transport Co. (No. 2)* (1987) 53 P & CR 215; see also 5.5).

Where there has been a long period of time between the review date and agreement or determination, this can cause practical financial problems for a tenant who may have substantial arrears to pay, and it may be wise to include a provision allowing the tenant to pay the arrears in instalments.

5.5 INTEREST

Given that very few new rents are agreed or determined until after a review date, landlords normally want to protect themselves against any financial disadvantage by including a provision in the lease that interest is paid on the shortfall between the old rent and the new rent. Such a provision may also have the effect of limiting the benefit to a tenant by unnecessarily delaying to agree a new rent and thereby enjoying the property at a lower than market value rent. If acting for a tenant, payment of interest may be unacceptable, particularly where any delay is not its fault. However, from the landlord's point of view, the tenant will have had the use of the money while he has not.

In the absence of an express provision, interest is not generally payable (*Trust House Forte Albany Hotels* v *Daejan Investments Ltd* [1980] 2 EGLR 123). However, if the reviewed rent is determined by arbitration, the Arbitration Act 1996, s. 46, confers a power on the arbitrator to award interest. Obviously, if the parties simply agree on the reviewed rent or an expert determines it, interest will not be payable in the absence of an express provision.

Most leases will contain a general interest provision for late payments under the lease which will generally have a penal rate of interest. A tenant should ensure that the rate of interest applicable to the shortfall is lower than that penal rate. Given the decision in *South Tottenham Land Securities Ltd* v *R & A Millett (Shops) Ltd* [1984] 1 All ER 614 (see 5.4), that in the absence of an express provision the rent will become payable on the next rent date following the determination, a tenant who pays the shortfall on the next payment day will not be liable for interest on arrears as there are technically no 'arrears' until the next payment day has passed. Therefore, if the landlord wants interest to be payable from the review date, there will have to be an express provision to that effect. It is also advisable from the tenant's point of view that the interest provision provides that interest is calculated so that a tenant only pays interest on the shortfall due on each rent day for the period from the rent day until the date the shortfall is actually paid, and not on all the shortfall from the review date to the date the shortfall is paid. If the latter provision applied it would result in a greater sum being payable where more than one rent day had passed since the review date.

Example 21
Example of a clause dealing with back-payments and interest

If the Rent payable during any review period has not been ascertained by the relevant review date, then the Tenant must pay to the Landlord, [within (*state period, e.g., 7 days*) of (*or as required*) on] the date on which the Rent is agreed or the arbitrator's award is received by him, any shortfall between the Rent that would have been paid for that period had it been ascertained on or before the relevant review date and the payments made by the Tenant on account [and any VAT payable thereon], and interest, at the base lending rate from time to time of the bank referred to in or nominated pursuant to clause (*insert clause number*), in respect of each instalment of rent due on or after that review date on the amount by which the instalment of the Rent that would have been paid had it been ascertained exceeds the amount paid by the Tenant on account, the interest to be payable for the period from the date on which the instalment was due up to the date of payment of the shortfall.

Note
See Appendix 3 for the full rent review provisions.

5.6   REVIEW OF RENT REVIEW

Over a long term, it is possible that circumstances will change and that rent review clauses will fail to reflect current practice. In a very long lease, the parties should consider whether a provision should be built in allowing them to reconsider either the terms of the entire rent review clause, or simply the rent review periods. Landlords will want any review to be at their discretion to avoid being forced into a change which is not to their advantage. On the other hand, tenants will want an element of control, and whether they get it will be a matter of negotiation between the parties. An example of provisions from the *Encyclopaedia of Forms and Precedents* allowing revision of the review date is set out in Appendix 9.

5.7   RENT 'FREEZE' PROVISIONS

During the early part of the 1970s the Government introduced legislation to control rents under business premises. The effect of these controls was to 'freeze' rent at the rate payable on a specified date. Although it seems unlikely that controls will be re-introduced, most leases will deal with the possibility. Landlords are concerned that statutory controls could prevent a review (although past legislation did not do so but limited the amount of rent payable) and therefore insert a provision which allows a rent review to take place after the rent 'freeze' has ceased to operate. Even if a review has not been prohibited and the control related only to the amount of rent, landlords will generally want to postpone the review as the comparables available to assess the open market rent will be depressed. Where such postponement is agreed, the tenant should ensure that the landlord has to initiate a review within a specified period of time after the end of the controls, otherwise the landlord could delay until such time as is more advantageous to him.

Rather than postponing the rent review until after the statutory controls have ceased, there could be a disregard of the effect of any controls or other statutory restrictions on rent. This option may be difficult in practice, as establishing what the open market rent is will be problematic where all lettings are subject to the statutory controls. The 1970s legislation restricted the amount of rent payable by providing that no rent was payable at a rate exceeding that payable on a specified date (whether or not that rate had been determined as to the amount). The effect of this was that if a rent review date was before the 'freeze' then the rent payable would be the rent that was contractually payable, whether or not the amount had been determined. If the rent review clause provided that the current rent was to be paid 'on account', the rent would be frozen at the reviewed figure and not the current one, as the reviewed rent was the one that was 'payable' even though it had not been determined. Modern rent review clauses provide that the current rent is payable 'on account' to deal with the possibility of a future 'rent freeze'.

Example 22
Example of a clause dealing with counter-inflation provisions

If at any review date a statute prevents, restricts or modifies the Landlord's right either to review the Rent in accordance with this Lease or to recover any increase in the Rent, then the Landlord may, when the restriction cr modification is removed, relaxed or varied — without prejudice to his rights, if any, to recover any rent the payment of which has only been deferred by statute — on giving not less than (*state minimum notice, e.g., 1 month's*) nor more than (*state maximum notice e.g., 3 months'*) notice to the Tenant [at any time within (*state period, e.g., 6 months*) of the restriction or modification being removed, relaxed or varied, time being of the essence,] require the Tenant to proceed with any review of the Rent that has been prevented or to review the Rent further where the Landlord's right was restricted or modified. The date of expiry of the notice is to be treated as a review date — provided that nothing in this paragraph is to be construed as varying any subsequent review date. The Landlord may recover any increase in the Rent with effect from the earliest date permitted by law.

Note
The words in square brackets are there to prevent the landlord postponing a review until such time as he feels is more financially advantageous to him.

5.8   STAMP DUTY IMPLICATIONS

Varying rent does not normally result in the payment of stamp duty under the Stamp Act 1891. If the lease provides for the rent to be reviewed and a memorandum is entered into to record the new rent, there will be no liability to duty under s. 77(5) of the 1891 Act. Accordingly, stamp duty is chargeable at rent review only if the document effecting the review actually varies the rent, and this will occur rarely (for example, where the lease did not contain rent review provisions but the parties have agreed to a review).

5.9   THE POSITION POST-REVIEW OF AN ORIGINAL TENANT AND GUARANTORS

5.9.1   Original tenants

If the lease was entered into before the Landlord and Tenant (Covenants) Act 1995 (which came into force on 1 January 1996) then the original tenant will continue to be liable to pay the rent throughout the term. Section 18 of that Act applies to both pre- and post-Act leases and provides that an original tenant remains liable for increased rent due under rent review provisions, provided the covenants in the lease are not varied after 1 January 1996. If the covenants are varied after that date then the original tenant is not liable to pay any increase resulting from the variation (s. 18(2)) provided that the landlord had absolute discretion in deciding whether or not to agree to the variation. Therefore, if rent increases under an existing rent review clause, this is not a variation and the original tenant will be liable. However, if some other term is altered (being a term which the landlord has an absolute right to refuse to vary) and the effect of that alteration is to increase the rent payable on a subsequent review, if the current tenant fails to pay the new rent, the original tenant will be liable to pay only the rent that would have been payable had there been no variation. For an example see *Blackstone's Guide to the Landlord and Tenant (Covenants) Act 1995*.

If the covenants are varied before 1 January 1996 the 1995 Act is not relevant and the common law will govern the position (*Friends Provident Life Office* v *British Railways Board* [1996] 1 All ER 336). This is similar to the position under the 1995 Act, in that the original tenant will not generally be liable for any variations not contemplated in the original lease (which a rent review is).

If the lease was granted after 1995, privity of contract has been abolished and an original tenant is no longer liable throughout the term. However, an original tenant may have entered into an authorised guarantee agreement, under which he has guaranteed the performance by his assignee of the covenants contained in the lease. Section 18 also applies here and the original tenant will not be liable to pay any amount referable to a variation of the original covenants.

5.9.2 Guarantors

A guarantor is a party to the lease and is someone who has guaranteed the obligations either of an original tenant or of an assignee. The generally accepted view is that since a rent review clause is provided for in the lease, a guarantor is liable not only for the original rent but also for any increase agreed or determined at review (*Torminster Properties Ltd* v *Green* [1983] 1 WLR 676). Section 18(3) of the Landlord and Tenant (Covenants) Act 1995 introduced new provisions, but under the common law a guarantor was discharged from liability if the lease was varied without his consent (*Holme* v *Brunskill* (1877) 3 QBD 495). A rent review clause which was already contained in a lease would not be seen as being a variation. Under

s. 18(3), if a variation is made after 1 January 1996 the position of the guarantor is similar to that of the original tenant, in that he will be liable for increases in rent due to the operation of the rent review provisions in the lease provided the covenants are not varied.

CHAPTER SIX

Alternative Methods of Review

6.1 ALTERNATIVE METHODS OF REVIEW

Reviews based on market rents can prove costly and time-consuming and will usually recur approximately every five years. Even in cases that may appear fairly simple, the parties often incur considerable expense as surveyors will have to be instructed to give advice on current market values. If matters cannot be agreed between the parties and a dispute arises, an even greater financial burden will ensue with arbitration and litigation costs. Accordingly, the question arises as to whether there is an alternative to rent reviews based on market rents which produces a quick and cost-effective method of reviewing rent. Obviously, the parties can avoid the question of review altogether by simply agreeing to short leases, but (as discussed in chapter 1 at 1.1) long leases have become the normal modern practice. A short lease may not in any event prove any better solution, as the issue of rent increase will have to be addressed if the tenant wants to renew the lease. Additionally, landlords will usually insist on the lease being contracted out of the security of tenure provisions contained in the Landlord and Tenant Act 1954, so there is no guarantee that the tenant will get a renewal.

The other alternatives are as follows:

(a) *Fixed rents.* The parties could, although it is not common, agree in advance what the increases are to be over the term of the lease. The problem with this is that the parties have to project rental growth in advance, and this is a very difficult thing to do with the unpredictability of the property market. Both parties are taking a risk by agreeing rents so far in advance, and one party could lose out. Accordingly, this method is very rarely encountered and is perhaps a viable alternative only when a lease is fairly short and of low value.

(b) *Premium rents*. This occurs where the tenant pays an inflated rent throughout the term. A rental figure will be agreed at the beginning of the term and that figure will be significantly greater than the current market rent. This means that the landlord will have a financial advantage at the start of the lease which will be off-set against the fact that there will not be a review; but as the term proceeds, the advantage will reduce as the market value increases. This method avoids the cost and uncertainty of a rent review, but is not commonly encountered due to the unpredictability of the property market. Few landlords or tenants want to take the risk of tying themselves into a long lease with a rent which may not reflect current market trends.

(c) *Index-linked rents*. Under this method the rent is linked to an index chosen by the parties and will increase or decrease in line with that index. Therefore it protects the parties from the effects of inflation. See 6.2 below.

(d) *Turnover rents*. Here the tenant pays rent based upon the amount of turnover of the tenant's business. See 6.3 below.

(e) *Equity rents or geared rents*. These apply where the tenant sublets the property and the landlord receives a percentage of the rents which the tenant receives from the subtenants. See 6.4 below.

(f) *Rents linked to head rent*. When a sublease is granted the parties will often link the rent to that payable under the headlease. See 6.5 below.

6.2 INDEX-LINKED RENTS

6.2.1 Introduction

This method of reviewing rent is rarely encountered in practice, even though it has an advantage over reviews based on market value in that the indexation is automatic and therefore should be more cost-effective. Under this method the rent is linked to an index chosen by the parties and will increase or decrease in line with that index, therefore protecting the parties from the effects of inflation. However, indexing only achieves a rent which is in line with inflation, it does not result in a market rent being determined, and all other factors which can effect rent will be ignored. Thus the rent will not take into account any change to the property or the locality, and rents can be higher or lower than current market rents. This can have important consequences for both parties: if the index falls and the rent is lower than current market rents, the landlord may then receive a lower than expected return and find it difficult to sell the freehold reversion and realise its full price; equally, if the index rises faster than current market values, the tenant may end up paying in excess of the going rate. As a result of such difficulties it has been suggested that index-linked rents work better when a lease is fairly short and rents are low, as it avoids the cost of normal rent review and there is less risk of the rents being totally out of line with the market rents.

6.2.2   The index

The parties must choose the index carefully as this is the sole factor that determines the new rental. Accordingly, the index must be one that is reliable, and the clause in the lease must deal with the possibility that the index chosen may cease to exist at some point in the future. A number of indices now exist but the most popular is the General Index of Retail Prices (RPI). It is published monthly by the Department of Employment and records changes in the retail prices of goods and services purchased by people in the United Kingdom. The items covered in the index are domestic in nature and include food, drink, clothing, fuel, household goods, transport and services. The benefit of this index is that the information is published monthly and is therefore easily accessible, and it is unlikely that it will cease to exist. However, the index is not fixed. For example, the items in the index may change, as in *Blumenthal* v *Gallery Five Ltd* (1971) 220 EG 33 and *Cumshaw Ltd* v *Bowen* [1987] 1 EGLR 30, where it was said that changes in the basket of items and the weighting in order to make the index more accurate were irrelevant. It would seem better logic to use an index based on property market rents rather than the RPI, but a reliable index does not currently seem to exist.

Another form of indexing mixes normal rent review provisions with a type of local indexing. This is illustrated in *Standard Life Assurance Co.* v *Oxoid Ltd* [1987] 2 EGLR 140, and could be used where the property is unusual and therefore comparables difficult to find. The mechanics of this type of clause are that a 'standard' property is defined and is subject to a normal rent review valuation. Once that is done, an agreed formula is then applied which results in the new rent.

6.2.3 Drafting index-linked clauses

6.2.3.1 *The basic rent and frequency of review*

The clause will refer to a 'basic rent', which will be the rent payable from the commencement of the lease until it is varied by reference to the index. To ensure that rental does not decrease, the lease can provide that if the new rent is not greater than the sum previously payable then it shall be deemed to be the same as the rental payable prior to the new rent being ascertained.

The parties have to agree on the frequency of the rent being reviewed. Adjustments every quarter or every year have the benefit of ensuring that the rent keeps in line with inflation. Less frequent adjustments lose that benefit but allow the tenant the ability to make longer-term financial projections. Constant adjustment will also mean that a considerable amount of time and effort will be spent in recalculating the rent.

6.2.3.2 *The base figure*

The index will have a base figure fixed at a chosen date, which will vary in line with inflation. The base figure may be recalculated from time to time, and since this would result in a drastic decrease in rent it should be expressly provided for in the lease (e.g., if the base rate was fixed at 100 in 1992 but rose to 400 in 1997, a base rate of 100 could be fixed as the new base figure from 1997). Providing for a recalculation of the base figure can be achieved in two main ways. The first way is by a mathematical conversion of the new base figure into the figure that would have applied if the base figure had not been recalculated. Some indices provide a conversion table which simplifies matters. The other way of providing for the recalculation of the base figure is to state that if the base figure is adjusted, indexation will be based not on the 'basic rent', but on the rent payable immediately before the adjustment, and indexation carries on with the adjusted base figure.

If the lease does not deal with the prospect of an adjustment to the base figure, a mathematical alteration will not prevent the index-linked clause operating (*Cumshaw* v *Bowen* [1987] 1 EGLR 30). In that case a lease was granted in 1960 and a service charge was to be calculated by reference to the RPI. The lease provided that if the index ceased to exist or was no longer available then the service charge was to be £100 per annum plus a fair proportion of any increase from time to time in the costs incurred by the lessors in providing the services. A dispute arose as to the amount of the service charge and the plaintiff contended that the index had either ceased to be published or was no longer available. The plaintiff's argument was based on the alterations that had been made to the index in

1962, i.e., changes were made to the commodities and services on which the index was based; the weightings given to the items in the index were revised; and the base reference on which subsequent changes in retail prices would be based was brought back to 100. Scott LJ said that he had to ask himself whether the index had ceased to be published or was no longer available. He held that neither of those things had occurred — the index was the same index to which the lease referred, notwithstanding that the mathematical base had been altered.

By way of contrast, in *Wyndham Investments* v *Motorway Tyres & Accessories* [1991] 2 EGLR 114, the provisions were interpreted more liberally. In that case the provisions were badly drafted, with the result that when the base figure was changed the mathematical alteration did not make sense. The lease provided that if the index ceased to exist, or if any event happened whereby it became impossible to implement then the rent was to be a fair and reasonable rent, and in the event cf disagreement as to the amount the rent was to be determined by arbitration. Dillon LJ held that because the formula provided in the lease did nct make sense, the only alternative was to rely on the fallback provision so that the rent would be a fair and reasonable rent assessed by arbitration. He said that both parties agreed that it was not possible, sensibly, to implement the index provisions by taking them in their literal meaning and reaching a ridiculous result.

The clause must deal with the possibility that the index chosen will cease to exist. This could be dealt with by providing an alternative index to be agreed between the parties, or failing agreement to be determined by a third party. Another method would be to revert to the normal rent review clause based on market rents.

What remains of critical importance when drafting index-linked clauses is to test the clause by doing the calculation to ensure that it works and is fair to your client.

An example of a clause from the *Encyclopaedia of Forms and Precedents* linking rent to an index is included in Appendix 10.

6.3   TURNOVER RENTS

6.3.1   Introduction

Turnover rents have become more popular in recent years. The underlying principle of a turnover rent is that the tenant pays rent based upon the amount of turnover of the tenant's business. Such rents are particularly popular in shopping centres, but have been used in cinemas, motorway service areas and airport buildings used to supply in-flight meals.

Turnover rents are not universally accepted, and this may partly be due to the institutional investors who have placed lower investment capital values where turnover rents are in operation because of the uncertainty attached to them.

6.3.2 The pros and cons of turnover tents

6.3.2.1 The tenant's position
A clear advantage of turnover rents for the tenant is that during any period of recession the rent will be lower, and thus the tenant will have some cushioning during leaner times. Also, if a tenant is starting up a business and building up trade the rent will reflect this. Turnover rents are based on reality, on the actual use to which the premises are put, and not on the 'hypothetical lease' which may or may not be based on the actual user. A further advantage for the tenant is that the leased property becomes to some extent a joint venture with the landlord who will make a direct gain from any increase in the tenant's income. This incentive may, in the case of shopping centres, for example, lead to the landlords exercising greater managerial control over the common parts to make the centre as commercially attractive as possible. Turnover rents may prevent landlords becoming complacent in the absence of direct competition, as it is in their interest to ensure that the centre keeps in touch with current trends and initiatives. Tenants, however, should be aware of a potential downside to such involvement by the landlords, in that if the landlords' pro-active role results in works being undertaken at the centre, this may increase any service charges payable by the tenants.

One of the disadvantages of turnover rents for the tenant is that they have a responsibility to provide financial information to the landlord, which ideally they would prefer remained confidential. It is possible to include a provision in the lease dealing with confidentiality. The clause could provide that the landlord can only use the information provided to calculate rent and cannot pass that information on to any other person or body without the tenant's permission. Another potential problem for tenants is the cost in gathering the information for the landlord; administratively, the provision of the information could prove time-consuming for the tenant's staff. Additionally, where turnover is based on 'gross' figures, no account is taken of the tenant's costs. A example of the potential danger for the tenant of turnover rents can be seen in *Tucker* v *Granada Motorway Services Ltd* [1979] 1 WLR 79, where an increase in duty on tobacco resulted in a reduction in profit but not in rent as rent was calculated on gross figures which included the duty. Therefore, from the tenant's point of view, 'turnover' should reflect 'net turnover', being the profit actually made by the tenant. This is likely to be resisted by the landlord as it could leave it vulnerable to a tenant's inefficiency.

6.3.2.2   The landlord's position

An advantage to the landlord of turnover rents is that the landlord can share in a tenant's success. Where, for example, a new shopping centre is built, rents may be low until the business is better established; turnover rents provide the landlord with the knowledge that he will benefit once business improves. Additionally, if the success of a new venture is initially underestimated, the landlord will not suffer for that underestimation. Turnover rents are also useful where comparables for market rent valuations are difficult to find.

One of the main difficulties with turnover rents for the landlord is the uncertainty involved; the landlord is completely reliant on the tenant's business skills and potential success, over which he has no direct control! Also, the landlord has to rely on the tenant providing information on its income in order to calculate the rent. The landlord could install its own tills, or could oblige the tenant to link into the landlord's system. Disputes can easily arise. The lease should contain detailed provisions to deal with the tenant's accountability (see 6.3.3).

As stated above, the landlord's management role will have to be pro-active, which will be costly but essential to the long-term profitability of the property.

6.3.3   Drafting turnover rents

6.3.3.1   Defining rent

Usually, a 'minimum' or 'base' rent will be payable, plus an additional rent which will be a percentage of turnover for a specified period. The base rent will be agreed between the parties and is usually fixed at around 75–80 per cent of the market value. The lower the base rent, the higher the percentage applied for the additional rent. Clearly, the minimum rent must be fixed at a level which the tenant can afford even if business is poor, but the landlord will want it at a level that ensures some profit and encourages the tenant to increase its business's profitability. Provisions can also be included which provide for the base rent to be reviewed at periodic intervals to a sum agreed by the parties or determined by a third party. The parties can also agree that the additional rent will apply only if turnover exceeds a certain figure, and could agree a maximum figure, above which turnover would be ignored.

The percentage applied to turnover varies and will have to be agreed between the parties. The percentage rate generally depends on the type of business carried on by the tenant and the profit margins associated with that business. Generally, for example, retailers who have large spaces and/or trade on high volume will have lower profit margins (such as supermarkets).

The parties do not have to agree one figure for the full term; the percentage rate could be varied to allow the tenant to become established.

6.3.3.2 Defining turnover

The next issue for the parties to agree is the definition of 'turnover', which will vary depending on the type of business. Careful drafting is needed here to avoid disputes in the future as to what 'turnover' actually means. The definition will usually encompass 'gross sales', 'gross receipts' or 'gross takings', but it should go on to give more detail as to what those terms mean. Clearly, detailed knowledge of the tenant's business is needed to make an accurate assessment of what the 'turnover' should be.

When dealing with retail property, the clause will also have to take into account items bought on credit and whether the payments are credited at the time of sale or at the time they are paid. Deductions will also have to be provided for, such as sales to employees, returned goods, exchanged goods, sale items/special offers and bad debts. The tenant will want to ensure that 'turnover' is based on the amount it receives rather than on the retail price. VAT will also have to be dealt with, and usually the VAT chargeable on the tenant's goods and services is excluded from 'turnover'.

One of the key elements of a turnover clause is provision by the tenant of financial information to the landlord. The lease must give the landlord adequate powers to inspect the tenant's accounts, and provide for an independent audit and deal with the costs involved in such an audit. However, the tenant will want to be protected from an over-zealous landlord by specifying the frequency and timing of the landlord's inspection of the tenant's books. On the other hand, the landlord may insist on spot checks at any reasonable time, which the landlord should pay for unless it discovers a material discrepancy in the tenant's accounts.

6.3.3.3 Calculating rent

The percentage rent cannot be determined until the turnover for the relevant period has been calculated. If the percentage rent is paid in arrears, the landlord's cash flow will be affected. Accordingly, the lease can provide for payments to be made on account with a later adjustment once turnover figures have been received. The payments on account will usually be based on earlier turnover periods, and accordingly the clause must deal with the reimbursement of any over-payment as well as the payment of any underpayment.

Rather than repaying any excess, the lease could alternatively provide that the sum is carried forward and put towards future payments.

A problem may arise for the landlord, however, in recovering rent when a lease is assigned. Where a lease is assigned the lease will usually provide that the turnover period will end on the date of the assignment. Therefore, the rent to be paid by the tenant will not be ascertained until some time after the assignment has taken place. If the lease was granted after the 1995 Act came into force (1 January 1996) then the impact of s. 5 of that Act has to be considered. Under s. 5 of the Landlord and Tenant (Covenants) Act 1995, a tenant is released from its obligations under the lease on an assignment. This section has to be read in conjunction with s. 24, which provides that where a person is released from a covenant under s. 5, that release does not affect any liability occurring before the release. However, it is questionable whether a payment which cannot be calculated until after the assignment can be said to be due. Also, the former tenant will have to produce the information to calculate the turnover rent, but the tenant will be under no obligation to do so because of the effect of s. 5. A possible solution to this problem would be to include a provision in the lease whereby on assignment the tenant pays a sum to the landlord which will cover the expected turnover rent, and the landlord agrees to repay any over-payment once the final calculations have been made. The difficulty with this solution, however, is that if the landlord did not repay any over-payment the former tenant would be unable to sue him, as under s. 5 of the Act the former tenant ceases to be entitled to the benefit of the landlord's covenants when released from its obligations under the tenancy. Given the difficulties of enforcement as between the former tenant and landlord, the only alternative seems to be that agreements are made between the former tenant and assignee and the assignee and the landlord. Accordingly, it has been suggested in an article by Frewin Jenkins and Sue Cullen ([2000] 45 EG 174) that the alienation provisions of the lease will need to include some provisions to deal with this situation:

> A requirement that the outgoing tenant pay to the landlord a sum equal to the highest possible amount of outstanding turnover rent for the turnover period ending on the assignment, such payment to be expressed as a fixed last payment of turnover rent due, subject to final calculation, and to be subject to reimbursement of any overpayment.
>
> A requirement that the assignee's covenants with the landlord to procure that the former tenant produces all the evidence necessary for the calculation of the last tranche of turnover rent, and, further, that the former tenant makes the relevant payment.

A requirement that, in the contract of assignment between the assignor and assignee, the assignor covenants with the assignee to produce all the evidence necessary to calculate the last tranche of turnover rent for the period ending with the assignment, and that the assignor covenants to make the necessary payment to the landlord.

A covenant on the part of the landlord in favour of the assignee that the landlord will repay to the former tenant any overpayment of turnover rent once the final amount has been agreed.

An example of a clause in which rent is based on turnover is included in Appendix 11.

6.3.4 The impact of turnover rents on other terms of the lease

6.3.4.1 Keep open clause

Given the landlord's reliance on the tenant's profitability (not only in relation to rent but also, if a shopping centre is involved, where empty units can reduce the general attractiveness of the centre), it will usually want a provision in the lease that the tenant continues to trade, and this can be achieved by a 'keep open' clause. The tenant will covenant to keep open and trade during normal trading hours. If this is done the landlord can claim damages against the tenant if the covenant is breached (*Transworld Land Co.* v *J. Sainsbury* [1990] 2 EGLR 53, which involved the assessment of damages for breach of such a covenant). A mandatory injunction will not be granted (*Co-operative Insurance Society Ltd* v *Argyll Stores (Holdings) Ltd* [1998] AC 1, HL). At present, the position is different in Scotland, where the remedy of specific implement is available to enforce keep open covenants. That is the case even post-*Argyll* as is illustrated in *Highland & Universal Properties Ltd* v *Safeway Properties Ltd* 2000 SLT 414, where a tenant's obligation to keep retail premises open for trading throughout normal work hours of business was held by the Inner House of the Court of Session to be enforceable in Scotland by specific implement. Accordingly, national retailers, such as Safeway, will be able to enforce keep open covenants north of the border, but will only be able to claim damages for breach of the keep open clause if the premises are in England. The *Safeway* decision is, however, under appeal to the House of Lords.

6.3.4.2 User

Other related concerns for the landlord will be the precise nature of the business, as a change may result in reduced profitability. It is usual for the tenant to covenant as to user; and the landlord could try to make that user clause very specific in that it could specify, for example, the items to be sold from the property. A tenant is unlikely to accept such limitations, and in any event it may prove counter-productive for the landlord as (particularly in the retail trade) the market is constantly changing and the retailer has to react to that. A more general clause under which the tenant covenants not substantially to alter the way the business is conducted may be sufficient to deal with the landlord's concerns.

6.3.4.3 *Anti-competition clause*

The landlord could also impose a covenant on the tenant to prohibit him from setting up a competing business within a certain radius of the property, or from relocating the business. On the other hand, the tenant may ask the landlord to covenant not to introduce competing businesses into the centre.

6.3.4.4 *Alienation clause*

Additionally, the landlord could prohibit assignments or sublettings so that a less profitable tenant cannot be substituted. The tenant is unlikely to accept an absolute prohibition and so a clause allowing assignment and subletting only with the landlord's consent is more usual. This can include a provision that consent will be granted only if the landlord's income would be maintained. However, where such a qualified covenant is drafted it must be remembered that consent cannot be unreasonably withheld (Landlord and Tenant Act 1927, s. 19(2)). Rather than assign or sublet, the tenant may grant licences or franchises, and the turnover clause must provide that the sales/receipts of the licences/franchises are included in the tenant's turnover. See also 6.3.3.3 above.

6.4 EQUITY RENTS OR GEARED RENTS

6.4.1 Introduction

Equity rents (also known as geared rents) exist where the tenant sublets the property and the landlord receives a percentage of the rents which the tenant receives from the subtenants. When the headlease is granted it is anticipated by the parties that the tenant will sublet the property, and often the tenant will not occupy any of the property itself. Equity rents are most commonly used in development leases where the landowner leases land to a developer tenant who then develops the site for the resulting benefit of both the landlord and the tenant. This arrangement benefits the landlord, in that he gets a share of whatever rents the tenant receives, and it benefits the tenant, in that he is paying rent only on income he actually

145

receives. However, there is clearly a risk for both parties as it can never be known in advance how profitable this method will be.

6.4.2   Drafting equity rent clauses

6.4.2.1   Introduction
Similar considerations apply as for turnover rents. Often there will be a base or minimum rent payable and then the equity rent which will be based on the tenant's income. It is possible for there to be no base rent and for all the rent to be geared, or the clause could limit the relevant income to income in excess of an agreed figure. As with turnover rents, the crucial thing will be to specify what 'income' actually is to limit potential conflict. The rents will clearly be the main 'income', and as such the headlease will usually state that the rent will be based on the open market value of the sublet property whether or not the open market value is actually achieved. The definition of 'income' need not be restricted to the rents payable under the subleases and should also include any other income arising from them, such as any licence or other occupancy fees, advertising fees, premiums paid for surrendering subleases and any damages payable for breaches under the subleases. If the definition fails to cover all potential types of 'income' then disputes can arise, as was seen in *Standard Life Co. Ltd v Greycoat Devonshire Square Ltd* [2000] EGCS 40. In that case the tenant paid a 'basic rent' and an 'additional rent'. The 'additional rent' was to be 24.0695 per cent of the gross rents payable by Greycoat in excess of £644,000. The gross rents were defined as 'the aggregate of all rent fees and other moneys from whatever source payable to the tenant in respect of the Rental Year directly or indirectly by virtue of its estate or interest in the demised premises'. The tenant surrendered its leases and paid a reverse premium and damages (for dilapidations). The dispute arose because Standard claimed that 24.0659 per cent of the damages (£116,803) was part of the gross rents payable by Greycoat. It was held that while the premium was part of the gross rents the damages were not, as the damages were compensation for damage inflicted on Greycoat's interest and it would be anomalous to allow such a benefit, given that Standard still had the benefit of the full repairing covenant.

6.4.2.2   Premiums
Within the income calculation the parties will have to consider how they deal with premiums. The tenant may grant subleases at low rents but with the payment of a premium. Given that the landlord's return is largely based on rents, the landlord will want any premiums to come within the

definition of 'income', and what has to be addressed is how this can be achieved. In *Freehold & Leasehold Shop Properties Ltd* v *Friends Provident Life Office* [1984] 2 EGLR 133, the court said that if the tenant sought to cheat the landlord by charging peppercorn rents and taking premiums, the court may be able to construe the lease to defeat his intention.

Rather than relying on construction by the courts, it is preferable to deal with the situation expressly. One possible way of doing this is to stipulate that a proportion of the premium is to be paid to the landlord (an express provision should avoid the prohibition in s. 144, LPA 1925). Another method is that the premium could be rentalised for the purposes of calculating the equity rent. Two further possibilities are: (i) the lease could contain a deeming provision whereby the sublet properties are deemed to be let at open market rents, or (ii) it could contain a prohibition against subletting unless at an open market rent. Both of those give the landlord consistency in his return, but the former clause could cause the tenant some problems if the deemed rent is subject to review as opposed to being fixed. If it can be reviewed then any review should be in line with the review under the headlease (see 6.4.2.6).

6.4.2.3   Unlet properties

A further issue to be agreed between the parties is the method of dealing with unlet properties. The landlord will not want his income to be reduced because of empty property and will argue that any risk should be borne by the tenant. However, the tenant will not want to pay equity rent on an unlet property, particularly if the reason for it is a slow property market rather than bad management on his part. Given that the rationale behind this type of arrangement is a joint venture, it seems unfair that the tenant should carry the cost alone. The matter will have to be negotiated, and the bargaining strengths of the parties will determine the issue. One solution that would appeal to the landlord would be an assumption that an unlet property is let and the rent is the open market rent for a hypothetical term. Obviously, if the property market is genuinely slow then this will be reflected in the open market value. In any event, the tenant should demand a reasonable 'rent-free' period to allow for a new subtenant to be found.

A problem of construction arose in *Ashworth Frazer* v *Gloucester City Council* [1997] 1 EGLR 104, where a development lease provided that the rent at review was to be the higher of £9,425 or a rent geared to 8 per cent of 'the rack rents receivable by the lessees in respect of the demised premises on the relevant date'. The problem was that the tenant had not sublet the site but had disposed of it by assignments, with each tenant holding directly from the Council. The respondent held one such site and argued that, given that there were no subtenancies, there were no 'rack rents receivable' and therefore nothing to which the 8 per cent figure could attach. The majority in the Court of Appeal held that the word 'receivable' meant 'capable of being received if sublet' and it was irrelevant that no subleases actually existed. A similar problem arose in *Coventry Motor Mart Ltd* v *Corner Coventry Ltd* [1997] EGCS 45, where rent was to be calculated by reference to rent paid by a subtenant but there were no subtenancies in existence at the time of review. Despite the absence of an actual subtenancy, it was held that the rent could be calculated by using a notional rent under a notional sublease.

A related issue is where the tenant occupies either all or part of the property itself. The lease should provide that the open market rental value of such areas is included in the calculation of income. Even where such an express provision was absent, the court was able to so hold because the language of the lease was capable of such construction (*British Railways Board* v *Elgar House Ltd* (1969) 209 EG 1313). The danger of not providing for a tenant occupying the property can be seen in *Fraser Pipestock Ltd* v *Gloucester City Council* [1995] 2 EGLR 90. There, the rent review clause provided that the yearly rent was to be a fair market rent to be determined under clause 4. Clause 4 provided that the yearly rent was to be either: (i) the rent of £9,425; or (ii) the rent payable during the previous rent period; or (iii) 8 per cent of the rack rents receivable by the lessee. The premises were not sublet but were in fact occupied by the tenant, a situation which the lease had not provided for. The landlords argued that since the premises were not sublet, the rent should be 8 per cent of what would be a market rent at the review date. The tenants argued that if there were no rack rents then the formula could not operate; and the landlords' response to that was that if it could not operate then the machinery to arrive at a fair market rent had broken down and the court should imply terms, or, alternatively, devise some valuation machinery to determine the fair market rent. It was held that 'receivable' meant the rent actually paid or payable; and given that the tenant was in occupation there was no rack rent and there would be a period in which no rent could be calculated by reference to the rack rent of a tenant in actual occupation. Clearly the machinery for determining the rent had broken down, but the court felt unable to imply a term or impose machinery because the parties had agreed an *ad hoc* method of arriving at a ground rent and the machinery that had broken down was not in reality machinery that was achieving a fair market rent.

6.4.2.4 Deductions

Deductions will be required by the tenant to be made from the gross income calculation, such as the costs involved in repairing, maintaining and managing the property, insurance premiums, rates, VAT and other taxes. The payment of any service charge by the subtenant will also have to be considered the tenant will want it to be ignored, but if the tenant charges the subtenant a management fee, the landlord could argue that that element should be included in the income calculation.

Other deductions will be the costs of re-letting (including any inducements), the cost of complying with statutory notices and any compensation payable to a subtenant under the Landlord and Tenant Act 1954 for non-renewal of a business tenancy. The danger of providing a list of deductions is that it does not cater for any change, and therefore it is good practice to provide that other deductions can be made with the head landlord's prior consent or if they are necessary to comply with the tenant's covenants. A further provision should cover the position where disputes arise and state that they will be referred to a third party.

6.4.2.5 Accountability

As with indexation, it is crucial that the tenant keeps good accounts showing what has been received and expended. The landlord will require an obligation from the tenant that proper records will be kept and that those records will be available for inspection. Such records will include copies of the counterpart leases and information on rent reviews.

6.4.2.6 Rent reviews

The headlease will also have to provide that all subleases have upwards only rent review clauses so that the landlord does not see a reduction in his return. If there are a number of subleases then the landlord will want reviews as close as possible to the rent review under the headlease, but it may be difficult for all the reviews to have taken place before or at the same time as that review. The difficulty then is what the rents will be for the purposes of the headlease — will the pre-review rents form the basis of the calculation, or will it be based on the rents that might be achieved at review? With the first possibility, the landlord will be at a disadvantage, and with the second the tenant will be. The approach by the courts does not help to clarify the position as each case is decided on its own facts. In *Buyneat Ltd* v *Tapnap Investments (UK) Ltd* [1992] 1 EGLR 283, the rent review clause provided that 'The ground rent shall represent one third of the then net rack rental value of the demised premises'. At the rent review date a number of rent reviews were awaiting determination, and the issue arose as to whether account should be taken of the rent reviews which were pending. It was held that account could not be taken of the pending rent reviews as it was not the court's function to re-make contracts. However, in *Commission for New Towns* v *Chesterfield Properties Ltd* [1992] 2

EGLR 123, the valuer was allowed to take into account future rent reviews because of the particular wording of the lease.

6.4.3   Other terms of the lease

6.4.3.1   Improvements
Usually equity rents are used when a land owner leases an undeveloped site which the tenant then develops. Accordingly, the value of those initial works should not be disregarded for assessing the rents of the sublets as the cost of those works would have been taken into account as part of the consideration for the land. The treatment of later improvements by the head tenant has to be considered as it will not want the landlord to benefit from increased rents on the subleases due to improvements which the head tenant has paid for. This could be provided for in the lease. The subleases will generally have the usual disregard of subtenant's improvements in the rent review clause, and since the tenant accounts only for rent which it receives, any improvements by the subtenants do not have to be expressly dealt with in the lease.

6.4.3.2   Covenants
The landlord will want a number of covenants to ensure that the property is fully let at open market rents, including:

(a)   a covenant not to let any property other than at the open market rent at the date of the lease;
(b)   a covenant not to grant rent-free periods or give other inducements without the landlord's consent;
(c)   a covenant to use best endeavours to keep the property fully let;
(d)   a covenant not to accept surrenders without the landlord's consent;
(e)   a covenant to provide the landlord with information on the sublettings and any rent reviews, which could perhaps include the right for the landlord to be involved in the rent review process.

6.4.3.3   Terms of subleases
The head landlord will usually want to have some say as to the terms of the subleases since these have a direct bearing on the head landlord's income. Generally, standard subleases will be agreed in advance, with the proviso that later variations can be agreed between the parties.

6.5   RENT LINKED TO HEAD RENT

When a sublease is granted the parties will often link the rent to that payable under the headlease. Where rent in a sublease is linked to a headlease then usually the rent review dates in the sublease will be the same as those in the headlease. Where the rent review dates are to coincide in the headlease and sublease, the draftsman must be careful to ensure that that occurs. It can be seen from the case of *Finger Lickin' Chicken Ltd* v *Ganton House Investments Ltd* [1989] EGCS 89 that confusion can easily arise. There, the headlease had rent reviews at the end of the 7th and 14th years of the term (which commenced on 31 August 1972), and the under-lease (which commenced on 1 March 1974) also contained rent reviews at the end of the 7th and 14th years 'of the said term'. The issue was whether 'the said term' referred to the headlease or to the sublease, and the court held that it was a reference to the sublease since there was no reference to the headlease. The wording was clear in that case; in cases where the wording is ambiguous it would make sense for the rent review dates to coincide.

Sometimes the only link between the rent review clauses will be the timing of the rent review, and the clause in the sublease will mirror the valuation formula of the headlease. This means that the sublease rent review operates independently of the headlease. In other leases the parties may provide that the subtenant will pay a percentage of the rent payable under the headlease. In the latter case the subtenant will need to be involved in the process of reviewing the head rent and will need to negotiate with the landlord to include provisions allowing it to be involved. The subtenant will ideally want the right to be notified of any agreement and to have the ability to challenge it. Whether the landlord will allow this will depend on the circumstances and the parties' respective bargaining strengths. Where the sublease rent review clause is independent but reflects the valuation formula of the headlease, the sublease rent review provisions will be similar but will often not be identical to the headlease as other factors may have to be considered (for example, if the premises which are the subject-matter of the sublease form only part of the premises comprised in the headlease, some assumptions and disregards may have to be varied as they may not be appropriate). The risk with this type of clause is that the rent payable under the sublease could differ after review from that payable under the headlease.

Problems can arise where the sublease rent review clause is linked to the rent review in the headlease. One such problem is the effect on the rent review in the sublease if the headlease is surrendered. The sublease could include a provision dealing with the situation, but if it does not then the rent review in the sublease may remain operative despite surrender, as in *R & A Millett (Shops) Ltd* v *Leon Allan International Fashions Ltd* [1989] 1 EGLR 138, CA, and *Lorien Textiles (UK) Ltd* v *SI Pension Trustees Ltd* [1981] 2 EGLR 100.

Trigger Notice Type of Review

Review triggered by notice

SCHEDULE (*INSERT NUMBER*): THE RENT AND RENT REVIEW

1 Definitions

For all purposes of this schedule the terms defined in this paragraph 1 have the meanings specified.

1.1 *'An arbitrator'*

References to 'an arbitrator' are references to a person appointed by agreement between the Landlord and the Tenant within (*state period, e.g., 21 days*) [(*if required*)— or such longer period as the parties agree in writing —] after the date of service of the Tenant's counternotice referred to in paragraph 2.2 AGREEMENT OF THE RENT or, in default of agreement within that period [(*if extension period allowed for*) or the longer period agreed], by the President on the application of either party.

1.2 *'The Assumptions'*

'The Assumptions' means—
1.2.1 the assumption that no work has been carried out on the Premises during the Term by the Tenant, his subtenants or their predecessors

in title [or any occupiers] that has diminished the rental value of the Premises [other than work carried out in compliance with clause (*insert clause number*) STATUTORY OBLIGATIONS],

1.2.2 the assumption that if the Premises have been destroyed or damaged they have been fully rebuilt or reinstated,

1.2.3 the assumption that the covenants contained in this Lease on the part of the [Landlord and the] Tenant have been fully performed and observed,

1.2.4 the assumption that the Premises are available to let by a willing landlord to a willing tenant in the open market by one lease ('the Hypothetical Lease') without a premium being paid by either party and with vacant possession,

1.2.5 the assumption that the Premises have already been fitted out and equipped by and at the expense of the incoming tenant so that they are capable of being used by the incoming tenant from the beginning of the Hypothetical Lease for all purposes required by the incoming tenant that would be permitted under this Lease,

1.2.6 the assumption that the Hypothetical Lease contains the same terms as this Lease, except the amount of the Initial Rent and any rent-free period allowed to the Tenant for fitting out the Premises for his occupation and use at the commencement of the Term, but including the provisions for rent review on the Review Dates, and except as set out in subparagraph 1.2.7,

1.2.7 the assumption that the term of the Hypothetical Lease is equal in length to [the Contractual Term (*or as required*) the Contractual Term remaining unexpired at the relevant review date (*or as required*) the Contractual Term remaining unexpired at the relevant review date or a period of . . . . . . years whichever is the greater (*or as required*) a period of . . . . . . years] and that such term begins on the relevant review date, that the rent commences to be payable on that date, and that the years during which the tenant covenants to decorate the Premises are at the same intervals after the beginning of the term of the Hypothetical Lease as those specified in this Lease [,

1.2.8 the assumption that the Hypothetical Lease will be renewed at the expiry of its term under the provisions of the 1954 Act] [, and

1.2.9 the assumption that every prospective willing landlord and willing tenant is able to recover VAT in full].

1.3 'The Disregards'

'The Disregards' means—

1.3.1   disregard of any effect on rent of the fact that the Tenant, his subtenants, or their predecessors in title [or any lawful occupier] have been in occupation of the Premises,

1.3.2   disregard of any goodwill attached to the Premises because the business of the Tenant, his subtenants, or their predecessors in title in their respective businesses is or was carried on there, [and]

1.3.3   disregard of any increase in rental value of the Premises attributable at the relevant review date to any improvement to the Premises carried out, with consent where required, otherwise than in pursuance of an obligation [except an obligation contained in clause (*insert clause number*) STATUTORY OBLIGATIONS] to the Landlord or his predecessors in title either—

(a)   by the Tenant, his subtenants, or their predecessors in title [or any lawful occupier] during the Term or during any period of occupation before the Term, or

(b)   by any tenant or subtenant of the Premises [or any lawful occupiers] before the commencement of the Term provided that the Landlord or his predecessors in title have not since the improvement was carried out had vacant possession of the relevant part of the Premises [, and

1.3.4   disregard of the taxable status of the Landlord or the Tenant for the purpose of VAT].

1.4   'The President'

The President' means the President for the time being of the Royal Institution of Chartered Surveyors or any person authorised by him to make appointments on his behalf.

1.5   'A review period'

References to 'a review period' are references to the period beginning on any review date and ending on the day before the next review date.

2   Ascertaining the Rent

2.1   The Rent

Until the First Review Date the Rent is to be the Initial Rent, and thereafter during each successive review period the Rent is to be a sum equal to [(*where the review is to be upwards only*) the greater of the rent payable under this Lease immediately before the relevant review date, or, if payment of rent has been suspended as provided for in this Lease, the rent that would have been payable had there been no such suspension, or] the revised rent ascertained in accordance with this schedule.

2.2 Agreement of the Rent

The Rent for any review period is to be either—

2-2.2.1 the Rent specified in a notice given by the Landlord to the Tenant at any time [not earlier than (*state period, e.g., 6 months*) before the review date to which it relates] ('a review notice'), or

2-2.2.2 the Rent agreed between the parties in writing within (*state period, e.g., 3 months*) after the date of service of a review notice in substitution for the sum specified in that review notice, or

2-2.2.3 at the election of the Tenant made in a written counternotice served on the Landlord within (*state period, e.g., 3 months*) after the date of service of a review notice, the Rent determined by an arbitrator.

Time is to be of the essence in relation to all stipulations as to time in this paragraph.

2.3 Open market rent

The sum to be determined by an arbitrator must be the sum at which he decides the Premises might reasonably be expected to be let in the open market at the relevant review date making the Assumptions but disregarding the Disregards.

2.4 Conduct of the arbitration

The arbitration must be conducted in accordance with the Arbitration Act 1996, except that if the arbitrator dies or declines to act the President may, on the application of either the Landlord or the Tenant, appoint another in his place.

2.5 Memoranda of agreement

Whenever the Rent has been ascertained in accordance with this schedule, memoranda to that effect must be signed by or on behalf of the Landlord and the Tenant and annexed to this document and its counterpart, and the Landlord and the Tenant must bear their own costs in this respect.

2.6 Reimbursement of costs

If, on publication of the arbitrator's award, the Landlord or the Tenant pays all his fees and expenses, the paying party may [, in default of payment within (*state period, e.g., 21 days*) of a demand to that effect,] recover such proportion of them, if any, as the arbitrator awards against the other [in the case of the Landlord as rent arrears or in the case of the Tenant by deduction from the Rent].

3   Payment of the Rent as ascertained

3.1   *Where the Rent is not ascertained by a review date*

If the Rent payable during any review period has not been ascertained by the relevant review date, then rent is to continue to be payable at the rate previously payable, such payments being on account of the Rent for that review period.

3.2   *Where a review date is not a quarter day*

If the Rent for any review period is ascertained on or before the relevant review date but that date is not a quarter day, then the Tenant must pay to the Landlord on that review date the difference between the Rent due for that quarter and the Rent already paid for it. (*adapt if the rent is not paid on the usual quarter days*)

3.3   *Back-payment where review delayed*

If the Rent payable during any review period has not been ascertained by the relevant review date, then the Tenant must pay to the Landlord, [within (*state period, e.g., 7 days*) of (*or as required*) on] the date on which the Rent is agreed or the arbitrator's award is received by him, any shortfall between the Rent that would have been paid for that period had it been ascertained on or before the relevant review date and the payments made by the Tenant on account [and any VAT payable thereon], and interest, at the base lending rate from time to time of the bank referred to in or nominated pursuant to clause (*insert clause number*) 'THE INTEREST RATE', in respect of each instalment of rent due on or after that review date on the amount by which the instalment of the Rent that would have been paid had it been ascertained exceeds the amount paid by the Tenant on account, the interest to be payable for the period from the date on which the instalment was due up to the date of payment of the shortfall.

4   Effect of counter-inflation provisions

If at any review date a statute prevents, restricts or modifies the Landlord's right either to review the Rent in accordance with this Lease or to recover any increase in the Rent, then the Landlord may, when the restriction or modification is removed, relaxed or varied — without prejudice to his rights, if any, to recover any rent the payment of which has only been deferred by statute — on giving not less than (*state minimum notice, e.g., 1 month's*) nor more than (*state maximum notice, e.g., 3 months'*) notice to the Tenant [at any time within (*state period, e.g., 6 months*) of the restriction or modification being removed, relaxed or varied, time being of the essence,] require the Tenant to proceed with any review of the Rent that has been prevented or to review the Rent further where the Landlord's right was restricted or modified. The date of expiry of the notice is to be treated as a review date — provided that nothing in this paragraph is to be construed as varying any subsequent review date. The Landlord may recover any increase in the Rent with effect from the earliest date permitted by law.

Note: The terms defined in clause 1 are only relevant to this Schedule. The other definitions referred to in this Schedule would be defined in the lease itself.

Law Society/RICS Model Forms

Introduction to Draft Clauses 1, 2 and 3, based on
Law Society/RICS Model Form of Rent Review Clause
(1985 edition)

Note: These forms were produced before the Arbitration Act 1996, therefore the references to the 1950 and 1979 Acts are out of date.

INTRODUCTION

The Law Society and the Royal Institution of Chartered Surveyors first published draft model forms of rent review clause relating to commercial leases in June 1979. Comments and criticisms from the professions and others were invited and received and recommended model forms and background notes relating thereto, which were published in March 1980, so far as possible took into account all the many points that had been made in correspondence to the Joint Committee set up to consider the matter.

The Joint Committee have revised the 1980 model forms of rent review clause in the light of recent case law and modern conveyancing practice and now publish the 1985 edition. The 1985 model forms supersede the 1980 model forms in their entirety. For greater convenience, these are set out in three principal variants, namely:

Variation A: determination in default of agreement by arbitration with alternative provisions for:

(a)   upwards only review; and

(b)   upwards or downwards review.

Variation B: determination in default of agreement by independent valuer acting as an expert with alternative provisions for:

(a)   upwards only review; and

(b)   upwards or downwards review.

Variation C: Determination in default of agreement to be either by arbitration or by independent valuer acting as expert (at the landlord's option) with alternative provisions for:

(a)   upwards only review; and

(b)   upwards or downwards review.

In the model forms, where words appear in italics, this denotes either that one of two alternatives is to be selected or that the inclusion is optional, and the notes applicable to the particular variation should be followed. The Joint Committee wish to emphasise that the model forms are published in order to assist those who possess professional expertise in the drafting of commercial leases. It will always be necessary to consider whether any of the variations set out below are appropriate to the particular case and, if considered to be so, what amendments may be required and which of the alternative clauses provided should be incorporated in the particular commercial lease. As these forms are designed to create specific legal rights and obligations, they are recommended for use only in accordance with the advice of somebody qualified as above.

Draft Rent Review Clause 1

MODEL FORM — VARIATION A

Determination in default of agreement by Arbitration with alternative provisions for (a) upwards only review, and (b) upwards or downwards review. [see *Introduction*]

... yielding and paying to the landlord yearly rents ascertained in accordance with the next four clauses hereof without any deduction by equal quarterly payments in advance on the usual quarter days the first payment (being an apportioned sum) to be made on the date hereof.

Clause 1. Definitions	In this lease 'review date' means the....................day of.....................in the year 19............and in every............year thereafter and 'review period' means the period starting with any review date up to the next review date or starting with the last review date up to the end of the term hereof
Clause 2.	The yearly rent shall be: (A) until the first review date the rent of £......and
Provisions for revision of rent in upwards only review	(B) *during each successive review period a rent equal to the rent previously payable hereunder or such revised rent as may be ascertained as herein provided whichever be the greater*
OR	
For revision of rent in upwards or down-wards review	(B) (i) *during each successive review period such revised rent as may be ascertained as herein provided and* (B) (ii) *in the event of a revised rent not being ascertained as herein provided the rent payable for the relevant review period shall be the rent payable immediately prior to the commencement of such period*
Clause 3. Ascertainment of amount by arbitrator	Such revised rent for any review period may be agreed at any time between the landlord and the tenant or (in the absence of agreement) determined not earlier than the relevant review date by an arbitrator such arbitrator to be nominated in the absence of agreement by or on behalf of the President for the time being of the Royal Institution of Chartered Surveyors on the application of the landlord or the tenant made not earlier than six months before the relevant review
(See Note 1)	*date but not later than the end of the relevant review period* and so that in the case of such arbitration the revised rent to be awarded by the arbitrator shall be such as he shall decide is the yearly rent at which the demised premises might reasonably be expected to be let at the relevant review date.

(A) On the following assumptions at that date:

    (i) That the demised premises:

(a) are available to let on the open market without a fine or premium with vacant possession by a willing landlord to a willing tenant for a term of [10 years or the residue then unexpired of the term of this lease (whichever be the longer)

(See Note 2)

(b) are to be let as a whole subject to the terms of this lease (other than the amount of the rent hereby reserved but including the provisions for review of that rent)

(c) are fit and available for immediate occupation

(d) may be used for any of the purposes permitted by the lease as varied or extended by any licence granted pursuant thereto

(See Note 3)

    (ii) That the covenants herein contained on the part of *the landlord and* the tenant have been fully performed and observed

    (iii) That no work has been carried out to the demised premises which has diminished the rental value and that in case the demised premises have been destroyed or damaged they have been fully restored

    (iv) That no reduction is to be made to take account of any rental concession which on a new letting with vacant possession might be granted to the incoming tenant for a period within which its fitting out works would take place

(B) But disregarding:

    (i) any effect on rent of the fact that the tenant its sub-tenants or their respective predecessors in title have been in occupation of the demised premises

    (ii) any goodwill attached to the demised premises by reason of the carrying on threat of the business of the tenant its subtenants or their predecessors in title in their respective businesses and

(See Note 4)

    (iii) any increase in rental value of the demised premises attributable to the existence at the relevant review date of any improvement to the demised premises or any part thereof carried out with consent where required otherwise than in pursuance of an obligation to the landlord or its predecessors in title except obligations requiring compliance with statutes or directions of Local Authorities or other bodies exercising powers under statute or Royal Charter either (a) by the tenant its sub-tenants or their respective predecessors in title during the said term or during any period of occupation prior thereto arising out of

(See Note 5)

an agreement to grant such term or *(b) by any tenant or sub-tenant of the demised premises before the commencement of the term hereby granted so long as the landlord or its predecessors in title have not since the improvement was carried out had vacant possession of the relevant part of the demised premises.*

Clause 4.

IT IS HEREBY FURTHER PROVIDED in relation to the ascertainment and payment of revised rent as follows:

Further provisions as to Arbitration

(A) The arbitration shall be conducted in accordance with the Arbitration Acts 1950 and 1979 or any statutory modification or re-enactment thereof for the time being in force with the further provision that if the arbitrator nominated pursuant to Clause 3 hereof shall die or decline to act the President for the time being of the Royal Institution of Chartered Surveyors or the person acting on his behalf may on the application of either the landlord or the tenant by writing discharge the arbitrator and appoint another in his place

As to memoranda of ascertainment

(B) When the amount of any rent to be ascertained as hereinbefore provided shall have been so ascertained memoranda thereof shall thereupon be signed by or on behalf of the landlord and the tenant and annexed to this lease and the counterpart thereof and the landlord and the tenant shall bear their own costs in respect thereof

As to interim payments and final adjustments upwards only review

(C) (i) *if the revised rent payable on and from any review date has not been agreed by that review date rent shall continue to be payable at the rate previously payable and forthwith upon the revised rent being ascertained the tenant shall pay to the landlord any shortfall between the rent and the revised rent payable up to and on the preceding quarter day together with interest on*

(See Note 6)

any shortfall at the seven day deposit rate of .... BANK such interest to be calculated on a day-to-day basis from the relevant review date on which it would have been payable if the revised rent had then been ascertained to the date of actual payment of any shortfall and the interest so payable shall be recoverable in the same manner as rent in arrear

OR

upwards or downwards review

(C) (i) *if the revised rent payable on and from any review date has not been agreed by that review date rent shall continue to be payable at the rate previously payable and forthwith upon the revised rent being ascertained, the tenant shall pay to the landlord any shortfall between the rent and the revised rent or as the case may be the landlord shall pay to the tenant any excess of the rent paid over the revised rent payable up to and on the*

162

preceding quarter day together with interest on any shortfall or as the case may be any excess at the seven (See Note 6) *day deposit rate of .... BANK such interest to be calculated on a day-to-day basis from the relevant review date on which it would have been payable if the revised rent had then been ascertained to the date of actual payment of any shortfall or any excess and the interest so payable shall be recoverable in the same manner as rent in arrear or as the case may be as a debt*

      (ii) for the purposes of this proviso the revised rent shall be deemed to have been ascertained on the date when the same has been agreed between the landlord and the tenant or as the case may be the date of the award of the arbitrator

  (D) If either the landlord or the tenant shall fail to pay any costs awarded against it in an arbitration under the provisions hereof within twenty-one days of the same being demanded by the arbitrator the other shall be entitled to pay the same and the amount so paid shall be repaid by the party chargeable on demand

Notes Applicable to Variation A

1. See paragraph 3, background notes (reprinted at the end of paragraph 15A-03).
2. See paragraph 6, background notes.
3. See paragraphs 8 and 9, background notes.
4. See paragraph 10, background notes.
5. It should be considered in each case whether these words are relevant.
6. Insert name of bank and see paragraph 13, background notes.

Draft Rent Review Clause 2

MODEL FORM — VARIATION B

Determination in default of agreement by independent valuer acting as an expert with alternative provisions for (a) upwards only review, and (b) upwards or downwards review. [see *Introduction*]

... yielding and paying to the landlord yearly rents ascertained in accordance with the next four clauses hereof without any deduction by equal quarterly payments in advance on the usual quarter days the first payment (being an apportioned sum) to be made on the date hereof.

Clause 1. Definitions	In this lease 'review date' means the...................day of......................in the year 19............and in every............year thereafter and 'review period' means the period starting with any review date up to the next review date or starting with the last review date up to the end of the term hereof
Clause 2.	The yearly rent shall be: (A) until the first review date the rent of £......and
Provisions for revision of rent in upwards only review	(B) *during each successive review period a rent equal to the rent previously payable hereunder or such revised rent as may be ascertained as herein provided whichever be the greater*
OR	
For revision of rent in upwards or down-wards review	(B) (i) *during each successive review period such revised rent as may be ascertained as herein provided and* (B) (ii) *in the event of a revised rent not being ascertained as herein provided the rent payable for the relevant review period shall be the rent payable immediately prior to the commencement of such period*
Clause 3. Ascertainment of amount by independent valuer	Such revised rent for any review period may be agreed at any time between the landlord and the tenant or (in the absence of agreement) determined not earlier than the relevant review date by an independent valuer (acting as an expert and not as an arbitrator) such valuer to be nominated in the absence of agreement by or on behalf of the President for the time being of the Royal Institution of Chartered Surveyors on the application of the landlord or the tenant made not earlier
(See Note 1)	than six months before the relevant review date *but not later than the end of the relevant review period* and so that in the case of such valuation the revised rent to be determined by the valuer shall be such as he shall decide is the yearly rent at which the demised premises might reasonably be expected to be let at the relevant review date.

(A)   On the following assumptions at that date:
    (i)   That the demised premises:

(a)   are available to let on the open market without a fine or premium with vacant possession by a willing landlord to a willing tenant for a term of [10] years or the residue then unexpired of the term of this lease (whichever be the longer)

(See Note 2)

(b)   are to be let as a whole subject to the terms of this lease (other than the amount of the rent hereby reserved but including the provisions for review of that rent)

(c)   are fit and available for immediate occupation

(d)   may be used for any of the purposes permitted by the lease as varied or extended by any licence granted pursuant thereto

(See Note 3)

    (ii)   That the covenants herein contained on the part of *the landlord and* the tenant have been fully performed and observed

    (iii)   That no work has been carried out to the demised premises which has diminished the rental value and that in case the demised premises have been destroyed or damaged they have been fully restored

    (iv)   That no reduction is to be made to take account of any rental concession which on a new letting with vacant possession might be granted to the incoming tenant for a period within which its fitting out works would take place

(B)   But disregarding:
    (i)   any effect on rent of the fact that the tenant its sub-tenants or their respective predecessors in title have been in occupation of the demised premises

    (ii)   any goodwill attached to the demised premises by reason of the carrying on threat of the business of the tenant its subtenants or their predecessors in title in their respective businesses and

(See Note 4)

    (iii)   any increase in rental value of the demised premises attributable to the existence at the relevant review date of any improvement to the demised premises or any part thereof carried out with consent where required otherwise than in pursuance of an obligation to the landlord or its predecessors in title except obligations requiring compliance with statutes or directions of Local Authorities or other bodies exercising powers under statute or Royal Charter either (a) by the tenant its sub-tenants or their respective predecessors in title during the said term or during any period of occupation prior thereto arising out of

(See Note 5)

an agreement to grant such term or *(b) by any tenant or sub-tenant of the demised premises before the commencement of the term hereby granted so long as the landlord or its predecessors in title have not since the improvement was carried out had vacant possession of the relevant part of the demised premises.*

Clause 4.

IT IS HEREBY FURTHER PROVIDED in relation to the ascertainment and payment of revised rent as follows:

As to independent valuation

(A)   (i)   the fees and expenses of the valuer including the cost of his nomination shall be borne equally by the landlord and the tenant who shall otherwise bear their own costs and

(ii)   the valuer shall afford the landlord and the tenant an opportunity to make representations to him and

(iii)   if the valuer nominated pursuant to Clause 3 hereof shall die or decline to act the President for the time being of the Royal Institution of Chartered Surveyors or the person acting on his behalf may on the application of either the landlord or the tenant by writing discharge the valuer and appoint another in his place

As to memoranda of ascertainment

(B)   When the amount of any rent to be ascertained as hereinbefore provided shall have been so ascertained memoranda thereof shall thereupon be signed by or on behalf of the landlord and the tenant and annexed to this lease and the counterpart thereof and the landlord and the tenant shall bear their own costs in respect thereof

Provision as to interim payments final adjustments upwards only review

(C)   (i)   *if the revised rent payable on and from any review date has not been agreed by that review date rent shall continue to be payable at the rate previously payable and forthwith upon the revised rent being ascertained, the tenant shall pay to the landlord any shortfall between the rent and the revised rent payable up to and on the preceding quarter day together with interest on*

(See Note 6)

any shortfall at the seven day deposit rate of .... BANK such interest to be calculated on a day-to-day basis from the relevant review date on which it would have been payable if the revised rent had then been ascertained to the date of actual payment of any shortfall and the interest so payable shall be recoverable in the same manner as rent in arrear

OR

upwards or downwards review

(C)   (i)   *if the revised rent payable on and from any review date has not been agreed by that review date rent shall continue to be payable at the rate previously payable and forthwith upon the revised rent being ascertained the tenant shall pay to the landlord any shortfall*

166

*between the rent and the revised rent or as the case may
be the landlord shall pay to the tenant any excess of the
rent paid over the revised rent payable up to and on the
preceding quarter day together with interest on any
shortfall or as the case may be any excess at the seven*

(See Note 6) *day deposit rate of .... BANK such interest to be
calculated on a day-to-day basis from the relevant
review date on which it would have been payable if the
revised rent had then been ascertained to the date of
actual payment of any shortfall or any excess and the
interest so payable shall be recoverable in the same
manner as rent in arrear or as the case may be as a debt*

(ii) for the purposes of this proviso the revised rent
shall be deemed to have been ascertained on the
date when the same has been agreed between the
landlord and the tenant or as the case may be the
date of the determination by the valuer

(D) If either the landlord or the tenant shall fail to pay the
moiety of the fees and expenses of the valuer under the
provisions hereof within twenty-one days of the same
being demanded by the arbitrator the other shall be
entitled to pay the same and the amount so paid shall
be repaid by the party chargeable on demand

Notes Applicable to Variation B

1. See paragraph 3, background notes (reprinted at the end of paragraph 15A-03).
2. See paragraph 6, background notes.
3. See paragraphs 8 and 9, background notes.
4. See paragraph 10, background notes.
5. It should be considered in each case whether these words are relevant.
6. Insert name of bank and see paragraph 13, background notes.

Draft Rent Review Clause 3

MODEL FORM — VARIATION C

Determination in default of agreement by arbitration or by independent valuer acting as an expert (at the landlord's option) with alternative provisions for (a) upwards only review, and (b) upwards or downwards review. [see *Introduction*]

... yielding and paying to the landlord yearly rents ascertained in accordance with the next four clauses hereof without any deduction by equal quarterly payments in advance on the usual quarter days the first payment (being an apportioned sum) to be made on the date hereof

Clause 1. Definitions	In this lease 'review date' means the...................day of......................in the year 19............and in every............year thereafter and 'review period' means the period starting with any review date up to the next review date or starting with the last review date up to the end of the term hereof
Clause 2.	The yearly rent shall be: (A)　until the first review date the rent of £......and
Provisions for revision of rent in upwards only review	*(B)　during each successive review period a rent equal to the rent previously payable hereunder or such revised rent as may be ascertained as herein provided whichever be the greater*
OR For revision of rent in upwards or down-wards review	*(B)　(i)　during each successive review period such revised rent as may be ascertained as herein provided and* *(B)　(ii)　in the event of a revised rent not being ascertained as herein provided the rent payable for the relevant review period shall be the rent payable immediately prior to the commencement of such period*
Clause 3. Ascertainment of amount by arbitratior or by independent valuer at the landlord's option [See Note 7)	Such revised rent for any review period may be agreed at any time between the landlord and the tenant or (in the absence of agreement) determined not earlier than the relevant review date at the option of the landlord either by an arbitrator or by an independent valuer (acting as an expert and not as an arbitrator) such arbitrator or valuer to be nominated in the absence of agreement by or on behalf of the President for the time being of the Royal Institution of Chartered Surveyors on the application of the landlord (in exercise of the saie option) made not earlier than six months
(See Note 1)	before the relevant review date *but not later than the end of the relevant review period* and so that in the case of such arbitration or valuation the revised rent to be awarded or determined by the arbitrator or valuer shall be such as he shall decide is the

yearly rent at which the demised premises might reasonably be expected to be let at the relevant review date.

(A) On the following assumptions at that date:

  (i) That the demised premises:

(See Note 2)

(a) are available to let on the open market without a fine or premium with vacant possession by a willing landlord to a willing tenant for a term of [10] years or the residue then unexpired of the term of this lease (whichever be the longer)

(b) are to be let as a whole subject to the terms of this lease (other than the amount of the rent hereby reserved but including the provisions for review of that rent)

(c) are fit and available for immediate occupation

(d) may be used for any of the purposes permitted by the lease as varied or extended by any licence granted pursuant thereto

(See Note 3)

  (ii) That the covenants herein contained on the part of *the landlord and* the tenant have been fully performed and observed

  (iii) That no work has been carried out to the demised premises which has diminished the rental value and that in case the demised premises have been destroyed or damaged they have been fully re-stored

  (iv) That no reduction is to be made to take account of any rental concession which on a new letting with vacant possession might be granted to the incoming tenant for a period within which its fitting out works would take place

(B) But disregarding:

  (i) any effect on rent of the fact that the tenant its sub-tenants or their respective predecessors in title have been in occupation of the demised premises

  (ii) any goodwill attached to the demised premises by reason of the carrying on threat of the business of the tenant its subtenants or their predecessors in title in their respective businesses and

(See Note 4)

  (iii) any increase in rental value of the demised premises attributable to the existence at the relevant review date of any improvement to the demised premises or any part thereof carried out with consent where required otherwise than in pursuance of an obligation to the landlord or its predecessors in title except obligations requiring compliance with statutes or directions of Local Authorities or other bodies exercising powers under statute or Royal Charter either (a) by the tenant its sub-tenants or their respective predeces-

(See Note 5)

sors in title during the said term or during any period of occupation prior thereto arising out of an agreement to grant such term or *(b) by any tenant or sub-tenant of the demised premises before the commencement of the term hereby granted so long as the landlord or its predecessors in title have not since the improvement was carried out had vacant possession of the relevant part of the demised premises.*

Clause 4.

IT IS HEREBY FURTHER PROVIDED in relation to the ascertainment and payment of revised rent as follows:

Further provisions as to arbitration

(A) (In the case of arbitration) the arbitration shall be conducted in accordance with the Arbitration Acts 1950 and 1979 or any statutory modification or re-enactment thereof for the time being in force with the further provision that if the arbitrator nominated pursuant to Clause 3 hereof shall die or decline to act the President for the time being of the Royal Institution of Chartered Surveyors or the person acting on his behalf may on the application of either the landlord or the tenant by writing discharge the valuer and appoint another in his place

As to independent valuation

(B) (In the case of determiantion by a valuer)

    (i) the fees and expenses of the valuer including the cost of his nomination shall be borne equally by the landlord and the tenant who shall otherwise bear their own costs and

    (ii) the valuer shall afford the landlord and the tenant an opportunity to make representations to him and

    (iii) if the valuer nominated pursuant to Clause 3 hereof shall die delay or become unwilling, unfit or incapable of acting or if for any other reason the President for the time being of the Royal Institution of Chartered Surveyors or the person acting on his behalf shall in his absolute discretion think fit he may on the application of either the landlord or the tenant by writting discharge the valuer and appoint another in his place

As to memoranda of ascertainment

(C) When the amount of any rent to be ascertained as hereinbefore provided shall have been so ascertained memoranda thereof shall thereupon be signed by or on behalf of the landlord and the tenant and annexed to this lease and the counterpart thereof and the landlord and the tenant shall bear their own costs in respect thereof

As to interim payments and final adjustments upwards only review

(D) (i) *If the revised rent payable on and from any review date has not been agreed by that review date rent shall continue to be payable at the rate previously payable and forthwith upon the revised rent being ascertained,*

170

the tenant shall pay to the landlord any shortfall between the rent and the revised rent payable up to and on the preceding quarter day together with interest on

(See Note 6) *any shortfall at the seven day deposit rate of .... BANK such interest to be calculated on a day-to-day basis from the relevant review date on which it would have been payable if the revised rent had then been ascertained to the date of actual payment of any shortfall and the interest so payable shall be recoverable in the same manner as rent in arrear*

OR

upwards or
downwards review

(D) (i) *if the revised rent payable on and from any review date has not been agreed by that review date rent shall continue to be payable at the rate previously payable and forthwith upon the revised rent being ascertained the tenant shall pay to the landlord any shortfall between the rent and the revised rent or as the case may be the landlord shall pay to the tenant any excess of the rent paid over the revised rent payable up to and on the preceding quarter day together with interest on any shortfall or as the case may be any excess at the seven*

(See Note 6) *day deposit rate of .... BANK such interest to be calculated on a day-to-day basis from the relevant review date on which it would have been payable if the revised rent had then been ascertained to the date of actual payment of any shortfall or any excess and the interest so payable shall be recoverable in the same manner as rent in arrear or as the case may be as a debt*

(ii) for the purposes of this proviso the revised rent shall be deemed to have been ascertained on the date when the same has been agreed between the landlord and the tenant or as the case may be the date of the determination by the valuer

(E) If either the landlord or the tenant shall fail to pay the moiety of the fees and expenses of the valuer under the provisions hereof within twenty-one days of the same being demanded by the arbitrator the other shall be entitled to pay the same and the amount so paid shall be repaid by the party chargeable on demand

As to notice by the
tenant to trigger
landlords application

(F) *Whenever a revised rent in respect of any review period has not been agreed between the landlord and the tenant before the relevant review date and where no agreement has been reached as to the appointment of an arbitrator or valuer nor has the*

(See note 7) *landlord made any application to the President for the time being of the Royal Institution of Chartered Surveyors as hereinbefore provided the tenant may serve on the landlord notice in writing referring to this provision and containing a*

(See note 8) *proposal as to the amount of such revised rent (which shall not be less than the rent payable immediately before the commencement of the relevant review period) and the amount so*

171

proposed shall be deemed to have been agreed by the landlord and the tenant as the revised rent for the relevant review period and sub-clause (D)(i) hereof shall apply accordingly unless the landlord shall make such application as aforesaid within three months after service of such notice by the tenant. Time shall be of the essence in respect of this provision.

Notes Applicable to Variation C

1. See paragraph 3, background notes (reprinted on the following page).
2. See paragraph 6, background notes.
3. See paragraphs 8 and 9, background notes.
4. See paragraph 10, background notes.
5. It should be considered in each case whether these words are relevant.
6. Insert name of bank and see paragraph 13, background notes.
7. See paragraph 2(b), background notes.
8. The words in parenthesis should only be included if the review provision is upwards only.

BACKGROUND NOTES

The following brief notes have been produced to provide information as to the background reasoning which led to the many variations included in the revised published rent review clauses and as to the phraseology used in them, the need for some of the differing provisions, and to explain why some of the revisions have been found necessary.

1. The clauses were drafted to embrace the widest range of business premises, varying from poor quality multi-tenanted buildings to lettings to single tenants of large and modern properties with sophisticated services and facilities.

2. In making revisions to the 1980 edition, the Joint Committee remained of the view that the revised model clauses should be able to reflect the market conditions prevailing at the time when the letting is negotiated. Thus, the following alternatives contained in the 1980 edition remain:

(a)   Provisions which cover (i) 'upwards only' and (ii) 'upwards/ downwards' rent reviews;

(b)(i)   Provision for the landlord to choose between an arbitrator and a valuer acting as an expert. In this case, it follows from the drafting that the landlord will also control the initiation of the review. Clause 4(F) of Variation C is therefore included to protect the tenant in the situation where he needs to avoid uncertainty or wants to assign after a rent review date and the landlord has not applied for the nomination of an arbitrator or valuer;

(ii)   Predetermined type of appointment, coupled with the more balanced right for either party to initiate the review.

3. In the light of the *Burnley* and *Cheapside* decisions, (*United Scientific Holdings Limited* v *Burnley Borough Council* and *Cheapside Land Development Company Limited* v *Messels Service Company* [1978] AC 904), the Joint Committee have continued to avoid, as far as possible, strict time-limits and notices, in order to give effect to the contract between the parties (i.e., a letting for a term of years with rent reviews at specified intervals) and remove the risk of that contract being frustrated by human error. There is however provision, as an alternative, for a time limit after which a review can no longer be initiated.

4. The Joint Committee also remained of the view that, in an inflationary economy and in often rapidly changing market conditions, it is wrong to expect a valuer or arbitrator to determine the rent in advance

of a review date. Hence, the referral process enables the appointment to take place prior to the review date, but requires that the revised rent may not be determined until the review date (save of course by mutual agreement).

5.   Amendments contained in the 1985 edition make it abundantly clear that the revised rent to be determined is in respect of a hypothetical letting of the premises actually demised at the relevant review date on certain assumptions and disregarding certain factors. The 1980 edition was on the same basis despite any appearances to the contrary.

6.   The Joint Committee have made significant revisions to the assumptions to be made in respect of the hypothetical lease to be considered when the revised rent is ascertained. As to the length of the hypothetical lease to be considered, recent market experience has suggested that neither 'the unexpired term' not 'a term equivalent to the original term' is entirely satisfactory. If the unexpired term is to be assumed, then at the later review dates a very limited unexpired length of term could depress the rent unfairly. However, the alternative assumption of a term equivalent to the original term of a long lease could equally be regarded as having a depreciating effect on rental value if obsolescence is thereby ignored. The Joint Committee were of the view that the unexpired term, subject to a minimum term (suggested to be 10 years or a figure closest thereto which represents a multiple of the 'review period'), was the most appropriate compromise.

7.   Assumptions that in the hypothetical letting the premises are to be let 'on the open market', 'with vacant possession' and 'as a whole' have all been retained. However, there may be occasional circumstances, such as when there are existing sub-tenancies at the start of the lease, where this should not necessarily apply. Furthermore, the original drafting of the 1980 edition would appear to cover more than adequately the problems raised in the case of *National Westminster Bank plc* v *Arthur Young McLelland Moores & Company* (1984) 273 EG 402, where it was held that if the revised rent were to be assessed on the basis of the provisions of the actual lease 'other than the rent . . . reserved,' the provisions relating to rent review are also to be disregarded.

8.   The assumption of landlord's covenants being fulfilled on review is included as an option in view of the uncertain position in law and the injustices which can occur either way. The Joint Committee were particularly concerned as to whether or not it should be assumed that the landlord had complied with his repairing obligations. If disrepair is recognised in assessing the rent, subsequent fulfilment of obligations by the landlord may be inhibited or he may conversely incur unnecessary expense (recoverable from the tenant) to avoid that situation. Conversely,

assumption of repair can disadvantage a tenant, not-withstanding any legal rights of redress. Unless therefore a review clause is specifically drafted to provide for a differential rent in the event of disrepair, the assumption to form the basis of valuation must remain a matter to be agreed by the parties in the circumstances.

9.	The Joint Committee considered it appropriate, in the light of difficulties arising from rent-free concessions in vacant possession lettings, to include an entirely new assumption that no account should be taken of any fitting-out period which might be allowed to a hypothetical tenant on a new letting. It was considered that if such a period were to be granted specifically for that purpose in the open market, it was a 'once off' concession made by the landlord to the tenant in respect of the full term of the lease and was not therefore a benefit that should be granted to the tenant at subsequent rent reviews.

10.	The disregards, referred to in Clause 3(B), include and extend the disregards referred to in section 34 of the Landlord and Tenant Act 1954 as amended. The Joint Committee gave extensive consideration to Clause 3(B)(iii) which deals with the disregard in respect of tenants' improvements. The basis adopted in the 1980 edition has been retained, subject only to minor variation. The alternative, as recommended by the ISVA, of undertaking a valuation 'rebus sic stantibus' thereafter making a 'fair allowance' to the tenant in respect of any alteration or improvement undertaken, was considered but rejected. Provision is now made for the landlord not to take the benefit of any increase in rental value resulting from obligations placed upon the tenant requiring compliance with enactments or directions of Government or Local Authorities. Furthermore, the provisions go beyond the Landlord and Tenant Act 1954 in protecting tenants against being charged rent on the improvements of their sub-tenants or predecessors in title. It is no longer suggested that the value of tenants' improvements over 21 years old may be taken into account by the landlord.

11.	In an arbitration, the parties have the right to appearance and the arbitrator must adjudicate. The independent valuer, however appointed, is not bound by the rules and procedures laid down by the Arbitration Acts and, unless the lease provides that he shall do so, may decline to receive any statement of facts or evidence from either of the parties to the dispute. In the 1985 edition of the model clauses, where reference is to an independent valuer, the Joint Committee have included a provision instead of an option which appeared in the 1980 edition that the valuer shall afford to each of the parties an opportunity to make representations.

12.	If in the case of determination by arbitration, the arbitrator shall die or decline to act, the revised model clause provide that the President of the

RICS may appoint another in his place. This should enable a further appointment to be made more quickly than by following the procedures laid down by the Arbitration Acts.

13.   In making revisions to the 1980 edition, the Joint Committee decided that it was now common practice for interest payments on arrears of increased rents to be included and as a result there has been an appropriate addition to the model clauses. In the view of the Joint Committee, the interest rate to be selected should equate to a deposit rate.

14.   Finally, Clause 4 provides for memoranda to be signed by or on behalf of the landlord and the tenant recording the amount of any reviewed rent ascertained. The form of memorandum recommended was published with the 1980 edition and is reprinted below for ease of reference.

MEMORANDUM

Lease dated:....................Premises:....................Parties:.................
....
BY THIS MEMORANDUM dated the .... day of .... 19.........
(as Landlord) and..(as
Tenant) desire to record the fact that the rent payable under the above-mentioned lease has been reviewed under the provisions of Clause......thereof and fixed in accordance with those provisions at £......................per year from the............................19............to the......................19............

For and on behalf of the (Landlord) (Tenant)

Automatic Rent Review Clauses

Revised rent to be determined by an arbitrator

SCHEDULE (*INSERT NUMBER*) THE RENT AND RENT REVIEW

1 Definitions

For all purposes of this schedule the terms defined in this paragraph 1 have the meanings specified.

1.1 *'An arbitrator'*

References to 'an arbitrator' are references to a person appointed by agreement between the Landlord and the Tenant or, in the absence of agreement within (*state period, e.g., 14 days*) of one of them giving notice to the other of his nomination, nominated by the President on the application of either made not earlier than (*state period, e.g., 6 months*) before the relevant review date or at any time thereafter to determine the rent under this schedule.

1.2 *'The Assumptions'*

'The Assumptions' means—
1.2.1   the assumption that no work has been carried out on the Premises during the Term by the Tenant, his subtenants or their predecessors

in title [or any occupiers] that has diminished the rental value of the Premises [other than work carried out in compliance with clause (*insert clause number*) STATUTORY OBLIGATIONS],

1.2.2 the assumption that if the Premises have been destroyed or damaged they have been fully rebuilt or reinstated,

1.2.3 the assumption that the covenants contained in this Lease on the part of the [Landlord and the] Tenant have been fully performed and observed,

1.2.4 the assumption that the Premises are available to let by a willing landlord to a willing tenant in the open market by one lease ('the Hypothetical Lease') without a premium being paid by either party and with vacant possession,

1.2.5 the assumption that the Premises have already been fitted out and equipped by and at the expense of the incoming tenant so that they are capable of being used by the incoming tenant from the beginning of the Hypothetical Lease for all purposes required by the incoming tenant that would be permitted under this Lease,

1.2.6 the assumption that the Hypothetical Lease contains the same terms as this Lease, except the amount of the Initial Rent and any rent-free period allowed to the Tenant for fitting out the Premises for his occupation and use at the commencement of the Term, but including the provisions for rent review on the Review Dates, and except as set out in subparagraph 1.2.7,

1.2.7 the assumption that the term of the Hypothetical Lease is equal in length to [the Contractual Term (*or as required*) the Contractual Term remaining unexpired at the relevant review date (*or as required*) the Contractual Term remaining unexpired at the relevant review date or a period of ...... years whichever is the greater (*or as required*) a period of ...... years] and that such term begins on the relevant review date, that the rent commences to be payable on that date, and that the years during which the tenant covenants to decorate the Premises are at the same intervals after the beginning of the term of the Hypothetical Lease as those specified in this Lease [,

1.2.8 the assumption that the Hypothetical Lease will be renewed at the expiry of its term under the provisions of the 1954 Act] [, and

1.2.9 the assumption that every prospective willing landlord and willing tenant is able to recover VAT in full].

1.3 '*The Disregards*'

'The Disregards' means—

1.3.1 disregard of any effect on rent of the fact that the Tenant, his subtenants, or their predecessors in title [or any lawful occupier] have been in occupation of the Premises,

1.3.2 disregard of any goodwill attached to the Premises because the business of the Tenant, his subtenants, or their predecessors in title in their respective businesses is or was carried on there, [and]

1.3.3 disregard of any increase in rental value of the Premises attributable at the relevant review date to any improvement to the Premises carried out, with consent where required, otherwise than in pursuance of an obligation [except an obligation contained in clause (*insert clause number*) STATUTORY OBLIGATIONS] to the Landlord or his predecessors in title either—

(a) by the Tenant, his subtenants, or their predecessors in title [or any lawful occupier] during the Term or during any period of occupation before the Term, or

(b) by any tenant or subtenant of the Premises [or any lawful occupiers] before the commencement of the Term provided that the Landlord or his predecessors in title have not since the improvement was carried out had vacant possession of the relevant part of the Premises [, and

1.3.4 disregard of the taxable status of the Landlord or the Tenant for the purpose of VAT].

1.4 'The President'

'The President' means the President for the time being of the Royal Institution of Chartered Surveyors or any person authorised by him to make appointments on his behalf.

1.5 'A review period'

References to 'a review period' are references to the period beginning on any review date and ending on the day before the next review date.

2 Ascertaining the Rent

2.1 The Rent

Until the First Review Date the Rent is to be the Initial Rent, and thereafter during each successive review period the Rent is to be a sum equal to [(*where the review is to be upwards only*) the greater of the rent payable under this Lease immediately before the relevant review date, or, if payment of rent has been suspended as provided for in this Lease, the rent that would have been payable had there been no such suspension, or] the revised rent ascertained in accordance with this schedule.

2.2   Agreement of the Rent

[Six months before each review date, time not being of the essence of the contract, the Landlord and the Tenant must [explore the possibility of (*or as required*) open negotiations with a view to] reaching a written agreement as to the Rent for the following review period and the Rent for that period may be agreed at any time or, in the absence of agreement, is to be determined by an arbitrator [not earlier than the relevant review date]. (*or as required*) The Rent for any review period may be agreed at any time or, in the absence of agreement, is to be determined by an arbitrator [not earlier than the relevant review date].]

2.3   Open market rent

The sum to be determined by an arbitrator must be the sum at which he decides the Premises might reasonably be expected to be let in the open market at the relevant review date making the Assumptions but disregarding the Disregards.

2.4   Conduct of the arbitration

The arbitration must be conducted in accordance with the Arbitration Act 1996, except that if the arbitrator dies or declines to act the President may, on the application of either the Landlord or the Tenant, appoint another in his place.

2.5   Memoranda of agreement

Whenever the Rent has been ascertained in accordance with this schedule, memoranda to that effect must be signed by or on behalf of the Landlord and the Tenant and annexed to this document and its counterpart, and the Landlord and the Tenant must bear their own costs in this respect.

2.6   Reimbursement of costs

If, on publication of the arbitrator's award, the Landlord or the Tenant pays all his fees and expenses, the paying party may [, in default of payment within (*state period, e.g., 21 days*) of a demand to that effect,] recover such proportion of them, if any, as the arbitrator awards against the other [in the case of the Landlord as rent arrears or in the case of the Tenant by deduction from the Rent].

3 Payment of the Rent as ascertained

3.1 *Where the Rent is not ascertained by a review date*

If the Rent payable during any review period has not been ascertained by the relevant review date, then rent is to continue to be payable at the rate previously payable, such payments being on account of the Rent for that review period.

3.2 *Where a review date is not a quarter day*

If the Rent for any review period is ascertained on or before the relevant review date but that date is not a quarter day, then the Tenant must pay to the Landlord on that review date the difference between the Rent due for that quarter and the Rent already paid for it. (*adapt if the rent is not paid on the usual quarter days*)

3.3 *Back-payment where review delayed*

If the Rent payable during any review period has not been ascertained by the relevant review date, then the Tenant must pay to the Landlord, [within (*state period, e.g., 7 days*) of (*or as required*) on] the date on which the Rent is agreed or the arbitrator's award is received by him, any shortfall between the Rent that would have been paid for that period had it been ascertained on or before the relevant review date and the payments made by the Tenant on account [and any VAT payable thereon], and interest, at the base lending rate from time to time of the bank referred to in or nominated pursuant to clause (*insert clause number*) 'THE INTEREST RATE', in respect of each instalment of rent due on or after that review date on the amount by which the instalment of the Rent that would have been paid had it been ascertained exceeds the amount paid by the Tenant on account, the interest to be payable for the period from the date on which the instalment was due up to the date of payment of the shortfall.

4 Effect of counter-inflation provisions

If at any review date a statute prevents, restricts or modifies the Landlord's right either to review the Rent in accordance with this Lease or to recover any increase in the Rent, then the Landlord may, when the restriction or modification is removed, relaxed or varied — without prejudice to his rights, if any, to recover any rent the payment of which has only been deferred by statute — on giving not less than (*state minimum notice, e.g., 1 month's*) nor more than (*state maximum notice, e.g., 3 months'*) notice to the Tenant [at any time within (*state period, e.g., 6 months*) of the restriction or modification being removed, relaxed or varied, time being of the essence,] require the Tenant to proceed with any review of the Rent that has been prevented or to review the Rent further where the Landlord's right was restricted or modified. The date of expiry of the notice is to be treated as a review date — provided that nothing in this paragraph is to be construed as varying any subsequent review date. The Landlord may recover any increase in the Rent with effect from the earliest date permitted by law.

Note: The terms defined in clause 1 are only relevant to this Schedule. The other definitions referred to in this Schedule would be defined in the lease itself.

Revised rent to be determined by an expert

SCHEDULE (*INSERT NUMBER*): THE RENT AND RENT REVIEW

1 Definitions

For all purposes of this schedule the terms defined in this paragraph 1 have the meanings specified.

1.1 'The Assumptions'

The Assumptions' means—

1.1.1 the assumption that no work has been carried out on the Premises during the Term by the Tenant, his subtenants or their predecessors in title [or any occupiers] that has diminished the rental value of the Premises [other than work carried out in compliance with clause (*insert clause number*) STATUTORY OBLIGATIONS],

1.1.2 the assumption that if the Premises have been destroyed or damaged they have been fully rebuilt or reinstated,

1.1.3 the assumption that the covenants contained in this Lease on the part of the [Landlord and the] Tenant have been fully performed and observed,

1.1.4 the assumption that the Premises are available to let by a willing landlord to a willing tenant in the open market by one lease ('the Hypothetical Lease') without a premium being paid by either party and with vacant possession,

1.1.5 the assumption that the Premises have already been fitted out and equipped by and at the expense of the incoming tenant so that they are capable of being used by the incoming tenant from the beginning of the Hypothetical Lease for all purposes required by the incoming tenant that would be permitted under this Lease,

1.1.6 the assumption that the Hypothetical Lease contains the same terms as this Lease, except the amount of the Initial Rent and any rent-free period allowed to the Tenant for fitting out the Premises for his occupation and use at the commencement of the Term, but including the provisions for rent review on the Review Dates, and except as set out in paragraph 1.1.7,

1.1.7 the assumption that the term of the Hypothetical Lease is equal in length to [the Contractual Term (*or as required*) the Contractual Term remaining unexpired at the relevant review date (*or as required*) the Contractual Term remaining unexpired at the relevant review date or a period of ...... years whichever is the greater (*or as required*) a period of ...... years] and that such term begins on the relevant

183

review date, that the rent commences to be payable on that date, and that the years during which the tenant covenants to decorate the Premises are at the same intervals after the beginning of the term of the Hypothetical Lease as those specified in this Lease [,

1.1.8 the assumption that the Hypothetical Lease will be renewed at the expiry of its term under the provisions of the 1954 Act][, and

1.1.9 the assumption that every prospective willing landlord and willing tenant is able to recover VAT in full]

1.2 'The Disregards'

'The Disregards' means—

1.2.1 disregard of any effect on rent of the fact that the Tenant, his subtenants, or their predecessors in title [or any lawful occupier] have been in occupation of the Premises,

1.2.2 disregard of any goodwill attached to the Premises because the business of the Tenant, his subtenants, or their predecessors in title in their respective businesses is or was carried on there, [and]

1.2.3 disregard of any increase in rental value of the Premises attributable at the relevant review date to any improvement to the Premises carried out, with consent where required, otherwise than in pursuance of an obligation [except an obligation contained in clause (*insert clause number*) STATUTORY OBLIGATIONS] to the Landlord or his predecessors in title either—

(a) by the Tenant, his subtenants, or their predecessors in title [or any lawful occupier] during the Term or during any period of occupation before the Term, or

(b) by any tenant or subtenant of the Premises [or any lawful occupiers] before the commencement of the Term, provided that the Landlord or his predecessors in title have not since the improvement was carried out had vacant possession of the relevant part of the Premises [, and

1.2.4 disregard of the taxable status of the Landlord or the Tenant for the purpose of VAT].

1.3 'An expert'

References to 'an expert' are references to an independent valuer appointed by agreement between the Landlord and the Tenant or, in the absence of agreement within (*state period, e.g., 14 days*) of one of them giving notice to the other of his nomination, nominated by the President on the application of either made not earlier than (*state period, e.g., 6 months*) before the relevant review date or at any time thereafter to determine the rent under this schedule.

1.4 *'The President'*

'The President' means the President for the time being of the Royal Institution of Chartered Surveyors or any person authorised by him to make appointments on his behalf.

1.5 *'A review period'*

References to 'a review period' are references to the period beginning on any review date and ending on the day before the next review date.

2 Ascertaining the Rent

2.1 *The Rent*

Until the First Review Date the Rent is to be the Initial Rent, and thereafter during each successive Review Period a sum equal to [(*where the review is to be upwards only*) the greater of the rent payable under this Lease immediately before the relevant review date, or, if payment of rent has been suspended as provided for in this Lease, the rent that would have been payable had there been no such suspension, or] the revised rent ascertained in accordance with this schedule.

2.2 *Agreement of the Rent*

[Six months before each review date, time not being of the essence of the contract, the Landlord and the Tenant must [explore the possibility of (*or as required*) open negotiations with a view to] reaching a written agreement as to the Rent for the following review period and the Rent for that period may be agreed at any time or, in the absence of agreement, is to be determined by an expert [not earlier than the relevant review date]. (*or as required*) The Rent for any review period may be agreed at any time or, in the absence of agreement, is to be determined by an expert [not earlier than the relevant review date].]

2.3 *Open market rent*

The sum to be determined by the expert must be the sum at which, acting as an expert and not as an arbitrator or quasi-arbitrator, he decides the Premises might reasonably be expected to be let in the open market at the relevant review date making the Assumptions but disregarding the Disregards.

2.4 *Conduct of the determination*

2.4.1 Fees and expenses

The fees and expenses of an expert [and any VAT payable on them], including the cost of his appointment, are to be borne equally by the Landlord and the Tenant, who must otherwise each bear their own costs.

2.4.2 Representations

An expert must afford each of the parties an opportunity to make written representations to him [and also an opportunity to make written counter-representations on any representations made to him by the other party] but is not to be in any way limited or fettered by such representations [and counter-representations] and is to be entitled to rely on his own judgment and opinion.

2.4.3 Replacement of an expert

If an expert dies or refuses to act or becomes incapable of acting [or if he fails to publish his determination within (state period, e.g., 4 months) of the date on which he accepted the appointment], either party may apply to the President to discharge him and appoint another in his place.

2.5 *Memoranda of agreement*

Whenever the Rent has been ascertained in accordance with this schedule, memoranda to that effect must be signed by or on behalf of the Landlord and the Tenant and annexed to this document and its counterpart, and the Landlord and the Tenant must bear their own costs in this respect.

2.6 *Reimbursement of costs*

If, on publication of an expert's determination, the Landlord or the Tenant pays all his fees and expenses, the paying party may [, in default of payment within (*state period, e.g., 21 days*) of a demand to that effect,] recover half of them from the other party [in the case of the Landlord as rent arrears or in the case of the Tenant by deduction from the Rent].

3 Payment of the Rent as ascertained

3.1 *Where the Rent is not ascertained by a review date*

If the Rent payable during any review period has not been ascertained by the relevant review date, then rent is to continue to be payable at the rate previously payable, such payments being on account of the Rent for that review period.

3.2 Where a review date is not a quarter day

If the Rent for any review period is ascertained on or before the relevant review date but that date is not a quarter day, then the Tenant must pay to the Landlord on that review date the difference between the Rent due for that quarter and the Rent already paid for it. (*adapt if the rent is not paid on the usual quarter days*)

3.3 Back-payment where review delayed

If the Rent payable during any review period has not been ascertained by the relevant review date, then the Tenant must pay to the Landlord, [within (*state period, e.g., 7 days*) of (*or as required*) on] the date on which the Rent is agreed or the expert's determination is received by him, any shortfall between the Rent that would have been paid for that period had it been ascertained on or before the relevant review date and the payments made by the Tenant on account [and any VAT payable thereon], and interest, at the base lending rate from time to time of the bank referred to in or nominated pursuant to clause (insert clause number) 'THE INTEREST RATE', in respect of each instalment of rent due on or after that review date on the amount by which the instalment of the Rent that would have been paid had it been ascertained exceeds the amount paid by the Tenant on account, the interest to be payable for the period from the date on which the instalment was due up to the date of payment of the shortfall.

4 Effect of counter-inflation provisions

If at any review date a statute prevents, restricts or modifies the Landlord's right either to review the Rent in accordance with this Lease or to recover any increase in the Rent, then the Landlord may, when the restriction or modification is removed, relaxed or varied — without prejudice to his rights, if any, to recover any rent the payment of which has only been deferred by statute — on giving not less than (*state minimum notice, e.g., 1 month's*) nor more than (*state maximum notice, e.g., 3 months'*) notice to the Tenant [at any time within (*state period, e.g., 6 months*) of the restriction or modification being removed, relaxed or varied, time being of the essence,] require the Tenant to proceed with any review of the Rent that has been prevented or to review the Rent further where the Landlord's right was restricted or modified. The date of expiry of the notice is to be treated as a review date — provided that nothing in this paragraph is to be construed as varying any subsequent review date. The Landlord may recover any increase in the Rent with effect from the earliest date permitted by law.

Note: The terms defined in clause 1 are only relevant to this Schedule. The other definitions referred to in this Schedule would be defined in the lease itself.

Rent Review Clause Requiring Valuation of Notional Premises

Revised rent to be determined by reference to hypothetical premises

SCHEDULE (*INSERT NUMBER*): THE RENT AND RENT REVIEW

1 Definitions

For all purposes of this schedule the terms defined in this paragraph 1 have the meanings specified.

1.1 *'An arbitrator'*

References to 'an arbitrator' are references to a person appointed by agreement between the Landlord and the Tenant or, in the absence of agreement within (*state period, e.g., 14 days*) of one of them giving notice to the other of his nomination, nominated by the President on the application of either made not earlier than (*state period, e.g., 6 months*) before the relevant review date or at any time thereafter to determine the rent under this schedule.

1.2 *'The Assumptions'*

'The Assumptions' means—

1.2.1   the assumption that the Hypothetical Premises were constructed in accordance with all statutes in force at the date of construction specified in paragraph 1.5 'THE HYPOTHETICAL PREMISES' and that they are in good and substantial repair and comply with all statutes in force at the relevant review date,

1.2.2   the assumption that the notional planning permission referred to in paragraph 1.5 'THE HYPOTHETICAL PREMISES' is available to all potential tenants interested in taking a lease of the Hypothetical Premises,

1.2.3   the assumption that no person other than the Landlord has had possession of the Hypothetical Premises since they were deemed to have been constructed and that no trade, business, profession or manufacture of any kind has ever been carried on in or from them,

1.2.4   the assumption that the Hypothetical Premises are available to let by a willing landlord to a willing tenant in the open market by one lease ('the Hypothetical Lease') without a premium being paid by either party and with vacant possession,

1.2.5   the assumption that the Hypothetical Premises have already been fitted out and equipped by and at the expense of the incoming tenant so that they are capable of being used by the incoming tenant from the beginning of the Hypothetical Lease for all purposes required by the incoming tenant that would be permitted under this Lease,

1.2.6   the assumption that the Hypothetical Lease contains the same terms as this Lease, except the amount of the Initial Rent and any rent-free period allowed to the Tenant for fitting out the Premises for his occupation and use at the commencement of the Term, but including the provisions for rent review on the Review Dates, and except as set out in paragraph 1.2.7,

1.2.7   the assumption that the term of the Hypothetical Lease is equal in length to [the Contractual Term (*or as required*) the Contractual Term remaining unexpired at the relevant review date (*or as required*) the Contractual Term remaining unexpired at the relevant review date or a period of . . . . . . years whichever is the greater (*or as required*) a period of . . . . . . years] and that such term begins on the relevant review date, that the rent commences to be payable on that date, and that the years during which the tenant covenants to decorate the Premises are at the same intervals after the beginning of the term of the Hypothetical Lease as those specified in this Lease [,

1.2.8   the assumption that the Hypothetical Lease will be renewed at the expiry of its term under the provisions of the 1954 Act] [, and

1.2.9   the assumption that every prospective willing landlord and willing tenant is able to recover VAT in full].

1.3 'The Code'

'The Code' means the Code of Measuring Practice issued by the Royal Institution of Chartered Surveyors and the Incorporated Society of Valuers and Auctioneers, as amended from time to time.

1.4 'The Disregards'

'The Disregards' means—
1.4.1 disregard of any effect on rent of the fact that the Tenant, his subtenants or their respective predecessors in title have been in occupation of the Premises [, and
1.4.2 disregard of the taxable status of the Landlord or the Tenant for the purpose of VAT].

1.5 'The Hypothetical Premises'

'The Hypothetical Premises' means (*give details of the notional premises, including date and method of construction, specification, location of site, location of building within the site, number of floors, floor areas (measured in accordance with the Code using whichever of the Code's definitions of area is used in paragraph 2.3 DETERMINATION OF THE REVISED RENT) broken down, if necessary, into areas of office space, factory space, storage space etc, number and location of car parking spaces, standard of decoration, presence or absence of lifts, air conditioning, central heating and other plant and machinery, toilet accommodation, together with details of the notional planning permission by which the Hypothetical Premises were erected and any deemed conditions subject to which it was notionally granted and any other matters of fact to be hypothesised that are capable of affecting the rental value of the Hypothetical Premises*)

1.6 'The President'

'The President' means the President for the time being of the Royal Institution of Chartered Surveyors or any person authorised by the President to make appointments on his behalf.

1.7 'A review period'

References to 'a review period' are references to the period beginning on any review date and ending on the day before the next review date.

2 Ascertaining the Rent

2.1 *The Rent*

Until the First Review Date the Rent is to be the Initial Rent, and thereafter during each successive review period the Rent is to be a sum equal to [(*where the review is to be upwards only*) the greater of the rent payable under this Lease immediately before the relevant review date, or, if payment of rent has been suspended as provided for in this Lease, the rent that would have been payable had there been no such suspension, or] the revised rent ascertained in accordance with this schedule.

2.2 *Agreement of the Rent*

[Six months before each review date, time not being of the essence of the contract, the Landlord and the Tenant must [explore the possibility of (*or as required*) open negotiations with a view to] reaching a written agreement as to the Rent for the following review period and the Rent for that period may be agreed at any time or, in the absence of agreement, is to be determined by an arbitrator [not earlier than the relevant review date]. (*or as required*) The Rent for any review period may be agreed at any time or, in the absence of agreement, is to be determined by an arbitrator [not earlier than the relevant review date].]

2.3 *Determination of the revised rent*

An arbitrator must determine the Rent for the Premises by—

2.3.1   determining the rent at which the Hypothetical Premises might reasonably be expected to be let in the open market at the relevant review date making the Assumptions but disregarding the Disregards,

2.3.2   determining the rate of rent for the Hypothetical Premises per square metre based on his determination made under subparagraph 2.3.1, and

2.3.3   determining the revised Rent for the Premises by multiplying the area of the Premises expressed in square metres and measured in accordance with the definition '[Net Internal Area]' of the Code by (insert agreed percentage) of the rate of rent per square metre for the Hypothetical Premises determined under subparagraph 2.3.2.

2.4 *Conduct of the arbitration*

The arbitration must be conducted in accordance with the Arbitration Act 1996, except that if an arbitrator dies or declines to act the President may on the application of either the Landlord or the Tenant appoint another in his place. The arbitrator's award must include a statement of the amount of the annual rent for the Hypothetical Premises determined by him under subparagraph 2.3.1 and the calculations made by him under subparagraphs 2.3.2 and 2.3.3.

2.5 *Memoranda of agreement*

Whenever the Rent has been ascertained in accordance with this schedule, memoranda to that effect must be signed by or on behalf of the Landlord and the Tenant and annexed to this document and its counterpart and the Landlord and the Tenant must bear their own costs in this respect.

2.6 *Reimbursement of costs*

If, on publication of the arbitrator's award, the Landlord or the Tenant pays all his fees and expenses, the paying party may [, in default of payment within (*state period, e.g., 21 days*) of a demand to that effect,] recover such proportion of them, if any, as the arbitrator awards against the other [in the case of the Landlord as rent arrears or in the case of the Tenant by deduction from the Rent].

3 Payment of the Rent as ascertained

3.1 *Where the Rent is not ascertained by a review date*

If the Rent payable during any review period has not been ascertained by the relevant review date, then rent is to continue to be payable at the rate previously payable, such payments being on account of the Rent for that review period.

3.2 *Where a review date is not a quarter day*

If the Rent for any review period is ascertained on or before the relevant review date but that date is not a quarter day, then the Tenant must pay to the Landlord on that review date the difference between the Rent due for that quarter and the Rent already paid for it. (*adapt if the rent is not paid on the usual quarter days*)

3.3 *Back-payment where review delayed*

If the Rent payable during any review period has not been ascertained by the relevant review date, then the Tenant must pay to the Landlord, [within (*state period, e.g., 7 days*) of (*or as required*) on] the date on which the

Rent is agreed or the arbitrator's award is received by him, any shortfall between the Rent that would have been paid for that period had it been ascertained on or before the relevant review date and the payments made by the Tenant on account [and any VAT payable thereon], and interest, at the base lending rate from time to time of the bank referred to in or nominated pursuant to clause (*insert clause number*) 'THE INTEREST RATE', in respect of each instalment of rent due on or after that review date on the amount by which the instalment of the Rent that would have been paid had it been ascertained exceeds the amount paid by the Tenant on account, the interest to be payable for the period from the date on which the instalment was due up to the date of payment of the shortfall.

4 Effect of counter-inflation provisions

If at any review date a statute prevents, restricts or modifies the Landlord's right either to review the Rent in accordance with this Lease or to recover any increase in the Rent, then the Landlord may, when the restriction or modification is removed, relaxed or varied — without prejudice to his rights, if any, to recover any rent the payment of which has only been deferred by statute — on giving not less than (*state minimum notice, e.g., 1 month's*) nor more than (*state maximum notice, e.g., 3 months'*) notice to the Tenant [at any time within (*state period, e.g., 6 months*) of the restriction or modification being removed, relaxed or varied, time being of the essence,] require the Tenant to proceed with any review of the Rent that has been prevented or to review the Rent further where the Landlord's right was restricted or modified. The date of expiry of the notice is to be treated as a review date — provided that nothing in this paragraph is to be construed as varying any subsequent review date. The Landlord may recover any increase in the Rent with effect from the earliest date permitted by law.

Note: The terms defined in clause 1 are only relevant to this Schedule. The other definitions referred to in this Schedule would be defined in the lease itself. For a determination by an expert see the relevant provisions in Appendix 3.

Rent Review Clause Based on a Vacant Site

Revised rent to be that for a vacant site without the buildings that have been or are to be erected on the premises

SCHEDULE (*INSERT NUMBER*): THE RENT AND RENT REVIEW

1 Definitions

For all purposes of this schedule the terms defined in this paragraph 1 have the meanings specified.

1.1 *'An arbitrator'*

References to 'an arbitrator' are references to a person appointed by agreement between the Landlord and the Tenant or, in the absence of agreement within (*state period, e.g., 14 days*) of one of them giving notice to the other of his nomination, nominated by the President on the application of either made not earlier than (*state period, e.g., 6 months*) before the relevant review date or at any time thereafter to determine the rent under this schedule.

1.2 *'The Assumptions'*

'The Assumptions' means—

1.2.1   the assumption that the Premises consist of a vacant site [in the condition shown by the schedule of condition annexed to this document] on which no buildings or works of any kind have been erected or carried out,

1.2.2   the assumption that the Premises have the benefit of the Planning Permission, but that the Planning Permission bears the same date as the relevant review date and not the actual date shown on it,

1.2.3   the assumption that the Premises are available to let by a willing landlord to a willing tenant in the open market by one lease ('the Hypothetical Lease') without a premium being paid by either party and with vacant possession;

1.2.4   the assumption that the Hypothetical Lease contains the same terms as this Lease, except the amount of the Initial Rent and any rent-free period allowed to the Tenant for fitting out the Premises for his occupation and use at the commencement of the Term, but including the provisions for rent review on the Review Dates, and except as set out in paragraph 1.2.5,

1.2.5   the assumption that the term of the Hypothetical Lease is equal in length to [the Contractual Term (*or as required*) the Contractual Term remaining unexpired at the relevant review date (*or as required*) the Contractual Term remaining unexpired at the relevant review date or a period of ...... years whichever is the greater (*or as required*) a period of ...... years] and that such term begins on the relevant review date, that the rent commences to be payable on that date, and that the years during which the tenant covenants to decorate the Premises are at the same intervals after the beginning of the term of the Hypothetical Lease as those specified in this Lease [,

1.2.8   the assumption that the Hypothetical Lease will be renewed at the expiry of its term under the provisions of the 1954 Act][, and

1.2.9   the assumption that every prospective willing landlord and willing tenant is able to recover VAT in full].

1.3   *'The Disregards'*

'The Disregards' means—

1.3.1   disregard of any effect on rent of the fact that the Tenant, his subtenants, or their predecessors in title [or any lawful occupier] have been in occupation of the Premises,

1.3.2   disregard of any goodwill attached to the Premises because the business of the Tenant, his subtenants, or their predecessors in title in their respective businesses is or was carried on there,

196

1.3.3   disregard of the effect of any statutes enacted after the date of this document that would have the effect of preventing or delaying the erection of [the Building] in accordance with the Planning Permission despite the actual and/or assumed existence of the Planning Permission, [and]

1.3.4   disregard of any possibility that the Premises may be used for a purpose or developed in a way otherwise than in accordance with the Planning Permission [, and

1.3.5   disregard of the taxable status of the Landlord or the Tenant for the purpose of VAT].

1.4   'The President'

'The President' means the President for the time being of the Royal Institution of Chartered Surveyors or any person authorised by the President to make appointments on his behalf.

1.5   'The Planning Permission'

The Planning Permission' means the planning permission of which a copy, together with copies of the application for it and the plans and documentation that accompanied that application, is annexed to this Lease.

1.6   'A review period'

References to 'a review period' are references to the period beginning on any review date and ending on the day before the next review date.

2   Ascertaining the Rent

2.1   The Rent

Until the First Review Date the Rent is to be the Initial Rent, and thereafter during each successive review period the Rent is to be a sum equal to [(*where the review is to be upwards only*) the greater of the rent payable under this Lease immediately before the relevant review date, or, if payment of rent has been suspended as provided for in this Lease, the rent that would have been payable had there been no such suspension, or] the revised rent ascertained in accordance with this schedule.

2.2   Agreement of the Rent

[Six months before each review date, time not being of the essence of the contract, the Landlord and the Tenant must [explore the possibility of (*or as required*) open negotiations with a view to] reaching a written agreement as to the Rent for the following review period and the Rent for that period may be agreed at any time or, in the absence of agreement, is to be determined by an arbitrator [not earlier than the relevant review date]. (*or as required*) The Rent for any review period may be agreed at any time or, in the absence of agreement, is to be determined by an arbitrator [not earlier than the relevant review date].]

2.3   *Open market rent*

The sum to be determined by an arbitrator must be the sum at which he decides the Premises might reasonably be expected to be let in the open market at the relevant review date making the Assumptions but disregarding the Disregards.

2.4   *Conduct of the arbitration*

The arbitration must be conducted in accordance with the Arbitration Act 1996, except that if the arbitrator dies or declines to act the President may, on the application of either the Landlord or the Tenant, appoint another in his place.

2.5   *Memoranda of agreement*

Whenever the Rent has been ascertained in accordance with this schedule, memoranda to that effect must be signed by or on behalf of the Landlord and the Tenant and annexed to this document and its counterpart, and the Landlord and the Tenant must bear their own costs in this respect.

2.6   *Reimbursement of costs*

If, on publication of the arbitrator's award, the Landlord or the Tenant pays all his fees and expenses, the paying party may [, in default of payment within (*state period, e.g., 21 days*) of a demand to that effect,] recover such proportion of them, if any, as the arbitrator awards against the other [in the case of the Landlord as rent arrears or in the case of the Tenant by deduction from the Rent].

3   Payment of the Rent as ascertained

3.1   *Where the Rent is not ascertained by a review date*

If the Rent payable during any review period has not been ascertained by the relevant review date, then rent is to continue to be payable at the rate previously payable, such payments being on account of the Rent for that review period.

3.2 Where a review date is not a quarter day

If the Rent for any review period is ascertained on or before the relevant review date but that date is not a quarter day, then the Tenant must pay to the Landlord on that review date the difference between the Rent due for that quarter and the Rent already paid for it. (*adapt if the rent is not paid on the usual quarter days*)

3.3 Back-payment where review delayed

If the Rent payable during any review period has not been ascertained by the relevant review date, then the Tenant must pay to the Landlord, [within (*state period, e.g., 7 days*) of (*or as required*) on] the date on which the Rent is agreed or the arbitrator's award is received by him, any shortfall between the Rent that would have been paid for that period had it been ascertained on or before the relevant review date and the payments made by the Tenant on account [and any VAT payable thereon], and interest, at the base lending rate from time to time of the bank referred to in or nominated pursuant to clause (*insert clause number*) 'THE INTEREST RATE', in respect of each instalment of rent due on or after that review date on the amount by which the instalment of the Rent that would have been paid had it been ascertained exceeds the amount paid by the Tenant on account, the interest to be payable for the period from the date on which the instalment was due up to the date of payment of the shortfall.

4 Effect of counter-inflation provisions

If at any review date a statute prevents, restricts or modifies the Landlord's right either to review the Rent in accordance with this Lease or to recover any increase in the Rent, then the Landlord may, when the restriction or modification is removed, relaxed or varied — without prejudice to his rights, if any, to recover any rent the payment of which has only been deferred by statute — on giving not less than (*state minimum notice, e.g., 1 month's*) nor more than (*state maximum notice, e.g., 3 months'*) notice to the Tenant [at any time within (*state period, e.g., 6 months*) of the restriction or modification being removed, relaxed or varied, time being of the essence,] require the Tenant to proceed with any review of the Rent that has been prevented or to review the Rent further where the Landlord's right was restricted or modified. The date of expiry of the notice is to be treated as a review date — provided that nothing in this paragraph is to be construed as varying any subsequent review date. The Landlord may recover any increase in the Rent with effect from the earliest date permitted by law.

Notes: The terms defined in clause 1 are only relevant to this Schedule. The other definitions referred to in this Schedule would be defined in the lease itself. For determination by an expert see the relevant provisions in Appendix 3.

APPENDIX SIX

Section 34, Landlord and Tenant Act 1954

(1)   The rent payable under a tenancy granted by order of the court under this Part of this Act shall be such as may be agreed between the landlord and the tenant or as, in default of such agreement, may be determined by the court to be that at which, having regard to the terms of the tenancy (other than those relating to rent), the holding might reasonably be expected to be let in the open market by a willing lessor, there being disregarded—

(a)   any effect on rent of the fact that the tenant has or his predecessors in title have been in occupation of the holding,

(b)   any goodwill attached to the holding by reason of the carrying on thereat of the business of the tenant (whether by him or by a predecessor of his in that business)

(c)   any effect on rent of an improvement to which this paragraph applies,

(d)   in the case of a holding comprising licensed premises, any addition to its value attributable to the licence, if it appears to the court that having regard to the terms of the current tenancy and any other relevant circumstances the benefit of the licence belongs to the tenant.

(2)   Paragraph (c) of the foregoing subsection applies to any improvement carried out by a person who at the time it was carried out was the tenant, but only if it was carried out otherwise than in pursuance of an obligation to his immediate landlord, and either it was carried out during the current tenancy or the following conditions are satisfied, that is to say,—

(a)   that it was completed not more than twenty-one years before the application for the new tenancy was made; and

(b)   that the holding or any part of it affected by the improvement has at all times since the completion of the improvement been comprised in tenancies of the description specified in section 23(1) of this Act; and

(c)   that at the termination of each of those tenancies the tenant did not quit.

(3)   Where the rent is determined by the court the court may, if it thinks fit, further determine that the terms of the tenancy shall include such provision for varying the rent as may be specified in the determination

(4)   It is hereby declared that the matters which are to be taken into account by the court in determining the rent include any effect on rent of the operation of the provisions of the Landlord and Tenant (Covenants) Act 1995.

Notes: Sub-section (1): numbered as such, and para (c) substituted, by the Law of Property Act 1969, s. 1(1).
Sub-sections (2),(3): inserted by the Law of Property Act 1969, ss. 1(1), 2.
Sub-section (4): inserted by the Landlord and Tenant (Covenants) Act 1995, s. 30(1), Sch 1, para 3.

Examples of Rent Review Memoranda

Memorandum of reviewed rent where review was concluded by agreement: for annexation to the lease and counterpart

MEMORANDUM

This memorandum is supplemental to a [lease (*or as appropriate*) sublease] dated (*date*) and made between (1) (*name of original landlord*) [and] (2) (*name of original tenant*) [and (3) (*name of guarantor*)] relating to (*describe the premises*).

Pursuant to and in accordance with the provisions of [clause (*insert clause number*) schedule (*insert schedule number*)] of the above-mentioned [lease (*or as appropriate*) sublease] the Landlord [now (*name of current landlord*)] and the Tenant [now (*name of current tenant*)] [and the Guarantor] have agreed that from [and including] (*date*) the reviewed yearly rent payable under the above-mentioned [lease (*or as appropriate*) sublease] is £ . . . . [exclusive of VAT][subject to further review in accordance with [clause (*insert clause number*) schedule (*insert schedule number*)] of the above-mentioned [lease (*or as appropriate*) sublease].

(*date*)

Signed by:
for and on behalf of:

Memorandum of reviewed rent where the review was concluded by agreement: for endorsement on the lease and counterpart

MEMORANDUM

Pursuant to and in accordance with the provisions of [clause (*insert clause number*) schedule (*insert schedule number*)] of the within-written [lease (*or as appropriate*) sublease] the Landlord [now (*name of current landlord*)] and the Tenant [now (*name of current tenant*)] [and the Guarantor] have agreed that from [and including] (*date*) the reviewed yearly rent payable under the within-written [lease (*or as appropriate*) sublease] is £ . . . . [exclusive of VAT][subject to further review in accordance with [clause (*insert clause number*) schedule (*insert schedule number*)] of the within-written [lease (*or as appropriate*) sublease].

(*date*)

Signed by:
for and on behalf of:

Memorandum of reviewed rent where the review was concluded by arbitration or expert determination: for annexation to the lease and counterpart

MEMORANDUM

This memorandum is supplemental to a [lease (*or as appropriate*) sublease] dated (*date*) and made between (1) (*name of original landlord*) [and] (2) (*name of original tenant*) [and (3) (*name of guarantor*)] relating to (*describe the premises*).

By a written [award (*or as appropriate*) determination] made on (*date*) by (*name of arbitrator or expert*) of (*address*) [acting as an [arbitrator under the Arbitration Act 1996 (*or as appropriate*) expert]] pursuant to and in accordance with [clause (*insert clause number*) schedule (*insert schedule number*)] of the above-mentioned [lease (*or as appropriate*) sublease] the yearly rent payable under the above-mentioned [lease (*or as appropriate*) sublease] was revised from and including (*date*) and is now £ . . . . per year [exclusive of VAT][subject to further review in accordance with [clause (*insert clause number*) schedule (*insert schedule number*)] of the above-mentioned [lease (*or as appropriate*) sublease]

(*date*)

Signed by:
for and on behalf of:

Memorandum of reviewed rent where the review was concluded by arbitration or expert determination: for endorsement on the lease and counterpart

MEMORANDUM

By a written [award (*or as appropriate*) determination] made on (*date*) by (*name of arbitrator or expert*) of (*address*) [acting as an [arbitrator under the Arbitration Act 1996 (*or as appropriate*) expert]] pursuant to and in accordance with [clause (*insert clause number*) schedule (*insert schedule number*)] of the within-written [lease (*or as appropriate*) sublease] the yearly rent payable under the within-written [lease (*or as appropriate*) sublease] was revised from and including (*date*) and is now £ .... per year [exclusive of VAT][subject to further review in accordance with [clause (*insert clause number*) schedule (*insert schedule number*)] of the within-written [lease (*or as appropriate*) sublease].

(*date*)

Signed by:
for and on behalf of:

Provisions for Payment of an Interim Rent

Increased interim rent to be paid after the review date has passed, pending ascertainment of the reviewed rent

SCHEDULE (*INSERT NUMBER*): THE RENT AND RENT REVIEW

1 Definitions

For all purposes of this schedule the terms defined in this paragraph 1 have the meanings specified.

1.1 *'An arbitrator'*

References to 'an arbitrator' are references to a person appointed by agreement between the Landlord and the Tenant or, in the absence of agreement within (*state period, e.g., 14 days*) of one of them giving notice to the other of his nomination, nominated by the President on the application of either made not earlier than (*state period, e.g., 6 months*) before the relevant review date or at any time thereafter to determine the rent under this schedule.

1.2 *'The Assumptions'*

'The Assumptions' means—

1.2.1   the assumption that no work has been carried out on the Premises during the Term by the Tenant, his subtenants or their predecessors in title [or any occupiers] that has diminished the rental value of the Premises [other than work carried out in compliance with clause (*insert clause number*) STATUTORY OBLIGATIONS],

1.2.2   the assumption that if the Premises have been destroyed or damaged they have been fully rebuilt or reinstated,

1.2.3   the assumption that the covenants contained in this Lease on the part of the [Landlord and the] Tenant have been fully performed and observed,

1.2.4   the assumption that the Premises are available to let by a willing landlord to a willing tenant in the open market by one lease ('the Hypothetical Lease') without a premium being paid by either party and with vacant possession,

1.2.5   the assumption that the Premises have already been fitted out and equipped by and at the expense of the incoming tenant so that they are capable of being used by the incoming tenant from the beginning of the Hypothetical Lease for all purposes required by the incoming tenant that would be permitted under this Lease,

1.2.6   the assumption that the Hypothetical Lease contains the same terms as this Lease, except the amount of the Initial Rent and any rent-free period allowed to the Tenant for fitting out the Premises for his occupation and use at the commencement of the Term, but including the provisions for rent review on the Review Dates, and except as set out in subparagraph 1.2.7,

1.2.7   the assumption that the term of the Hypothetical Lease is equal in length to [the Contractual Term (*or as required*) the Contractual Term remaining unexpired at the relevant review date (*or as required*) the Contractual Term remaining unexpired at the relevant review date or a period of . . . . . . years whichever is the greater (*or as required*) a period of . . . . . . years] and that such term begins on the relevant review date, that the rent commences to be payable on that date, and that the years during which the tenant covenants to decorate the Premises are at the same intervals after the beginning of the term of the Hypothetical Lease as those specified in this Lease [,

1.2.8   the assumption that the Hypothetical Lease will be renewed at the expiry of its term under the provisions of the 1954 Act] [, and

1.2.9   the assumption that every prospective willing landlord and willing tenant is able to recover VAT in full].

1.3 *'The Disregards'*

'The Disregards' means—

1.3.1 disregard of any effect on rent of the fact that the Tenant, his subtenants, or their predecessors in title [or any lawful occupier] have been in occupation of the Premises,

1.3.2 disregard of any goodwill attached to the Premises because the business of the Tenant, his subtenants, or their predecessors in title in their respective businesses is or was carried on there, [and]

1.3.3 disregard of any increase in rental value of the Premises attributable at the relevant review date to any improvement to the Premises carried out, with consent where required, otherwise than in pursuance of an obligation [except an obligation contained in clause (*insert clause number*) STATUTORY OBLIGATIONS] to the Landlord or his predecessors in title either—

(a)   by the Tenant, his subtenants, or their predecessors in title [or any lawful occupier] during the Term or during any period of occupation before the Term, or

(b)   by any tenant or subtenant of the Premises [or any lawful occupiers] before the commencement of the Term provided that the Landlord or his predecessors in title have not since the improvement was carried out had vacant possession of the relevant part of the Premises [, and

1.3.4 disregard of the taxable status of the Landlord or the Tenant for the purpose of VAT].

1.4   'The Interim Rent'

'The Interim Rent' means, in relation to any review period, a rent equal to whichever is the lesser of [twice] the Passing Rent or the Passing Rent plus (*state percentage, e.g., 50%*) of the amount by which the rent specified in the relevant interim rent notice exceeds the Passing Rent.

1.5   'The Passing Rent'

In relation to any review period,'the Passing Rent' means the rent payable during the previous review period or, if payment of rent has been suspended pursuant to the provision for suspension contained in this Lease, the rent that would have been payable had there been no such suspension.

1.6   'The President'

'The President' means the President for the time being of the Royal Institution of Chartered Surveyors or any person authorised by the President to make appointments on his behalf.

1.7 'A review period'

References to 'a review period' are references to the period beginning on any review date and ending on the day before the next review date.

2 Ascertaining the Rent

2.1 The Rent

Until the First Review Date the Rent is to be the Initial Rent, and thereafter during each successive review period the Rent is to be a sum equal to [(where the review is to be upwards only) the greater of the rent payable under this Lease immediately before the relevant review date, or, if payment of rent has been suspended as provided for in this Lease, the rent that would have been payable had there been no such suspension, or] the revised rent ascertained in accordance with this schedule.

2.2 Agreement of the Rent

[Six months before each review date, time not being cf the essence of the contract, the Landlord and the Tenant must [explore the possibility of (*or as required*) open negotiations with a view to] reaching a written agreement as to the Rent for the following review period and the Rent for that period may be agreed at any time or, in the absence of agreement, is to be determined by an expert [not earlier than the relevant review date]. (*or as required*) The Rent for any review period may be agreed at any time or, in the absence of agreement, is to be determined by an expert [not earlier than the relevant review date].]

2.3 Open market rent

The sum to be determined by an arbitrator must be the sum at which he decides the Premises might reasonably be expected to be let in the open market at the relevant review date making the Assumptions but disregarding the Disregards.

2.4 Conduct of the arbitration

The arbitration must be conducted in accordance with the Arbitration Act 1996, except that if the Arbitrator dies or declines to act the President may on the application of either the Landlord or the Tenant appoint another in his place.

2.5 *Memoranda of agreement*

Whenever the Rent has been ascertained in accordance with this schedule, memoranda to that effect must be signed by or on behalf of the Landlord and the Tenant and annexed to this document and its counterpart, and the Landlord and the Tenant must bear their own costs in this respect.

2.6 *Reimbursement of costs*

If, on publication of the arbitrator's award, the Landlord or the Tenant pays all his fees and expenses, the paying party may [, in default of payment within (*state period, e.g., 21 days*) of a demand to that effect,] recover such proportion of them, if any, as the arbitrator awards against the other [in the case of the Landlord as rent arrears or in the case of the Tenant by deduction from the Rent].

3 Payment of the Rent as ascertained

3.1 *Where the Rent is not ascertained by a review date*

If the Rent payable during any review period has not been ascertained by the relevant review date, then rent is to continue to be payable at the rate of the Passing Rent, or of the Interim Rent if the Landlord serves an interim rent notice, such payments being on account of the Rent for that Review Period.

3.2 *Interim rent notice*

The Landlord may, at any time, whether before or after a review date, but in relation to any particular review period not after the Rent for that review period has been ascertained, by notice to the Tenant ('an interim rent notice') require that, if the Rent for the relevant review period has not been ascertained on or before the relevant review date, the Tenant must pay the Interim Rent and not the Passing Rent until the Rent has been ascertained. The notice must contain a statement of the Landlord's opinion of the rent at which the Premises might reasonably be expected to be let in the open market at the relevant review date, making the Assumptions but disregarding the Disregards.

3.3 *Payment of the Interim Rent: notice served before the review date*

If the Landlord serves an interim rent notice before a review date, the Tenant must pay the Interim Rent from that review date until the Rent for that review period is ascertained.

3.4 *Payment of the Interim Rent: notice served after the review date*

If the Landlord serves an interim rent notice after a review date, the Tenant must pay the Interim Rent from [the next quarter day] until the Rent for the relevant review period is ascertained.

3.5 *Where a review date is not a quarter day*

If the Rent for any review period is ascertained on or before the relevant review date but that date is not a quarter day, then the Tenant must pay to the Landlord on that review date the difference between the Rent due for that quarter and the Rent already paid for it. (*adapt if the rent is not paid on the usual quarter days*)

3.6 *Back-payment where review delayed*

If the Rent payable during any review period has not been ascertained by the relevant review date, then the Tenant must pay to the Landlord, [within (*state period, e.g., 7 days*) of (*or as required*) on] the date on which the Rent is agreed or the arbitrator's award is received by him, any shortfall between the Rent that would have been paid for that period had it been ascertained on or before the relevant review date and the payments made by the Tenant on account [and any VAT payable thereon], and interest, at the base lending rate from time to time of the bank referred to in or nominated pursuant to clause (*insert clause number*) 'THE INTEREST RATE', in respect of each instalment of rent due on or after that review date on the amount by which the instalment of the Rent that would have been paid had it been ascertained exceeds the amount paid by the Tenant on account, the interest to be payable for the period from the date on which the instalment was due up to the date of payment of the shortfall.

3.7 *Refund of excess interim payments*

If the aggregate rent, including the Interim Rent if any, paid by the Tenant on account of the Rent for any review period before the Rent is ascertained exceeds the aggregate rent payable for that period, the Landlord must repay to the Tenant the amount of the excess, but without interest, on the day on which the Tenant would have been due to pay a shortfall had there been one.

4 Effect of counter-inflation provisions

If at any review date a statute prevents, restricts or modifies the Landlord's right either to review the Rent in accordance with this Lease or to recover any increase in the Rent, then the Landlord may, when the restriction or modification is removed, relaxed or varied — without prejudice to his rights, if any, to recover any rent the payment of which has only been deferred by statute — on giving not less than (*state minimum notice, e.g., 1 month's*) nor more than (*state maximum notice, e.g., 3 months'*) notice to the Tenant [at any time within (*state period, e.g., 6 months*) of the restriction or modification being removed, relaxed or varied, time being of the essence,] require the Tenant to proceed with any review of the Rent that has been prevented or to review the Rent further where the Landlord's right was restricted or modified. The date of expiry of the notice is to be treated as a review date — provided that nothing in this paragraph is to be construed as varying any subsequent review date. The Landlord may recover any increase in the Rent with effect from the earliest date permitted by law.

Note: The terms defined in clause 1 are only relevant to this Schedule. The other definitions referred to in this Schedule would be defined in the lease itself.

Provisions Allowing Review of Rent Review

Revision of the review dates at an unspecified date in the future

1 DEFINITIONS AND INTERPRETATION ...

1.1 'The Review Dates'

'The First Review Date' means (*date*). 'The Review Dates' means the First Review Date and every (*insert ordinal, e.g., 5th*) anniversary of that date during the [Contractual] Term [— and any other date that may from time to time be specified pursuant to paragraph 4 EFFECT OF COUNTER-INFLATION PROVISIONS —] subject to revision in accordance with schedule (*insert number*) THE RENT AND RENT REVIEW Part B REVISION OF THE REVIEW DATES. References to 'a review date' are references to any one of the Review Dates.

SCHEDULE (*INSERT NUMBER*): THE RENT AND RENT REVIEW

1 Definitions

For all purposes of this schedule the terms defined in this paragraph 1 have the meanings specified.

1.1 *'An arbitrator'*

References to 'an arbitrator' are references to a person appointed by agreement between the Landlord and the Tenant or, in the absence of agreement within (*state period, e.g., 14 days*) of one of them giving notice to the other of his nomination, nominated by the President on the application of either made not earlier than (*state period, e.g., 6 months*) before the relevant review date or at any time thereafter to determine the rent under this schedule.

1.2 *'The Assumptions'*

'The Assumptions' means—

1.2.1   the assumption that no work has been carried out on the Premises during the Term by the Tenant, his subtenants or their predecessors in title [or any occupiers] that has diminished the rental value of the Premises [other than work carried out in compliance with clause (*insert clause number*) STATUTORY OBLIGATIONS],

1.2.2   the assumption that if the Premises have been destroyed or damaged they have been fully rebuilt or reinstated,

1.2.3   the assumption that the covenants contained in this Lease on the part of the [Landlord and the] Tenant have been fully performed and observed,

1.2.4   the assumption that the Premises are available to let by a willing landlord to a willing tenant in the open market by one lease ('the Hypothetical Lease') without a premium being paid by either party and with vacant possession,

1.2.5   the assumption that the Premises have already been fitted out and equipped by and at the expense of the incoming tenant so that they are capable of being used by the incoming tenant from the beginning of the Hypothetical Lease for all purposes required by the incoming tenant that would be permitted under this Lease,

1.2.6   the assumption that the Hypothetical Lease contains the same terms as this Lease, except the amount of the Initial Rent and any rent-free period allowed to the Tenant for fitting out the Premises for his occupation and use at the commencement of the Term, but including the provisions for rent review on the Review Dates, and except as set out in subparagraph 1.2.7,

1.2.7   the assumption that the term of the Hypothetical Lease is equal in length to [the Contractual Term (*or as required*) the Contractual Term remaining unexpired at the relevant review date (*or as required*) the Contractual Term remaining unexpired at the relevant review date or a period of . . . . . . years whichever is the greater (*or as required*) a

214

period of ...... years] and that such term begins on the relevant review date, that the rent commences to be payable on that date, and that the years during which the tenant covenants to decorate the Premises are at the same intervals after the beginning of the term of the Hypothetical Lease as those specified in this Lease [,

1.2.8 the assumption that the Hypothetical Lease will be renewed at the expiry of its term under the provisions of the 1954 Act] [, and

1.2.9 the assumption that every prospective willing landlord and willing tenant is able to recover VAT in full].

1.3 'The Disregards'

'The Disregards' means—

1.3.1 disregard of any effect on rent of the fact that the Tenant, his subtenants, or their predecessors in title [or any lawful occupier] have been in occupation of the Premises,

1.3.2 disregard of any goodwill attached to the Premises because the business of the Tenant, his subtenants, or their predecessors in title in their respective businesses is or was carried on there, [and]

1.3.3 disregard of any increase in rental value of the Premises attributable at the relevant review date to any improvement to the Premises carried out, with consent where required, otherwise than in pursuance of an obligation [except an obligation contained in clause (insert clause number) STATUTORY OBLIGATIONS] to the Landlord or his predecessors in title either—

(a) by the Tenant, his subtenants, or their predecessors in title [or any lawful occupier] during the Term or during any period of occupation before the Term, or

(b) by any tenant or subtenant of the Premises [or any lawful occupiers] before the commencement of the Term provided that the Landlord or his predecessors in title have not since the improvement was carried out had vacant possession of the relevant part of the Premises [, and

1.3.4 disregard of the taxable status of the Landlord or the Tenant for the purpose of VAT].

1.4 'The President'

'The President' means the President for the time being of the Royal Institution of Chartered Surveyors or any person authorised by him to make appointments on his behalf.

1.5 'A review period'

References to 'a review period' are references to the period beginning on any review date and ending on the day before the next review date.

PART A: THE REVIEW PROVISIONS

2 Ascertaining the Rent

2.1 *The Rent*

Until the First Review Date the Rent is to be the Initial Rent, and thereafter during each successive review period the Rent is to be a sum equal to [(*where the review is to be upwards only*) the greater of the rent payable under this Lease immediately before the relevant review date, or, if payment of rent has been suspended as provided for in this Lease, the rent that would have been payable had there been no such suspension, or] the revised rent ascertained in accordance with this schedule.

2.2 *Agreement of the Rent*

[Six months before each review date, time not being of the essence of the contract, the Landlord and the Tenant must [explore the possibility of (*or as required*) open negotiations with a view to] reaching a written agreement as to the Rent for the following review period and the Rent for that period may be agreed at any time or, in the absence of agreement, is to be determined by an arbitrator [not earlier than the relevant review date]. (*or as required*) The Rent for any review period may be agreed at any time or, in the absence of agreement, is to be determined by an arbitrator [not earlier than the relevant review date].]

2.3 *Open market rent*

The sum to be determined by an arbitrator must be the sum at which he decides the Premises might reasonably be expected to be let in the open market at the relevant review date making the Assumptions but disregarding the Disregards.

2.4 *Conduct of the arbitration*

The arbitration must be conducted in accordance with the Arbitration Act 1996, except that if the arbitrator dies or declines to act the President may, on the application of either the Landlord or the Tenant, appoint another in his place.

2.5 *Memoranda of agreement*

Whenever the Rent has been ascertained in accordance with this schedule, memoranda to that effect must be signed by or on behalf of the Landlord and the Tenant and annexed to this document and its counterpart, and the Landlord and the Tenant must bear their own costs in this respect.

2.6 *Reimbursement of costs*

If, on publication of the arbitrator's award, the Landlord or the Tenant pays all his fees and expenses, the paying party may [, in default of payment within (*state period, e.g., 21 days*) of a demand to that effect,] recover such proportion of them, if any, as the arbitrator awards against the other [in the case of the Landlord as rent arrears or in the case of the Tenant by deduction from the Rent].

3 Payment of the Rent as ascertained

3.1 *Where the Rent is not ascertained by a review date*

If the Rent payable during any review period has not been ascertained by the relevant review date, then rent is to continue to be payable at the rate previously payable, such payments being on account of the Rent for that review period.

3.2 *Where a review date is not a quarter day*

If the Rent for any review period is ascertained on or before the relevant review date but that date is not a quarter day, then the Tenant must pay to the Landlord on that review date the difference between the Rent due for that quarter and the Rent already paid for it. (*adapt if the rent is not paid on the usual quarter days*)

3.3 *Back-payment where review delayed*

If the Rent payable during any review period has not been ascertained by the relevant review date, then the Tenant must pay to the Landlord, [within (*state period, e.g., 7 days*) of (*or as required*) on] the date on which the Rent is agreed or the arbitrator's award is received by him, any shortfall between the Rent that would have been paid for that period had it been ascertained on or before the relevant review date and the payments made by the Tenant on account [and any VAT payable thereon], and interest, at the base lending rate from time to time of the bank referred to in or nominated pursuant to clause (*insert clause number*) 'THE INTEREST

RATE', in respect of each instalment of rent due on or after that review date on the amount by which the instalment of the Rent that would have been paid had it been ascertained exceeds the amount paid by the Tenant on account, the interest to be payable for the period from the date on which the instalment was due up to the date of payment of the shortfall.

4   Effect of counter-inflation provisions

If at any review date a statute prevents, restricts or modifies the Landlord's right either to review the Rent in accordance with this Lease or to recover any increase in the Rent, then the Landlord may, when the restriction or modification is removed, relaxed or varied — without prejudice to his rights, if any, to recover any rent the payment of which has only been deferred by statute — on giving not less than (*state minimum notice, e.g., 1 month's*) nor more than (*state maximum notice, e.g., 3 months'*) notice to the Tenant [at any time within (*state period, e.g., 6 months*) of the restriction or modification being removed, relaxed or varied, time being of the essence,] require the Tenant to proceed with any review of the Rent that has been prevented or to review the Rent further where the Landlord's right was restricted or modified. The date of expiry of the notice is to be treated as a review date — provided that nothing in this paragraph is to be construed as varying any subsequent review date. The Landlord may recover any increase in the Rent with effect from the earliest date permitted by law.

PART B: REVISION OF THE REVIEW DATES

5   Definitions

The terms defined in this paragraph 5 have the meanings specified for all purposes of this part of this schedule.

5.1   *'The Existing Review Dates'*

'The Existing Review Dates' means the review dates specified in clause 1.1 'THE REVIEW DATES'.

5.2   *'A frequency revision notice'*

References to 'a frequency revision notice' are references to a notice served by the Landlord under paragraph 6 A FREQUENCY REVISION NOTICE.

5.3 'The New Review Dates'

'The New Review Dates' means the review dates ascertained in accordance with this part of this schedule. References to 'a new review date' are references to any one of the New Review Dates.

6 A frequency revision notice

The Landlord may, once only but at any time [during the Contractual Term] after the [third (*or as required*)] of the Existing Review Dates, serve a notice on the Tenant requiring the Existing Review Dates occurring subsequently to be revised and specifying new review dates to be substituted for them.

7 Arbitration in default of agreement of new dates

If the Landlord and the Tenant have not reached a written agreement as to the New Review Dates within (*state period, e.g., 3 months*) after the date of service of a frequency revision notice, the matter is to be referred to an arbitrator who must determine what rent review dates would have been agreed between a willing landlord and a willing tenant negotiating in the open market for the grant of a new lease of the Premises for a term equal to the residue of the Contractual Term remaining unexpired on the date of service of the frequency revision notice on the terms of this Lease except for the Rent payable on that date, the Existing Review Dates, and this part of this schedule and references to this part of this schedule.

8 Conduct of the arbitration

The arbitration is to be conducted in accordance with the Arbitration Act 1996.

9 Reimbursement of fees

If, on publication of an arbitrator's award, the Landlord or the Tenant pays all his fees and expenses, that party may recover such proportion of them, if any, as the arbitrator awards against the other.

10 Election to retain the Existing Review Dates

The Landlord may, by written notice given within (*state period, e.g., 28 days*) after the publication of an arbitrator's award, elect that the New Review Dates are to be the same as the Existing Review Dates for the residue of the Contractual Term and not the New Review Dates specified in the award. Such an election is to be final and binding on both parties. If no such notice is served in time, time being of the essence in this respect, the New Review Dates are to be those specified in the arbitrator's award.

11 Memoranda of the New Review Dates

Memoranda recording the agreement between the parties, the arbitrator's award, or the Landlord's election, as the case may be, must be signed by or on behalf of the parties and annexed to this document and its counterpart, and the parties must each bear their own costs in this respect.

12 Reviews arising during the change of dates

12.1 *Review during change of dates*

If, during the period after service of a frequency revision notice but before the New Review Dates are ascertained ('the Period of Uncertainty'), an Existing Review Date would, but for the service of the frequency revision notice, occur, the Rent payable for that part of the Period of Uncertainty following the Existing Review Date is to be the Rent payable for the review period immediately preceding that Existing Review Date unless the Landlord properly elects under paragraph 10 ELECTION TO RETAIN THE EXISTING REVIEW DATES that the New Review Dates are to be the same as the Existing Review Dates, in which case the provisions of PART A of this schedule are to apply to the Existing Review Date except that the interest payable under paragraph 3.3 BACK-PAYMENT WHERE RE-VIEW IS DELAYED is to be payable only from the day occurring (*state period, e.g., 3 months*) after the date of the Landlord's election.

12.2 *Retrospective application of review provisions*

If the parties agree, or an arbitrator's award — not being rendered nugatory by an election made by the Landlord under paragraph 10 ELECTION TO RETAIN THE EXISTING REVIEW DATES — provides, that a new review date, or more than one of them, would have occurred during the Period of Uncertainty, then the provisions of Part A of this schedule are to apply to that new review date, or those dates, except that the interest payable under paragraph 3.3 BACK-PAYMENT WHERE REVIEW IS DELAYED is to be payable only from the day occurring (*state period, e.g., 3 months*) after the date of the agreement or the arbitrator's award, as the case may be.

Note: The terms defined in clause 1 are only relevant to this Schedule. The other definitions referred to in this Schedule would be defined in the lease itself. For determination by an expert see the relevant provisions in Appendix 3.

Index-linked Rent Review Clause

**Rent to be increased on review dates by reference to the
Index of Retail Prices**

SCHEDULE [1]: THE RIGHTS RESERVED

1-2 Access on renewal

The right to enter the Premises with the Surveyor at [any time (*or as
required*) convenient hours and on reasonable prior notice] to inspect [and
measure] them for all purposes connected with any pending or intended
step under Part II of the 1954 Act.

SCHEDULE [2]: THE RENT AND RENT REVIEW

2-1 Definitions

For all purposes of this schedule the terms defined in this paragraph 2-1
have the meanings specified.

2-1.1 *'The Base Figure'*

The Base Figure' means (*insert the Index figure for the month preceding the
grant of the lease or otherwise as has been agreed*).

2-1.2 'The Index'

'The Index' means the ['all Items' index figure] of the Index of Retail Prices published by the Office for National Statistics.

2-1.3 'A review period'

References to 'a review period' means a period beginning on any review date and ending on the day before the next review date, and qualified uses of the term are to be construed accordingly.

2-2 Ascertaining the Rent

2-2.1 The Rent

Until the First Review Date the Rent is to be the Initial Rent, and thereafter during each successive review period the Rent is to be a sum equal to [(where the review is upwards only) the greater of] the rent payable under this Lease immediately before the relevant review date or, if payment of rent has been suspended as provided in this Lease, the rent that would have been payable had there been no such suspension, or the revised rent that is ascertained in accordance with this schedule.

2-2.2 The revised rent

The Rent for any review period is to be determined at the relevant review date by multiplying the Initial Rent by the Index for the month preceding the relevant review date and dividing the result by the Base Figure.

2-2.3 Changes in the Index

If the reference base used to compile the Index changes after the date of this Lease the figure taken to be shown in the Index after the change is to be the figure that would have been shown in the Index if the reference base current at the date of this lease had been retained.

2-2.4 Arbitration of problems

If it becomes impossible to calculate the Rent for any Review Period by reference to the Index because of any change in the methods used to compile the Index after the date of this Lease or for any other reason whatever, or if any dispute or question whatever arises between the parties as to the amount of the Rent for any review period or the construction or effect of this schedule, then the Rent for that review period or the disputed matter is to be determined by an arbitrator to be appointed either by agreement between the parties or, in the absence of agreement, by the President for the time being of the Royal Institution of Chartered Surveyors, or any person authorised by him to make appointments on his behalf, on the application of either the Landlord or the Tenant. This is to be deemed to be a submission to arbitration within the meaning of the Arbitration Act 1996. The arbitrator is to have full power to determine, on such dates as he considers appropriate, what the increase in the Index would have been had it continued on the basis assumed for the operation of this rent review and in view of the information assumed to be available for it. If that determination is also impossible, the arbitrator must determine a reasonable rent for the Premises on such dates as he considers appropriate, having regard to the purposes and intent of the provisions in this Lease for the review of the Rent.

2-2.5 *Notice of the Rent payable*

The Landlord must, before each review date, give notice to the Tenant of the amount of the Rent for the next review period.

2-2.6 *Memoranda of the Rent payable*

Whenever the Rent has been ascertained in accordance with this schedule, memoranda to that effect must be signed by or on behalf of the Landlord and the Tenant and annexed to this document and its counterpart and the Landlord and the Tenant must bear their own costs in this respect.

Note: The terms defined in clause 1 are only relevant to this Schedule. The other definitions referred to in this Schedule would be defined in the lease itself.

Turnover Rent

Rent linked to turnover

1   DEFINITIONS AND INTERPRETATION

1.1   'A turnover period'

References to 'a turnover period' are references to the period of one year commencing on each (*day*) of (*month*).

1.2   'The Turnover Rent'

'The Turnover Rent' means the rent ascertained in accordance with schedule (insert schedule number) THE TURNOVER RENT.

1.3   'The Turnover Rent Percentage'

'The Turnover Rent Percentage' means ... %.

(*insert further definition and interpretation clauses as required*)

2   DEMISE

(*insert demise as required*) ... yielding and paying to the Landlord—

2.1 the Initial Rent without any deduction or set off by equal quarterly payments in advance on the usual quarter days in every year and proportionately for any period of less than a year, the first such payment, being a proportionate sum in respect of the period from and including the Rent Commencement Date to and including the day before the quarter day next after the Rent Commencement Date, to be paid on the date of this Lease, and

2.2 by way of further rent the Turnover Rent, payable in accordance with schedule (*insert schedule number*) THE TURNOVER RENT.

(*insert covenants and other provisions as required*)

SCHEDULE (*insert schedule number*): THE TURNOVER RENT

1 The Gross Turnover

'The Gross Turnover' means the aggregate of all sums received or receivable for all goods sold, leased, hired or otherwise disposed of or for services rendered at, in, from or on the Premises by the Tenant or any other person, and all sums received or receivable by the Tenant for the use and/or occupation of the Premises or any part of the Premises by any other person, but excluding—

1.1 VAT, purchase tax, and any similar sales or excise tax imposed directly on the Tenant in respect of the supply of goods or services and actually paid or accounted for by the Tenant to the taxing authorities,

1.2 any sum refunded or credit given to his customers in respect of defective or unsatisfactory goods or services, provided that the sum or credit must not exceed the sale price of the goods or the charge for the services, and

1.3 ... % of any sum received by the Tenant for services performed otherwise than at the Premises but where the orders are received at the Premises.

2 Turnover Rent

The Turnover Rent for a turnover period is to be the Turnover Rent Percentage of the Gross Turnover for the year immediately preceding that turnover period.

3 Certificate of the Gross Turnover

Within (*state period, e.g., 30 days*) after the end of a turnover period, the Tenant must deliver to the Landlord a certificate, signed by a professionally qualified accountant appointed by the Tenant, certifying the amount of the Gross Turnover during that turnover period. If the Tenant fails to supply a certificate under the provisions of this paragraph, or any dispute arises between the Landlord and the Tenant as to the amount of the Gross Turnover or the Turnover Rent, then the Gross Turnover and the Turnover Rent are to be determined by a member of the Institute of Chartered Accountants in England and Wales appointed by the President of the Institute, acting as an expert and not as an arbitrator, whose decision is to be binding on the Landlord and the Tenant.

4   Inspection of accounts

The Tenant must make the books, documents and records that are, or in the opinion of the Landlord ought to be, kept by him for the purpose of ascertaining and verifying the Gross Turnover, or that in the opinion of the Landlord are or may be relevant for that purpose, available for inspection at all reasonable times by the Landlord or his agent duly authorised for that purpose in writing. The Tenant must bear the cost of the inspection if any material discrepancy is discovered.

5   Payment and interim provisions

5.1   Payment

The Turnover Rent [and any VAT payable thereon] must be paid without deduction, by equal quarterly payments in advance, on the usual quarter days.

5.2   Payment on account

If the Turnover Rent for a turnover period has not been determined on or before the first quarter day during that turnover period, the Tenant must pay to the Landlord on that and any subsequent quarter days before the Turnover Rent is determined, a sum on account of the Turnover Rent equal to the Turnover Rent that was payable on the quarter day immediately preceding the beginning of that turnover period ('the Sum on Account').

5.3   Back-payment of a shortfall

On determination of the Turnover Rent, the Tenant must pay the difference between the Sum on Account and what would have been payable had the Turnover Rent been determined on or before the first quarter day of the turnover period ('the Actual Sum') [immediately (*or as required*) on the next quarter day].

[5.4   Set-off against the Rent

Where the Sum on Account exceeds the Actual Sum the Tenant may deduct the difference from the Rent due on the next quarter day.]

[5.5   Interest

If the Turnover Rent is determined by an accountant because the Tenant has failed to supply a certificate or in the event of a dispute, and if the Actual Sum exceeds the Sum on Account, the Tenant must pay interest for the period from the quarter day upon which the instalment was due up to the date of payment on the difference between each instalment of the Sum on Account and what would have been payable on each quarter day had the Turnover Rent for that turnover period been determined.]

6   Open Market Rent

If the Turnover Rent for a turnover period is less than £ (*insert sum*) the Landlord may by notice in writing within (*insert period of time e.g., one month*) of the determination of the Turnover Rent for a turnover period (time not being of the essence) require that the Initial Rent and the Turnover Rent for that year be substituted for the amount which the Premises might reasonably be expected to be let in the open market at the beginning of the turnover period in question making the following assumptions but disregarding the following disregards ('the Open Market Rent').

6.1   The Assumptions

6.1.1   the assumption that no work has been carried out on the Premises during the Term by the Tenant, his subtenants or their predecessors in title [or any occupiers] that has diminished the rental value of the Premises [other than work carried out in compliance with clause (*insert clause number*) STATUTORY OBLIGATIONS],

6.1.2   the assumption that if the Premises have been destroyed or damaged they have been fully rebuilt or reinstated,

6.1.3   the assumption that the covenants contained in this Lease on the part of the [Landlord and the] Tenant have been fully performed and observed,

6.1.4   the assumption that the Premises are available to let by a willing landlord to a willing tenant in the open market by one lease ('the Hypothetical Lease') without a premium being paid by either party and with vacant possession,

6.1.5   the assumption that the Premises have already been fitted out and equipped by and at the expense of the incoming tenant so that they are capable of being used by the incoming tenant from the beginning of the Hypothetical Lease for all purposes required by the incoming tenant that would be permitted under this Lease,

6.1.6   the assumption that the Hypothetical Lease contains the same terms as this Lease, except the amount of the Initial Rent and any rent-free period allowed to the Tenant for fitting out the Premises for his occupation and use at the commencement of the Term, but including the provisions for rent review on the Review Dates, and except as set out in subparagraph 6.1.7,

6.1.7   the assumption that the term of the Hypothetical Lease is equal in length to [the Contractual Term (*or as required*) the Contractual Term remaining unexpired at the relevant review date (*or as required*) the Contractual Term remaining unexpired at the relevant review date or a period of . . . . . . years whichever is the greater (*or as required*) a period of . . . . . . years] and that such term begins on the relevant review date, that the rent commences to be payable on that date, and that the years during which the tenant covenants to decorate the Premises are at the same intervals after the beginning of the term of the Hypothetical Lease as those specified in this Lease [,

6.1.8   the assumption that the Hypothetical Lease will be renewed at the expiry of its term under the provisions of the 1954 Act] [, and

6.1.9   the assumption that every prospective willing landlord and willing tenant is able to recover VAT in full].

6.2   The Disregards

6.2.1   disregard of any effect on rent of the fact that the Tenant, his subtenants, or their predecessors in title [or any lawful occupier] have been in occupation of the Premises,

6.2.2   disregard of any goodwill attached to the Premises because the business of the Tenant, his subtenants, or their predecessors in title in their respective businesses is or was carried on there, [and]

6.2.3   disregard of any increase in rental value of the Premises attributable at the relevant review date to any improvement to the Premises carried out, with consent where required, otherwise than in pursuance of an obligation [except an obligation contained in clause (*insert clause number*) STATUTORY OBLIGATIONS] to the Landlord or his predecessors in title either—

(a)   by the Tenant, his subtenants, or their predecessors in title [or any lawful occupier] during the Term or during any period of occupation before the Term, or

(b) by any tenant or subtenant of the Premises [or any lawful occupiers] before the commencement of the Term provided that the Landlord or his predecessors in title have not since the improvement was carried out had vacant possession of the relevant part of the Premises [, and

6.2.4 disregard of the taxable status of the Landlord or the Tenant for the purpose of VAT].

6.3 Agreement for Open Market Rent

The Open Market Rent may be agreed at any time, or in the absence of agreement, is to be determined by an arbitrator. An arbitrator will be a person appointed by agreement between the Landlord and the Tenant or, in the absence of agreement within (*state period, e.g., 14 days*) of one of them giving notice to the other of his nomination, nominated by the President for the time being of the Royal Institution of Chartered Surveyors or any person authorised by him to make appointments on his behalf on the application of either the Landlord or the Tenant.

6.4 Conduct of the arbitration

The arbitration must be conducted in accordance with the Arbitration Act 1996, except that if the arbitrator dies or declines to act the President may, on the application of either the Landlord or the Tenant, appoint another in his place.

6.5 Memorandum of agreement

Whenever the Open Market Rent has been ascertained in accordance with this clause, memoranda to that effect must be signed by or on behalf of the Landlord and the Tenant and annexed to this document and its counterpart, and the Landlord and the Tenant must bear their own costs in this respect.

6.6 Reimbursement of costs

If, on publication of the arbitrator's award, the Landlord or the Tenant pays all his fees and expenses, the paying party may [, in default of payment within (*state period, e.g., 21 days*) of a demand to that effect,] recover such proportion of them, if any, as the arbitrator awards against the other [in the case of the Landlord as rent arrears or in the case of the Tenant by deduction from the Open Market Rent].

6.7 Open Market Rent not ascertained

The Open Market Rent will not have been ascertained by the beginning of the turnover period in question, therefore the rent is to continue to be payable at the rate previously payable, such payments being on account of the Open Market Rent for the year in question.

6.8 Back-payment

Once the Open Market Rent has been ascertained then the Tenant must pay to the Landlord, [within (*state period, e.g., 7 days*) of (*or as required*) on] the date on which the Open Market Rent is agreed or the arbitrator's award is received by him, any shortfall between the Open Market Rent that would have been paid for that period had it been ascertained at the beginning of the turnover period in question and the payments made by the Tenant on account [and any VAT payable thereon], and interest, at the base lending rate from time to time of the bank referred to in or nominated pursuant to clause (*insert clause number*) 'THE INTEREST RATE', in respect of each instalment of rent due on or after the beginning of the turnover period in question on the amount by which the instalment of the Open Market Rent that would have been paid had it been ascertained exceeds the amount paid by the Tenant on account, the interest to be payable for the period from the date on which the instalment was due up to the date of payment of the shortfall.

6.9 Effect of counter-inflation provisions

If at any time a statute prevents, restricts or modifies the Landlord's right either to review the rent in accordance with this Lease or to recover any increase in the rent, then the Landlord may, when the restriction or modification is removed, relaxed or varied — without prejudice to his rights, if any, to recover any rent the payment of which has only been deferred by statute — on giving not less than (*state minimum notice, e.g., 1 month's*) nor more than (*state maximum notice, e.g., 3 months'*) notice to the Tenant [at any time within (*state period, e.g., 6 months*) of the restriction or modification being removed, relaxed or varied, time being of the essence,] require the Tenant to proceed with any review of the rent that has been prevented or to review the rent further where the Landlord's right was restricted or modified. The date of expiry of the notice is to be treated as a review date — provided that nothing in this paragraph is to be construed as varying any subsequent review date. The Landlord may recover any increase in the rent with effect from the earliest date permitted by law.

Notes: This is a fairly simple form of turnover clause which provides for a basic rent and an additional rent to be paid. It gives the landlord the right to vary the lease and have a review to the open market if the turnover rent falls below a certain level. If the parties fail to agree on an open market rent then the rent is determined by an arbitrator. For determination by an expert see the relevant provisions in Appendix 3.

Index